Bismarck and Germany 1862–1890

Bismarck and Germany 1862–1890

Third edition

David G. Williamson

LONDON AND NEW YORK

First published 1986 by Pearson Education Limited
Second edition 1998
Third edition 2011

Published 2013 by Routledge
2 Park Square, Milton Park, Abingdon, Oxon OX14 4RN
711 Third Avenue, New York, NY 10017, USA

Routledge is an imprint of the Taylor & Francis Group, an informa business

ISBN: 978–1–4082–2318–5 (pbk)

British Library Cataloguing in Publication Data
A CIP catalogue record for this book can be obtained from the British Library

Library of Congress Cataloging in Publication Data
Williamson, D.G.
    Bismarck and Germany, 1862–1890 / David G. Williamson.—3rd ed.
        p. cm.
    Includes bibliographical references and index.
    ISBN 978-1-4082-2318-5 (pbk.)
    1. Germany—History—1871–1918. 2. Germany—History—1848–1870.
3. Bismarck, Otto, Fürst von, 1815–1898. I. Title.
    DD220.W48 2010
    943.08—dc22

                                                            2010017041

Set 10/13.5pt Berkeley Book by 35

Introduction to the series

History is a narrative constructed by historians from traces left by the past. Historical enquiry is often driven by contemporary issues and, in consequence, historical narratives are constantly reconsidered, reconstructed and reshaped. The fact that different historians have different perspectives on issues means that there is also often controversy and no universally agreed version of past events. *Seminar Studies in History* was designed to bridge the gap between current research and debate, and the broad, popular general surveys that often date rapidly.

The volumes in the series are written by historians who are not only familiar with the latest research and current debates concerning their topic, but who have themselves contributed to our understanding of the subject. The books are intended to provide the reader with a clear introduction to a major topic in history. They provide both a narrative of events and a critical analysis of contemporary interpretations. They include the kinds of tools generally omitted from specialist monographs: a chronology of events, a glossary of terms and brief biographies of 'who's who'. They also include bibliographical essays in order to guide students to the literature on various aspects of the subject. Students and teachers alike will find that the selection of documents will stimulate discussion and offer insight into the raw materials used by historians in their attempt to understand the past.

Clive Emsley and Gordon Martel
Series Editors

For P.G.R.B.R. Williamson 1950–2009

Contents

Publisher's acknowledgements

We are grateful to the following for permission to reproduce copyright material:

Documents 3 and 6 reprinted from *The Social and Political Conflict in Prussia, 1858–61* by Eugene N. Anderson by permission of the University of Nebraska Press. Copyright 1954 by the University of Nebraska. Copyright renewed 1982 by the University of Nebraska Press; Document 4 from HAMEROW, THEORDORE S.; THE SOCIAL FOUNDATIONS OF GERMAN UNIFICATION, 1858–1871, IDEAS AND INSTITUTIONS. © 1969 Princeton University Press, 1997 renewed PUP Reprinted by permission of Princeton University Press; Documents 5 and 10 from HAMEROW, THEORDORE S.; THE SOCIAL FOUNDATIONS OF GERMAN UNIFICATION, 1858–1871, © 1972 Princeton University Press, 2000 renewed PUP Reprinted by permission of Princeton University Press; Document 13 from *The Schleswig-Holstein Question*, Harvard Historical Studies, Harvard University Press (Steefel, L.D. 1932) p. 52, originally from *Die Gesammelten Werke, IV*, No. 17 (Bismarck); Document 17 from *From Bismarck to Hitler. The Problem of Continuity in German History*, Longman (J.C. Röhl (ed) 1970) pp. 20–1; Document 20 from BISMARCK by Alan Palmer used by permission of Campbell Thomson & McLaughlin Ltd on behalf of the author; Documents 25 and 47 from KENNAN, GEORGE F.; THE DECLINE OF BISMARCK'S EUROPEAN ORDER. © 1979 Princeton University Press, Reprinted by permission of Princeton University Press; Documents 29, 33 and 34 excerpts from pp. 142–3, 180–2, 186–7 from THE AGE OF BISMARCK: DOCUMENTS AND INTERPRETATIONS, EDITED by THEORDORE S. Hamerow. Copyright © 1973 by Theodore S. Hamerow. Reprinted by permission of HarperCollins Publishers; Document 30 from *Free Trade and Protection in Germany, 1868–1879*, Steiner (Lambi, I.N. 1963) p. 133; Document 35 from *Das Ruhelose Reich-Deutschland, 1866–1918*, Severin and Siedler (Stürmer, M. 1983) p. 41; Document 39 from LIDTKE, VERNON L.; THE OUTLAWED PARTY. © 1966 Princeton University Press, 1994 renewed PUP Reprinted by permission of Princeton University Press; Document 50 from Wehler, H-U. Bismarck's Imperialism, 1862–1890, *Past and Present*, 1970, August, No. 48, pp. 122–3 by permission of the Past and Present Society.

Map 2 'Prussia and the Unification of Germany, 1871' from *A History of Prussia*, Longman (Koch, H.W. 1978); Map 3 'Germany's colonial empire in Africa and Asia' from *Recent History Atlas, 1860–1960*, Weidenfield & Nicolson (Gilbert, M. 1966) p. 23, with permission of A P Watt Ltd on behalf of Sir Martin Gilbert.

Plate 1, Photo: akg-images/ullstein bild; Plates 2, 6, 7, 8, 11, Photo: akg-images; Plates 3, 4, 5, 9, 10, The Bridgeman Art Library.

In some instances we have been unable to trace the owners of copyright material, and we would appreciate any information that would enable us to do so.

Chronology

1814	Napoleon abdicates.
	Vienna Congress convened.
1815	
1 April	Bismarck born at Schönhausen.
9 June	German Confederation set up.
18 June	Napoleon's final defeat at Battle of Waterloo.
1817	Nationalist festival organized at Wartburg by the German Student Associations.
1819	Kotzebue's murder by Karl Sand.
	The Karlsbad Decrees.
1832–35	Bismarck is a student at Göttingen and Berlin.
1833	Establishment of *Zollverein*.
1840	Frederick William IV becomes King of Prussia.
1847	Meeting of United Diet in Berlin.
	Bismarck becomes member of the Diet.
1848	
18 March	Uprising in Berlin.
21/22 March	Frederick William IV promises political reforms and a parliament.
1 May	Elections to German National Parliament in Frankfurt.
1849	
3 April	Frederick William rejects offer of Imperial Crown from Frankfurt Delegation.
7 May	Prussia rejects Imperial Constitution.
14 May	Prussian delegates recalled from Frankfurt.

1850

March Bismarck elected member of Erfurt Parliament.

November Prussia retreats over Hesse-Kassel affair – Olmütz Agreement.

1851 German Confederation restored.
Bismarck appointed Prussian envoy at Frankfurt.

1853 *Zollverein* renewed for 12 years.

1854–56 Crimean War.

1858

October William appointed Regent.
Von Moltke becomes Chief of Staff.

1859

March Bismarck appointed ambassador to St Petersburg.

April–July Franco-Piedmontese war against Austria.

1860

February Von Roon introduces military reforms into Prussian *Landtag*.

1861

January Death of Frederick William IV. William I becomes King of Prussia.

June Progressive Party founded.

1862

May Prussian *Landtag* elections.

23 Sept. Bismarck appointed minister-president.

30 Sept. 'Blood and iron' speech.

1863

8 Feb. Alvensleben Convention.

March March Patent: Schleswig to be integrated into Denmark.

May Prussian *Landtag* dissolved after rejection of army reforms.

August Bismarck persuaded William not to attend congress in Frankfurt to discuss Austrian reform plans.

October German Confederation votes for war against Denmark.

24 Dec. Confederation troops enter Holstein.

1864

Feb.–July	Austro-Prussian war against Denmark.
3–4 Feb.	*Landtag* rejects war credits bill.
18 April	Battle of Düppel.
August	Schönbrunn Convention.
30 October	Treaty of Vienna.

1865	Constitutional conflict deepens.
16 May	Renewal of *Zollverein*.
August	Convention of Gastein.
October	Bismarck meets Napoleon at Biarritz.

1866

April	Prussian alliance with Italy.
14 June	Austro-Prussian war starts.
3 July	Prussian victory at Königgratz.
23 August	Treaty of Prague.

1867

12 Feb.	North German Constituent *Reichstag* opened.
April	Constitution of North German *Reichstag* approved.
April–May	Luxemburg Crisis.
12 June	National Liberal Party formed.

1868

March	Customs Union Parliament meets.
September	Deposition of Queen Isabella. Search for a successor begins.

1870

July	Hohenzollern candidacy for Spanish throne made public.
13 July	Bismarck releases edited version of Ems telegram.
19 July	France declares war on Prussia.
1–2 Sept.	Battle of Sedan.
Oct.–Nov.	Bismarck negotiates German unity with south German states.

1871

18 Jan.   Second Empire proclaimed at Versailles.

March   Elections to *Reichstag.*

10 May   The Treaty of Frankfurt.

1871–73   Boom fuelled by the French indemnity and currency reform.

1872

January   Adalbert Falk appointed Prussian minister of culture.
             Kulturkampf begins.

December   Bismarck resigns as Prussian minister-president.

1873   The Stock Exchange Crash and beginning of the Great Depresssion.

May   The May Laws.

October   The League of the Three Emperors.

October   Bismarck again becomes Prussian minister-president.

1875

April–May   The War in Sight Crisis.

July   Revolt against Turkish rule in Bosnia and Herzegovina.
         Foundation of the *Reichsbank.*

1876   The Central Association of German Industrialists for Tax and
          Economic Reform founded.

July   Foundation of German Conservative Party.

1877

24 April   Russia declares war on Turkey.
             Bismarck offers Bennigsen ministerial post and vice-chancellorship.

1878

3 March   Treaty of San Stefano.

11 May   Attempted assassination of Emperor William by Hödel.

24 May   Anti-Socialist bill rejected by the *Reichstag.*

2 June   Second assassination attempt by Karl Nobiling.

11 June	*Reichstag* dissolved.
June–July	Berlin Congress.
October	Revised Anti-Socialist Law approved by *Reichstag*.

1879	'Second foundation of the *Reich*'.
12 July	Tariffs on iron and grain.
6 October	Dual Alliance with Austria.

1880	Industrial production sinks to the levels of 1872–73.
	Secessionists leave National Liberal Party.

1881

March	First Accident Insurance bill introduced.
June	Three Emperors' Alliance.
October	Three-quarters of newly elected *Reichstag* hostile to Bismarck.

1882

20 May	Triple Alliance between Italy, Austria and Germany.

1883

30 October	German-Austro-Romanian Defensive Alliance.

1884

March	*Freisinnige Partei* formed.
6 July	Accident Insurance Act.
September	Renewal of Three Emperors' Alliance.
November	Berlin Congo Conference opened.

1884–85	Foundations of German colonial empire laid.

1885

March	Expulsion of Jewish and Polish aliens from Prussia.
September	Bulgarian crisis begins with revolution in Eastern Roumelia.

1886

April   Settlement law financing land purchases from Poles in eastern provinces.

14 July   Boulanger becomes French minister of war.

1887

February   *Kartell* Elections.

24 March   Mediterranean Agreement.

16 May   Boulanger dismissed.

18 June   Reinsurance Treaty.

1888

March   Crown Prince Frederick succeeds to the throne.

15 June   Frederick's death and William II's accession.

1889

January   Old Age Pensions introduced.

1890

20 March   Bismarck resigns; Caprivi appointed chancellor.
Anti-Socialist Laws lapse.

1891

April   Bismarck elected to *Reichstag*.

1894

January   Bismarck pays ceremonial visit to Berlin.

1898

30 July   Bismarck's death.

Who's who

Alexander, Prince Joseph of Battenberg (1857–1893): Prince of Bulgaria from 29 April 1879 to 7 September 1886.

Alexander II, Tsar (1818–81): Emperor of the Russian Empire from 3 March 1855 until his assassination in 1881 by the terrorist movement, 'The People's Will'. He was a reformer domestically although his critics argued that he was not radical enough. In foreign affairs, he was primarily interested in the Balkans.

Alexander III, Tsar (1845–1894): Emperor of Russia from 13 March 1881 until his death in 1894. In reaction to his father's assassination he was a firm autocrat, and throughout his reign he followed a policy of repression. When the Reinsurance Treaty was allowed to lapse in 1890, he turned to France and in 1893 signed the Franco-Russian alliance.

Andrassy, Count Gyula (1823–1890): In the revolutions of 1848–49 he was a Hungarian patriot and went into exile until 1858. In 1867 he was appointed prime minister of Hungary and he replaced Beust as foreign minister in 1871.

Arndt, Ernst Moritz (1769–1860): German nationalist author and poet.

Bennigsen, Rudolf von (1824–1902): Civil servant and the leader of the Liberal opposition in Hanover. He became president of the *Nationalverein* and played a major role in founding the National Liberal Party in 1866, which he was for the next thirty years to lead. He cooperated with Bismarck in creating the infrastructure of the newly founded *Reich*, but in 1877 rejected Bismarck's offer of the vice-chancellorship, as Bismarck and the Emperor refused to make further concessions. In 1887 he was instrumental in the rejection of the first Anti-Socialist bill. In 1883 he resigned his seat but returned to the *Reichstag* in 1887 to support the *Kartel*.

Bernstorff, Albrecht Graf von (1809–1873): Prussian diplomat who served in Vienna and London. Appointed foreign minister in 1861, he revived the

Radowitz Plan, but he resigned a year later in protest against the violation of the constitution by the government.

Beust, Friedrich Ferdinand (1809–1886): Saxon and Austrian politician. He held various portfolios in the Saxon ministry and served as premier (1853–66), but his opposition to Bismarck forced his resignation after Saxony's defeat in the Austro-Prussian War. He then became Austrian foreign minister (1866), prime minister (Feb. 1867), and chancellor (June 1867). He negotiated the *Ausgleich* (compromise) of 1867, which resulted in the establishment of the Austro-Hungarian monarchy. Created a count in 1868, Beust was dismissed in 1871, but later served as ambassador in London (1871–78) and Paris (1878–82).

Bismarck, Otto von (1815–1898): Born into an old *Junker* family in Brandenburg. He entered politics in 1847, and made a reputation for himself as an extreme counter-revolutionary when he supported the Prussian king during the revolutionary turmoil of the years 1848–49. As a reward he served as Prussian ambassador to the German Confederation. He became minister-president of Prussia in 1862 and, after defeating first Denmark, then Austria and France, created the German *Reich* in 1871. As *Reich* chancellor and foreign minister, 1871–90, he pursued with some exceptions a cautious foreign policy which aimed at the isolation of France and the avoidance of a European war. In home affairs he cooperated with the National Liberals, 1871–78, and waged the *Kulturkampf* against the Catholics. In 1878 he ended his support for free trade, broke with the Liberals and introduced the Anti-Socialist Law aimed at the SPD. In his last decade of power he virtually lost control of the *Reichstag*, but in 1887 managed to patch together an alliance between the National Liberals and the Conservatives. One of Bismarck's greatest achievement during the 1880s was his welfare legislation. In March 1890 he was forced to resign by Kaiser Wilhelm II. By the time of his death he had already become a legend.

Bleichröder, Gerson von (1822–1893): Jewish German banker and son of Samuel Bleichröder, who founded the Bleichröder Bank in 1803 in Berlin. Bleichröder was responsible for the private banking transactions of Otto von Bismarck and the transfer of credits and placing of loans on behalf of the Prussian state and the German Empire. He was ennobled in 1872.

Boulanger, General Georges (1837–1891): Entered politics in 1884 and was an effective and charismatic war minister. He appealed to those who wanted revenge against Germany. In 1889 it seemed as if he might stage a coup, but he lost his nerve and fled to Brussels. In the end he committed suicide on the grave of his mistress.

Delbrück, Rudolf von (1817–1903): Spent most of his career in the Prussian ministry of commerce, the foreign trade section of which he directed after 1848. He was responsible for extending the *Zollverein* and for using it as an instrument of Prussian statecraft, particularly in negotiations with Austria. In 1871 Bismarck appointed him head of the *Reich* chancellery where he was effectively vice-chancellor. Later in the decade his free trade ideas became unpopular and he resigned in 1876. In 1878 he entered the *Reichstag* and opposed the imposition of tariffs.

Disraeli, Benjamin (1804–1881): Conservative leader in the House of Commons for twenty years. British prime minister, 1868 and 1874–80. He was an ardent imperialist who believed that patriotism and nationalism could overcome class divisions.

Falk, Adalbert (1827–1900): Entered the Prussian state service. In 1858 he was elected a deputy, joining the Old Liberal party. In 1868 he became a privy-councillor in the ministry of justice. In 1872 he was made minister of education, and was responsible for drafting and implementing the May Laws against the Catholics. In 1879 his position became untenable, owing to the death of Pope Pius IX and Bismarck's desire to end the *Kulturkampf*. He resigned his office, but retained his seat in the *Reichstag* until 1882.

Ferdinand of Coburg, Tsar of Bulgaria (1861–1948): Son of Prince August of Saxe-Coburg and his wife Clémentine of Orléans, daughter of King Louis Philippe I of France. He grew up in the Austro-Hungarian Empire and was consequently seen by the Russians essentially as an Austrian puppet. He remained on the Bulgarian throne until October 1918.

Ferry, Jules (1832–1893): Prime minister of France, 1880–01 and 1883–85. His main interests were education and colonial development. He acquired Tunisia and Indo-China for France.

Fichte, Johann (1762–1814): Philosopher, German nationalist and professor at Berlin University. Famous for his Addresses (*Reden*) to the German Nation, 1807–08.

Francis Joseph (1830–1916): Emperor of Austria, 1848–1916. His political ideas were formed during the autocratic regime of Schwarzenberg (q.v.), He was determined to preserve the power of Austria but presided over the collapse of Austrian power in both Italy and Germany. In 1867 Austria was transformed into the Dual monarchy of Austria-Hungary.

Frederick III (1831–1888): Fought with distinction in the Schleswig, Austro-Prussian and Franco-Prussian wars. He married Princess Victoria, the daughter of Queen Victoria, and was a great admirer of the British constitution, as well as having close links with the German Liberals. On the death of William I, Frederick, having by then been the Crown Prince for twenty-seven years, ascended the throne for a mere 99 days as he was suffering from cancer of the larynx. He died on 15 June 1888.

Frederick William III (1770–1840): The historian James Sheehan describes him 'at best an ordinary man, who found himself living in extraordinary times'. Before 1806 he attempted to acquire territory by negotiating with the French, but this policy ended in ruins when Prussia entered the war against France and was defeated at Jena. He gave only half-hearted support to the Reform Party in Prussia and played a relatively minor part in the war and subsequent peace negotiations of 1813–15. Thereafter he cooperated closely with Austria to enforce the settlement of 1815.

Frederick William IV (1795–1861): Because of his interests in neo-gothic architecture and his old-fashioned political values he was known as 'the romantic upon the throne'. Although he bitterly opposed constitutional reform, he quickly surrendered to the demands of the revolution in 1848, but by the autumn he was already moving to reverse these concessions. He refused to accept the crown of a united Germany from the Frankfurt parliament but he did support plans by his foreign minister, Joseph Radowitz (q.v.), for creating a Prussian led *Kleindeutschland*. He was forced by Austria to give this up in 1850 and to agree to the restoration of the Confederation. Until 1858 he pursued a determinedly counter-revolutionary policy in Prussia, when he was incapacitated by a stroke.

Gentz, Friedrich (1764–1832): German political journalist, writer and confidential adviser of Metternich.

Giers, Nicholas de (1820–1895): Russian foreign minister during the reign of Alexander III. He attempted to establish more friendly relations with the cabinets of Berlin, Vienna and Rome. However, when the Reinsurance Treaty lapsed in 1890, he played a key part in negotiating the Franco-Russian Alliance.

Goltz, Robert Heinrich Ludwig von der (1817–1869): Prussian civil servant and diplomat. He was Bismarck's successor both at St Petersburg and then Paris as Prussian ambassador.

Gramont, Antoine, Duke of (1819–1880): French diplomat and statesman whose belligerent attitudes as foreign minister in 1870 helped push France into a disastrous war with Prussia.

Guizot, François (1787–1874): French historian, orator, and statesman. He was prime minister from September 1847 to February 1848, and outraged the French Liberals by refusing to extend the franchise or reform the political system.

Helldorf-Bedra, Otto Heinrich von (1833–1908): Leader of the German Conservatives in the *Reichstag*.

Herder, Gottfried von (1774–1803): Court preacher at Weimar, teacher, theologian, philosopher and philologist.

Hohenlohe, Prince Chlodwig zu Hohenlohe–Schillingfurst (1819–1901): Bavarian aristocrat, who had, as a younger man, worked in the Prussian civil service. After the defeat of Bavaria in 1866, he became minister-president in Munich and attempted to Prussianize Bavaria. In 1873 he became German ambassador in Paris, and in 1885 Governor of Alsace-Lorraine. He was *Reich* chancellor, 1894–1900.

Isabella II, Queen of Spain (1830–1904): Queen of Spain 1833–68. Liberal opposition to her authoritarianism, scandalous reports about her private life, and her arbitrary political interference led to the revolution of 1868, which drove her into exile in Paris.

Kotzebue, August von (1761–1831): German dramatist and man of letters. In 1816 he was attached to the Russian foreign ministry and sent to Mannheim from where he reported on German affairs to Russia.

Kusserow, Heinrich von (1836–1900): Prussian and then later *Reich* diplomat, as well as a Liberal deputy in the *Reichstag* (1871–74). In 1885 he was put in charge of the colonial department of the foreign office, but his unbridled enthusiasm for colonies soon irritated Bismarck, who then sent him as Prussian envoy to the Hansa cities and the Mecklenburgs.

Lagarde, Paul de (1827–1891): German Biblical scholar and orientalist. He was also active in politics. He belonged to the Prussian Conservative party, and was a violent anti-Semite. His *Deutsche Schriften* (1878–81) became a nationalist text.

Lasker, Eduard (1829–1884): As a student he took part in the October uprising in Vienna, 1848. After studying law he then entered the Prussian judicial service. In 1865 he was elected to the Prussian *Landtag* and joined the Progressive party. In 1867 he played a key part in the formation of the National Liberal Party. In 1880 he joined the Seccession, but died in New York in 1884.

Lassalle, Ferdinand (1825–1864): Descended from a prosperous Jewish family. He was imprisoned in 1849 for his part in the revolution in Düsseldorf. In May 1863 he founded the General German Workers' Association.

Leo XIII (1810–1903): Pope from1878 to 1903 in succession to Pope Pius IX. In contrast to the latter he sought to modernize the thinking of the

Roman Catholic Church and come to terms with the modern world. Hence his desire to end the *Kulturkampf*.

Leopold, Prince of Hohenzollern (1835–1905): Head of the Swabian branch of the House of Hohenzollern. In 1861 he had married Antonia of Portugal, daughter of Queen Maria II of Portugal. After the Spanish Revolution of 1868 that overthrew Queen Isabella II, Leopold was offered the Spanish crown by the new government. This offer was supported by the Prussian prime minister, Bismarck, but opposed by the French emperor, Napoleon III, which led to Leopold declining the offer.

Louis-Philippe I (1773–1850): Called himself 'King of the French' from 1830 to 1848 in what was known as the July Monarchy.

Lüderitz, Franz Adolf (1834–1886): Born in Bremen, where he was a tobacco importer with his father. In 1881, he established a factory at Lagos, and in 1883 acquired land in southwest Africa which he placed under the protection of the German Empire in 1884. He drowned in the Orange River in 1886.

Ludwig II (1845–1886): King of Bavaria from 1864 until shortly before his death. He was as an eccentric whose main interest was the history of art and architecture, and he commissioned the construction of several extravagant fantasy castles.

Manteuffel, Edwin Freiherr von (1809–1885): Cousin of the Prussian statesman, Otto von Manteuffel. He entered the Prussian army in 1827. He became the aide de camp to Frederick William IV. In 1857 he was promoted to major general and chief of the Prussian Military Cabinet. He strongly supported William's plans for the reorganization of the army and was bitterly attacked by the Progressive Liberal Karl von Twesten, whom he challenged to a duel. He served in the Danish, Austrian and French campaigns. From June 1871 to 1873 he commanded the army of occupation in northern France. He was promoted to field marshal, and in 1879 became Governor-General of Alsace-Lorraine.

Metternich, Prince Clemens von (1773–1859): Originally a Rhinelander, who became an Austrian diplomat. In 1809 he was appointed Austrian foreign minister. At first he hoped to come to terms with Napoleon and so avoid having to introduce radical reforms at home, as Prussia had been compelled to do. In 1813 he belatedly joined the alliance against France, and a year later presided brilliantly over the Congress of Vienna (1814–15) where he witnessed the triumph of his conservative policies of monarchical restoration and defensive alliances against aggression and revolution. He became Austrian chancellor in 1821 and, until forced to resign in 1848, he used his formidable skills to defend the 1815 settlement.

Miquel, Johannes (1829–1901): Initially a member of the Communist League, but by the 1850s he had become a Liberal. He was a founding member of the *Nationalverein* and was elected to the Hanoverian *Landtag* in 1864. In 1867 he won a seat in the Prussian *Landtag*, but it was not until 1887 that he entered the *Reichstag*. Three years later he became Prussian finance minister. He had been both Mayor of Osnabrück (1865–70 and 1876–79) and Lord Mayor of Frankfurt (1879).

Moltke, Field-Marshal Helmuth von (1800–1891): Entered the Prussian army in 1822, and became chief of the Prussian General Staff in 1857. In collaboration with Roon (q.v.) and Bismarck he radically reorganized the Prussian army. He was responsible for the strategic planning of the Danish, Austrian and French campaigns. From 1870 to 1888 he was the chief of the Great German General staff.

Motteler, Julius (1838–1907): One of the founding members of the SPD in 1875. He became a *Reichstag* deputy and in 1879, as a result of the Anti-Socialist Law, emigrated to Zurich where he organized the smuggling of banned SPD literature into the *Reich*. When under pressure from Bismarck, the Swiss expelled him, he fled to London. From 1903–07 he again became a *Reichstag* deputy.

Napoleon III (1803–1871): Nephew of Napoleon I. President of the Third Republic, 1848–52. On 2 December 1851 he extended his presidential power through a *coup d'état* and a year later declared himself Emperor. Like Bismarck in 1867, he introduced universal manhood suffrage. Until the late 1860s the French Chamber had little power, and Napoleon consolidated his regime by appealing to the bourgeoisie, exploiting nationalism and appeasing the working classes with welfare reforms. In many ways his domestic policies served as a model for Bismarck.

Obruchev, General-Adjutant Nikolai (1830–1904): Military statistician, planner and chief of the Imperial Russian General Staff. He played a major role in planning for the Russo-Turkish War of 1877–78.

Peters, Carl (1856–1918): German explorer, journalist and philosopher, instrumental in the founding of German East Africa and helped trigger the European 'Scramble for Africa'. He founded the Society for German Colonization in 1884. In 1891 he was appointed *Reichskommissar* for German East Africa but his brutal action against the local population provoked an uprising. He was recalled to Berlin and in 1887 found guilty of misusing official power in East Africa.

Pius IX (1792–1878): Pope from June 1846 until his death. He convened the First Vatican Council in 1869, which decreed Papal infallibility. He was hostile to Italian unity and looked to France for protection against Italian nationalism. In 1864 he published the *Syllabus Errorum*, which was deeply critical of contemporary liberalism.

Radowitz, General Joseph von (1797–1853): Conservative Prussian statesman and leader of the political Right in the Frankfurt parliament. He was a close friend of Friedrich William IV (q.v.) and is best known for his proposal to unify Germany under Prussian leadership by means of a negotiated agreement among the reigning German princes – the Radowitz Plan. In September 1851 he was appointed minister of foreign affairs, but resigned in November, owing to the king's refusal to go to war with Austria.

Richter, Eugen (1838–1906): German politician and journalist. Entered the *Reichstag* in 1867 as a member of the Progressives, and from 1869 he was also a member of the Prussian Lower House. He was a bitter critic of Bismarck and from 1884 led the *Deutsche Freisinnige Partei*.

Roon, General Albrecht Graf von (1803–1879): Joined the Prussian army in 1816 as a cadet, and in 1835 entered the General Staff. In 1848 he served under Prince William and played a key role in suppressing the disturbances in Baden. Once William became Regent, Roon was appointed as a member of a Commission to report on the reorganization of the army. In 1859 he became Prussian minister of war and introduced the Army bill to modernize the Prussian armed forces. This ran into opposition from the Liberals, and on Roon's advice Bismarck was appointed to implement it. Roon served under the command of Moltke (q.v.) in the Austro-Prussian war and was in attendance on King William in the Franco-Prussian war. He was briefly prime minister of Prussia 1871–72 and was promoted to field marshal in 1873.

Schleiermacher, Friedrich (1769–1834): Philosopher and protestant theologian.

Schulze-Delitzsch, Hermann von (1808–1883): German Liberal politician and economist. He was a member of the Prussian *Landtag* from 1861, of the North German *Reichstag* from 1867, and of the German *Reichstag* from 1871 until his death.

Schwarzenberg, Felix Fürst zu (1800–1852): Austrian minister-president and foreign minister 1848–52. Advised Franz Joseph I during the introduction of Neo-absolutism, and through the Olmütz Agreement of 1850 re-established the German Confederation.

Skobelev, General Mikhail (1843–1882): Charismatic Russian general, famous for his conquest of Central Asia and heroism during the Russo-Turkish War of 1877–78.

Stahl, Friedrich Julius (1802–1861): Lawyer, politician and conservative philosopher. He was born in Munich, of Jewish parentage.

Stoecker, Adolf (1835–1909): Chaplain to the Imperial Court, *Reichstag* and Prussian *Landtag* deputy. He was fanatically anti-Semitic and founded the Christian Social Workers' Party in 1878, renamed the Christian Social Party in 1881.

Strousberg, Bethel (1823–1884): Jewish industrialist and railway entrepreneur. In 1872, he was forced into liquidation after a ruinous settlement with the Romanian government on account of unfulfilled railway contracts and was declared bankrupt in 1875.

Treitschke, Heinrich von (1834–1896): Strong advocate of a *Kleindeutschland* led by Prussia. In 1871 he was appointed Professor of History at Berlin University. He sat as a National Liberal in the *Reichstag* and became an ardent supporter of Bismarck and German imperialism. His major work was *The History of Germany in the Nineteenth Century* in which he strongly criticized Austria and the south German states.

Waldersee, Field Marshal Alfred Graf von (1832–1904): Chief of the Imperial German General Staff from 1888 to 1891.

Weber, Maximilian (1864–1920): German lawyer, politician, historian, and one of the founding fathers of sociology.

William 1 (1797–1888): Frederick William IV's younger brother. He was a bitter enemy of the 1848 revolutionaries and highly critical of the Olmütz agreement. In 1858 he became regent as a result of his brother's stroke. He appointed a Liberal ministry and the Liberals became the dominant party in the *Landtag*. However William's ambition was to reform the army. When these reforms were opposed by the Liberals, he was prepared to violate the constitution to raise the necessary money to finance the reform and expansion of the army, 1861–62. He appointed Bismarck minister-president to carry out this policy. Thereafter William supported him in his domestic and foreign policies until he died in 1888.

Windthorst, Ludwig (1812–1891): Studied law and became minister of justice in the Hanoverian government. He was an opponent of *kleindeutsch* nationalism and leader of the Centre Party until 1890. He attempted to create an alliance between German Catholics, the Polish, Danish and Alsatian ethnic minorities and the Guelphs, who were all opponents of a Prussian-led *Kleindeutschland*. He was a brilliant debater and could more that hold his own with Bismarck in the *Reichstag*.

Wirth, Johann (1798–1848): Lawyer, German nationalist and writer.

Glossary

Agrarian League: Extra-parliamentary organization founded in 1893. Formed to combat the free-trade policies of Chancellor Caprivi.

Bielefeld school of historiography: Based at Bielefeld University, where H.J. Wehler was Professor of History, 1971–96. This is one of the leading historical centres of structuralism in Germany.

Bundesrat: Federal Council or upper house of the German parliament in which the German states were represented according to their size and power.

Confederation: Union of individual states in which the independence of each state is preserved, as in the German Confederation. It contrasts with a federation (Q.V.).

Constituent Reichstag: Parliament elected to draw up and approve a constitution.

Corporatism: The attempt to defuse class hatred and unify society by giving both employers and workers a joint role in the running of welfare agencies, industry, etc. In the 1930s Mussolini attempted to create a corporate state in Italy.

Cortes: The Spanish Parliament.

Deutsche Freisinnige Partei (Freisinn): The German Free Thought Party formed from the Progressives and Liberal Union, 1884 (the former Seccessionists).

Deutsche Reformverein: Founded in reaction to the *Nationalverein* on 26 October 1862 to campaign for the creation of a *Grossdeutschland*. It had a membership of about 1500.

East Elbian: Germany east of the Elbe: a predominantly rural area dominated by the great estates owned by the *Junkers*.

Eastern Question: The diplomatic and political problems caused by the decay of the Turkish Empire.

Entente: Friendly understanding between two states.

Federation: A system of government in which several states or regions form a unity but still manage to remain self-governing in internal affairs.

Free Conservative Party: Fifteen deputies broke from the Conservative Party in July 1866 and supported Bismarck's policy of reconciliation with the Liberals. This group became known as the Free Conservatives. The Party won 39 seats in the elections of 1867 to the North German Constituent *Reichstag*.

The German Confederation (Bund): Created in 1815 by the Vienna Settlement and dissolved in 1867 after Prussia's defeat of Austria.

Grossdeutschland: A united Germany including the German-speaking countries of the Austrian Empire.

Gründerjahre: The years when the Second *Reich* was established, circa 1871–73. These were characterized by rapid economic expansion, stocks and shares boom and subsequent crash.

Guelph: The family name of the ruling house of Hanover, which was deposed in 1866 by Bismarck. The Guelph Party was a Hanoverian particularist party.

Holy Roman Empire: Originally composed of the German and north Italian Territories of Otto I who was crowned Emperor by the Pope in 962. From 1273 onwards the Empire was increasingly dominated by the Habsburgs. It was dissolved in 1806 by Napoleon.

Hohenzollern monarchy: Ruling dynasty of Kingdom of Prussia, and then Germany, 1701–1918.

Iron budget: The military budget for Prussia's and, after 1871 Germany's, armed forces.

Joint stock company: A corporation or business partnership involving two or more legal persons. Certificates of part ownership (shares) are issued by the company in return for each financial contribution, which the shareholders are free to sell.

Junker: Prussian nobleman and landowner.

Kaiser: Emperor of Germany.

Kartell: Cartel or manufacturers' association to control and regulate production. Also an alliance of political parties.

Kleindeutschland: United Germany without Austria.

Kolonialverein: Colonial Association founded in 1882. Its membership was roughly about 15,000 and was drawn mainly from political, financial and commercial circles.

Kulturkampf: Struggle between cultures. A term used to describe Bismarck's conflict with the Catholic Church, 1872–87.

Landtag(e): Elected assembly(ies) at the level of the individual German states.

Landwehr: Set up in February 1813 to comprise all men not serving in the regular army. In 1815 the *Landwehr* was reorganized to amalgamate with the regular army, but in peacetime keep its character as a militia. Increasingly the Liberals saw it in the words of General Leopold von Boyen 'the happy union of the warrior and civilian society'.

Laissez-faire: Policies which seek to minimize or eliminate all aspects of government intervention in the economy.

Left Centre: Sometimes called the Bockum-Dolffs Caucus from the name of its leader. Composed of moderate Liberals, mainly from the Rhineland.

Liberalism: Belief in national self-determination, constitutional government, individual and economic freedom.

Liberum veto: The right to veto.

Manchesterism: General term for the political, economic and social movements of the nineteenth century that originated in Manchester, such as free trade and liberalism.

Matricular contribution: Fixed contribution paid by the German states to the central government. The term comes originally from the Holy Roman Empire where member states were given a list of money and troops to be supplied annually.

Mittelstaaten: The medium-sized states in the German Confederation: Bavaria, Württemberg, Baden, Hessen-Darmstadt, Saxony and Hanover. Their attempts to form an independent third force or Trias between Prussia and Austria proved unsuccessful.

Mitrailleuse: First machine-gun to be used in major combat, during the Franco-Prussian War of 1870–71.

National Liberal Party: Founded in 1867, its membership was drawn from the propertied and educated elite of German society. It's most influential period was 1867–79 when it cooperated with Bismarck as his chief parliamentary ally. In 1879 he broke with it over the tariff question and the demands of the party's leaders for a greater participation in government. It was weakened by the defection of the South German protectionists and then in 1880 by the secession of the party's liberal wing. In 1884 it announced in the Heidelberg Declaration its readiness to cooperate with the government. It participated in *Kartell*, 1897–90.

Nationalism: In Germany from 1815 until 1890 nationalism took on several different forms varying from a sense of linguistic and cultural identity to the desire for political union. In the 1880s it was increasingly metamorphosing into an aggressive imperialism aimed at making Germany a colonial power.

Nationalverein: The National Association, founded in 1859.

Neo-absolutist regime: An autocratic system of government as established by Schwarzenberg in Austria in 1849.

'*New orthodoxy*': Name given to historical interpretation of the Second *Reich*, which was adopted by Hans-Ulrich Wehler (see Bielefeld school) and other historians, arguing that the key to understanding Bismarckian Germany was that it had industrialized without undergoing a 'bourgeois revolution'.

Old Liberals: In late June 1849 after the dissolution of the Frankfurt Parliament a group of moderate Liberals met in Gotha. They concluded that the unification of Germany was more important than the 'form' of its attainment. In other words they supported the use of Prussian power to secure unification. By 1861 they were known as the 'Constitutionalists'.

Pan-German League: An extremist political pressure group which was officially founded in 1891. Its members believed in the unification of all Germans in Europe within one state. Consequently for the Pan-German League the unification of 1871 was just a starting point.

Pan Slav: Initially a programme based on the brotherhood of Slav nations, and then increasingly synonymous with Greater Russian nationalism.

Pints: Pre-metric measurement primarily for liquids, but was also used for dry substances such as potatoes.

Pograms: Organized attacks on Jewish settlements in Russia.

Political particularism: The principle that each state should have the maximum independence within the German Confederation.

Progressive Party: The German Progressive Party was founded in 1861 in Prussia. Its programme was both liberal and national.

Rapprochement: Establishing harmonious relations between two states.

Reich: The German Empire or state after 1871.

Reichstag: The lower house of the North German Confederation (1867–1870) and of the German *Reich*, 1867–1945.

Reichsbank: The German Central Bank, 1875–1945, responsible for the issue of currency.

Reichsfeinde: Enemies of the state.

Reichsfreunde: Friends of the state.

Sammlung: A concentration or coalition of forces and groups.

Sacraments: The core of Catholic teaching is the seven sacraments: Baptism, Confirmation, Eucharist, Penance, Anointing of the Sick, Holy Orders, and Matrimony.

Seccession: The break-away of twenty-seven *Reichstag* deputies led by Lasker in 1880 from the National Liberals. Later known as the 'Liberal Union'.

Septennat: Septennial military (or iron) budget.

Sonderweg: Literally unique path or development. Scholars such as Hans-Ulrich Wehler, using Britain and France as models, have argued that industrialization in Germany was not accompanied by 'modernization or democratization'. Hence Germany took its own 'special path'. This is disputed, especially by historians D. Blackbourne and G. Eley.

SPD (Sozialdemokratische Partei Deutschlands): The German Social Democratic Party was formed through the amalgamation of Ferdinand Lassalle's General German Workers' Association and Bebel's Social Democratic Workers' Party at the unity congress at Gotha in 1875. Despite Bismarck's Anti-Socialist Law, the SPD survived to become the largest party in the *Reichstag* in 1912.

Staatsstreich: A *coup d'état*.

Tariffs: Taxes placed on imported goods to protect the home economy.

Three class voting system: Remained in place until 1918. The voters were not divided by estate or class, but by the amount of taxes they paid. In 1849 4.7% belonged to the first category, 12.6% to the second and 82.7% to the third. Each class chose a third of the electors, who in turn chose the actual delegates. The voting system did not necessarily guarantee conservative majority. In the 1860s liberal majorities were regularly returned.

Ultramontane: Political party in favour of the absolute spiritual authority of the pope.

Volk: A people sharing a common ethnic origin, language and culture, but not necessarily belonging to the same state.

Weltpolitik: Literally world policy; in other words, a global pursuit of German political interests and the intention to create a colonial empire.

Wilhelmsstrasse: The German equivalent to Whitehall in London, the centre of government in Berlin.

Zentrum: (Centre Party) Founded by Ludwig Windhorst to defend Catholic interests in a united and predominantly Protestant country. It survived the *Kulturkampf* strengthened.

Zollverein: The German Customs Union formed in 1833 with a membership of eighteen states. By 1852 only the two Mecklenburgs, the Hansa cities and Holstein remained outside. The Austrian Empire, however, remained excluded.

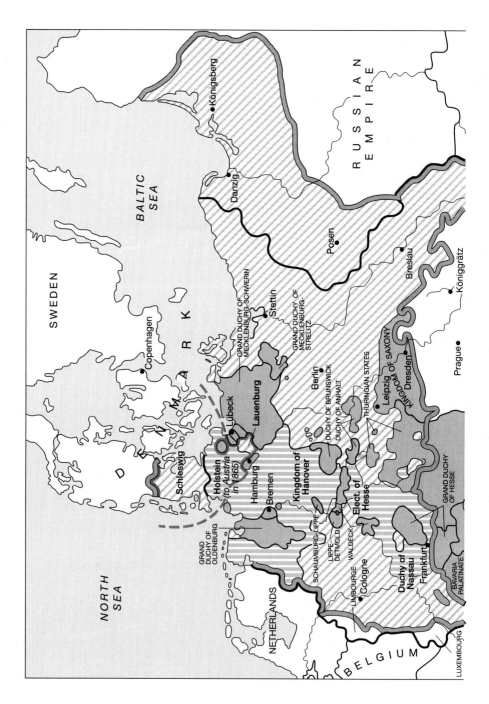

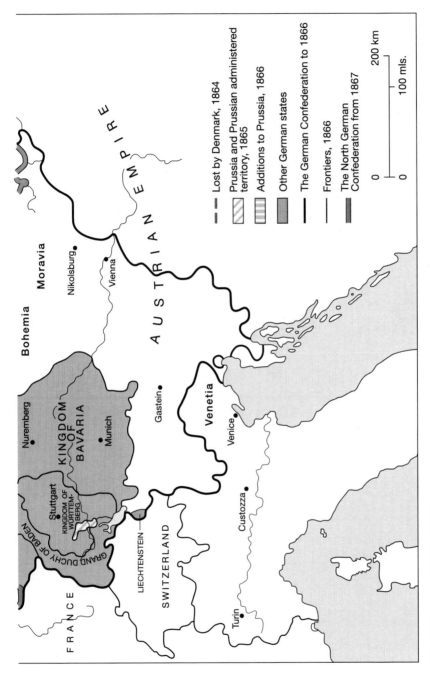

Map 1 Germany 1864–1866

Lost by Denmark, 1864

Prussia and Prussian administered territory, 1865

Additions to Prussia, 1866

Other German states

The German Confederation to 1866

Frontiers, 1866

The North German Confederation from 1867

200 km

100 mls.

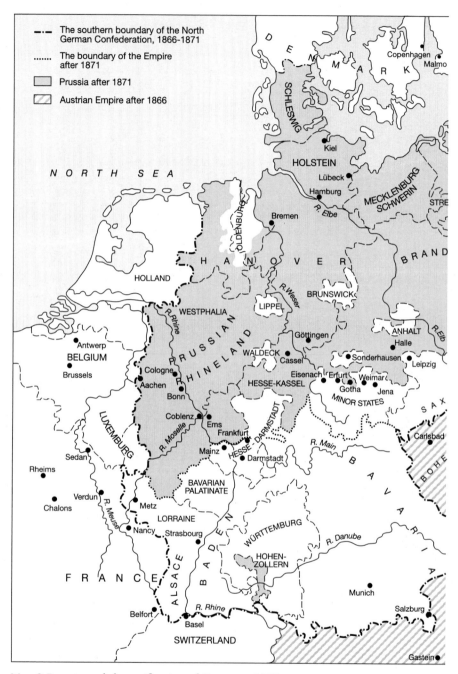

Map 2 Prussia and the unification of Germany, 1871

Source: H.W. Koch, *A History of Prussia*, Longman, 1978, with permission of Pearson Education Ltd

SWEDEN

BALTIC SEA

● Memel

● Königsberg

POMERANIA

Danzig ●

EAST PRUSSIA

WEST PRUSSIA

LITZ

P

● Stettin

ENBURG

● Berlin

POSEN

R. Vistula

● Warsaw

RUSSIAN POLAND

● Breslau

SILESIA

● Dresden

MIA

ONY

● Teplitz

Sadowa ● ● Königgrätz

● Prague

Troppau ●

GALICIA

MORAVIA

● Olmütz

A U S T R I A

Nikolsburg ●

H U N G A R Y

Pressburg ●

● Vienna

R. Danube

Buda ●● Pest

| 0 | | 100 km. |
| 0 | | 100 mls. |

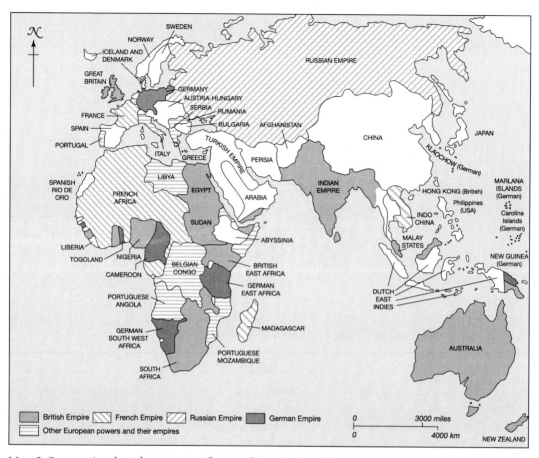

Map 3 Germany's colonial empire in Africa and Asia (adapted from M. Gilbert, *Recent History Atlas, 1860–1960*, Weidenfeld & Nicolson, 1966, p. 23, with permission of A P Watt Ltd on behalf of Sir Martin Gilbert)

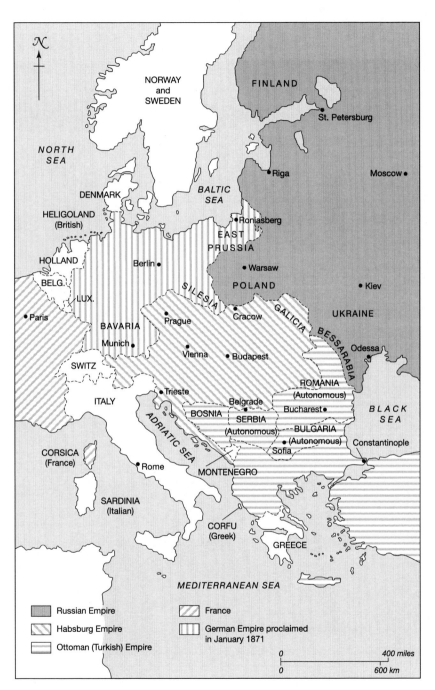

Map 4 Central and eastern Europe in 1871

Part 1

THE SETTING

1

The Background, 1815–1862

THE GERMAN CONFEDERATION

After the destruction of the **Holy Roman Empire** by Napoleon in 1806 and the collapse of subsequent French attempts to reorganize central Europe in 1814 when the Napoleonic armies were driven back over the French frontiers, the Great Powers created at the Congress of Vienna in 1815 the German Confederation. This reorganized German Central Europe into a confederation of 39 states dominated by Austria and Prussia, which was to survive until its destruction at the hands of Bismarck in 1866.

Apart from Austria and Prussia, the most important members of the **Confederation** were the *Mittelstaaten*, the medium-sized states of Saxony Bavaria, Hanover, Württemberg and the Grand Duchies of Hessen and Baden. The great majority of states, including the four city states of Hamburg, Bremen, Lübeck and Frankfurt were small territorial units. Twenty-one of the member states had populations of under 100,000, while Liechenstein had a population of barely 5000.

The prime aim of the German Confederation was to safeguard the internal and external security of each member state. It had only one statutory institution – the Diet – in which each state was represented by its ambassador. This, however only met when there were important matters to discuss, such as constitutional reform or security. Day-to-day business was dealt with in the *Engerer Rat*, a small standing committee in which 17 votes were distributed amongst the 39 states.

It soon became clear that the Confederation was an intensely conservative organization. Neither Prince Metternich of Austin nor Frederick William III, King of Prussia, were prepared to see it evolve into an effective **federation**. This betrayal of the national ideal (see page **6**) led to protests by students and intellectuals and to the assassination of August von Kotzebue, a political agent employed by the Russian legation in Mannheim in 1819. Metternich, with Prussian support, seized the chance to announce a series of repressive

Holy Roman Empire Original composed of the German and north Italian territories of OTTOI, who was crowned Emperor by the Pope in 962. From 1273 onwards the Empire was increasingly dominated by the Habsburgs.

Confederation Union of individual states in which the independence of each state is preserved.

Mittelstaaten The medium-sized states in the German Confederation.

Federation A system of government in which several states or regions form a unity but still manage to remain self-governing in internal affairs.

decrees and at a specially summoned conference at Karlsbad, which he then represented as a fait accompli to the Confederation. Until the revolutions of 1848 the Confederation became what James Sheehan has called 'a kind of counter revolutionary holding company through which Metternich could coordinate governmental action against his political enemies' (Sheehan, 1989: 409) [**Doc. 1, p. 120**].

Until 1848 the Confederation was effectively dominated by the dual hegemony of Austria and Prussia. As long as the two states cooperated and Prussia did not challenge Austria's Presidency of the Diet, their power could not be challenged, but their hegemony rested on the uneasy balance, which was only workable as long as Prussia had no ambition to dominate Germany.

Austro-Prussian cooperation tended to mask the fact that Prussia was best placed to seize the leadership of Germany. Brendan Simms goes so far as to claim that in the longer term 'the new geopolitical configuration of Central Europe after 1815 almost predetermined Prussia's victory in the struggle for mastery in Germany' (Simms, 1998: 116). Unlike Austria, Prussia had no interests in Italy or the Balkans. The Rhineland territory she acquired at the Congress of Vienna gave her a vital interest in defending western Germany and in creating a customs union which would knit together economically her western and eastern territories. In both these areas Prussian interests converged increasingly not only with the emerging national movement but also with the economic and defensive needs of the *Mittelstaaten*.

THE *ZOLLVEREIN*

In 1815 German trade was crippled by the lack of free movement. Each state levied its own tariffs. For instance, merchants moving goods from the Swiss frontier to Berlin faced ten sets of **tariffs** and transit dues. The negotiation of a customs union should have been one of the initial tasks of the Confederation, but **political particularism** and widely divergent economies of the different states ensured that no progress was made.

Tariffs Taxes placed on imported goods to protect the home economy.

Political particularism The principle that each state should have the maximum independence within the German Confederation.

The only option at first was for groups of states within the Confederation to negotiate regional customs unions. Prussia with its new western territories separated from its heartlands in the east had a 7500 km customs boundary studded with small enclaves belonging to other states. To remedy this, Prussia introduced in 1818 a law aiming to create an integrated Prussian customs system and to force the small states surrounded by Prussian territory to join. Over the next fifteen years Prussia, through a mixture of threats and concessions, managed to go far towards creating what can be called a 'separate confederation with regard to customs policy' (Nipperdey, 1996:

316). In 1833 the **Zollverein** came into being and by 1842 only eleven German states (not counting Austria) were not included in the union.

Metternich viewed these events with alarm, and warned the Emperor that there was being created 'a smaller rival confederation . . . which all too quickly will become accustomed to following its own objectives with its own means' (Wehler, 1996: 131). In 1841 he even urged Austria's entry into the Zollverein, but fear of Prussian economic competition and the divisive effects on the Austrian Empire of excluding her non-German Habsburg territories from entry ensured that nothing came of this initiative.

The Zollverein has 'long played an almost mythical role in explanations of Prussia's eventual rise to political and economic supremacy in Germany' (Voth, 2001: 110). The nationalist historian Treitschke saw it as heralding the ultimate conflict between Austria and Prussia, which ended on the field of Königgrätz – a view largely echoed by post-1945 West German historians such as Böhme who saw it as the economic blueprint for a united Germany (Böhme, 1966). The Zollverein certainly increased Prussian influence over the other German states, and isolated Austria economically within the Confederation, but *politically* it did not forge a united Germany. In 1866 most of the smaller German states joined Austria against Prussia (see page **37**), and it was only the Prussian defeat of Austria at the battle of Königgrätz that enabled Bismarck to destroy the Confederation and drive Austria from Germany.

Zollverein The German Customs Union formed in 1833 with a membership of eighteen states. By 1853 only the two Mecklenburgs, the Hansa cities and Holstein remained outside. The Austrian Empire, however, remained excluded.

THE GROWTH OF GERMAN NATIONALISM

At the end of the eighteenth century there was no single concept of German **nationalism**. Some German intellectuals identified Germany with the old Holy Roman Empire, others like Johann Herder perceived Germany to be primarily a cultural nation defined by its literature and language. It was the defeat of Prussia and Austria and occupation by the French, 1806–13, that gave birth to the German nationalist movement, but even then there was no uniform 'national' reaction against the French occupation. Some Germans looked to the Rhineland Confederation, which Napoleon had formed in 1806 as a future nucleus for the 'German nation'. The more conservative minded patriots, such as Friedrich Gentz, were drawn to Vienna, while others were attracted by appeals for an uprising of the German **Volk** against the French invader that were persuasively articulated in Berlin by the philosopher, J.G. Fichte. The theologian, Friedrich Schleiermacher, and liberal man of letters, Ernst Arndt, also began to call for the creation of a nation state. The latter, with his call for a single monarchical German state

Nationalism In Germany from 1815 until 1890 nationalism took on several different forms varying from a sense of linguistic and cultural identity to the desire for political union. In the 1880s it was increasingly metamorphosing into an aggressive imperialism aimed at making Germany a colonial power.

Volk A people sharing a common ethnic origin, language and culture, but not necessarily belonging to the same state.

with its own army, laws and parliament anticipated the ideal of the nineteenth-century German liberals.

How much public support was there in reality for these ideas? Much of the German population in the Rhineland Confederation remained loyal to the French, or at least lukewarm towards their liberators in 1813–14. In March 1813 when Prussia declared war on France, attempts were made to harness the new wave of patriotism, but in reality Frederick William was interested primarily in Prussian rather than German patriotism. As Sheehan has pointed out 'the *Volk*'s role in its own "liberation" was, at best, a minor one. Napoleon was defeated by regular armies, not patriotic poets and quaintly attired gymnasts' (Sheehan, 1989: 398). In retrospect, however, the War of Liberation of 1813–14 became a powerful myth, which inspired later generations of nationalists.

After the War of Liberation and the disappointments of the Vienna settlement of 1815, the ambitions of the nationalist movement were initially kept alive by the gymnastic societies and the student fraternities (*Burschenschaften*). The former set out deliberately to encourage a feeling of Germanness and managed to win the loyalty of a whole generation of school and university students. By 1820 there were 150 different gymnastic societies, with 12,000 members. In many ways they were 'the prototype of a political party' (Nipperdey, 1996: 244), and pioneered the rally and mass public meeting as a new form of public event. The latter, which were formed at the universities to create a new pan-German ethos of friendship and honour, were nationalist and liberal in orientation. [**Doc. 1, p. 120**]. The young Bismarck himself briefly joined one of these radical fraternities at Göttingen university in 1832.

This first phase of nationalist agitation was brought to an end by the Karlsbad Decrees (see page **4**), but Metternich did not succeed in stamping out the nationalist message. German nationalism was part of a powerful pan-European and even American movement. It was thus inspired and so strengthened by both the example of the Greek uprising against the Turks in the 1820s and the Polish revolt of 1830 in Russian Poland. The threat of a French invasion of the Rhineland in 1840 also triggered a large-scale nationalist reaction, the spirit of which was caught by Nikolas Becker's Rhineland song, *Der deutsche Rhein*, which was sung to over 200 different tunes throughout Germany. Similarly the ongoing threat by the Danish crown to integrate the Duchies of Schleswig into the Danish state (see page **28**) caused growing concern amongst the German nationalists. In July 1844 12,000 people flocked to the Schleswig-Holstein singing festival and the 'battle hymn' *Schleswig-Holstein meerumschlungen*' (Schlewig-Holstein embraced by the sea) became as popular as the Rhineland song. By 1848 about 250,000 Germans were organized in various nationalist organizations.

Thanks to the improvement in communications, the press and the increasingly frequent inter-regional festivals their tentacles had spread throughout Germany.

THE GROWTH OF LIBERALISM

Up to the 1870s, at least, nationalism belonged, as Hans-Ulrich Wehler puts it with **Liberalism** 'like a pair together' (Wehler, 1996: 397). Both Liberalism and Nationalism desired a united self-governing Germany. Liberalism was strongest in south Germany, where local *Landtage* gave Liberal politicians a platform for their views. In the aftermath of the French revolution of 1830 the Liberals in Brunswick, Hesse-Kassel, Saxony and Hanover were able to exploit local disturbances and fear of the mob to persuade the rulers to grant constitutions. In the Palatinate the journalist, Johann Wirth, set up the *Presseverein* (press union) as a pressure group to campaign for liberal ideals throughout German speaking Europe. By 1832 it had already had five thousand members and over a hundred branches in Bavaria. In May it organized a large-scale 'political festival' in the ruins of the old castle near Hambach, which inspired a series of similar meetings throughout Germany. Its organizers called for a united liberal and democratic Germany, but more radical proposals to create a revolutionary committee to work towards unification were rejected as being too utopian.

Liberalism Belief in national self-determination, constitutional government, individual and economic freedom.

Landtag(e) Elected assembly(ies) at the level of the individual German states.

By 1840 Liberalism was becoming a popular movement and its division into a left and right wing was becoming discernible. Its left wing was increasingly pressing for a strong parliamentary system in which the state would of necessity bow to parliament, while right-wing liberals were more pragmatic and looked to the state as a potential ally against too disruptive a pace of economic and social change.

CONSERVATIVE ACCEPTANCE OF NATIONALISM

Initially it appeared that Conservatism was doomed to remain a reactionary anti-modernist movement totally opposed to the development of nationalism and the modern state. Yet by the 1840s there were signs that these two traditional enemies were drawing closer to each other. The conservative philosopher, Friedrich Stahl, recognized the need for a constitution and a elected parliament, provided that the Crown still actually determined policy.

Joseph von Radowitz, the councillor and friend of Freidrich Wilhelm IV of Prussia was also beginning to argue that to survive, the Prussian monarchy and state needed to accept the 'idea of nationality [which] was the most powerful force of the present time' (Nipperdey, 1996: 336).

CATHOLICISM AND NATIONALISM

There was considerable tension between Catholicism and Nationalism. The Catholic paper, *Historische-politische Blätter*, observed that there was 'a vastly more profound bond' between a Catholic German and a Catholic African than between the latter and a German atheist (Nipperdey, 1996: 243). The Catholics also distrusted Prussia and instinctively looked to Catholic Vienna rather than to Protestant Berlin to take the lead in German affairs.

After the French Revolution the Catholic Church became fiercely critical of the claims of the modern state and liberal individualism. As early as the 1830s small groups of Catholic deputies began to join forces in the south German *Landtage*, but it was the arrest of the Archbishop of Cologne in 1838 by the Prussian authorities for opposing regulations on mixed marriages between Protestants and Catholics that acted as a catalyst for the development of Catholicism as a political force. Political Catholicism was in itself a coalition of forces. On the one hand there were the Conservatives, who regarded unquestioning faith in the institutions of the Catholic Church as the key to opposing liberalism. On the other hand there were Catholics, mainly in the Rhineland, who supported liberal demands for individual freedom and a constitution, while there was also a growth in social Catholicism, which urged controls on *laissez-faire* capitalism.

Laissez-faire Policies which seek to minimize or eliminate all aspects of government intervention in the economy.

THE 1848 REVOLUTIONS

In March 1848 the structure that had been created in 1815 collapsed with a suddenness that surprised even its bitterest opponents. In each German state the threat of revolution compelled the ruler to call elections for an elected *Landtag*. The Liberals then seized the initiative to summon a 'pre-parliament' of 'trusted men from all German peoples' to plan elections for a constituent assembly, which met in Frankfurt in May 1848. It set up a 'Provisional Central Power' in the expectation that it would rapidly oversee the creation of a united Germany. Yet this was to prove a false dawn and three years later the Confederation was restored [**Doc. 2, p. 120**].

Its failure all too clearly illustrated the problems that German unification would encounter. The Provisional Central Power was in reality hardly a government. It had no armed force or professional bureaucracy, and no means of raising taxes. In the final analysis it was still dependent on the individual German states, particularly both Austria and Prussia. It was, too, unsure of what constituted 'the German nation'. The general assumption was that the territory of the German Confederation would form the basis of the new united Germany, but the problem here was that the northern, eastern and southern borders of the Confederation did not mark a clear-cut ethnic divide. Germans were mixed up with Danes, Poles, Czechs, Slovaks, Slovenes, Croats, Italians and Dutch (see Map 1). So inevitably the process of creating a new German state would cause acute international and ethnic tension and could only take place with the approval of the Great Powers. This became clear when Britain, France and Russia vetoed the inclusion of the Dutch province of Limburg and then the Danish province of Schleswig in a prospective German state.

Central to the future of Germany was the attitude of Austria and Prussia. By the autumn of 1848 the uprisings in the Austrian territory of Bohemia and northern Italy had been defeated. In the spring of 1849 Schwarzenberg, the new Austrian chancellor, formally rejected the idea of a German federation. This left the Frankfurt Assembly with no option but to create a **Kleindeutschland** and offer the crown to the Prussian king. But this too ran into difficulties when Frederick William IV refused point-blank to accept what he considered a 'dog collar with which they wish to lash me to the revolution of 1848'. In reaction to this the Assembly attempted to speak over the heads of the individual state governments to the German people by unilaterally setting a date for national elections. In protest at this, Austria, Prussia, Hanover and Baden recalled their delegates, and the rump assembly moved to Stuttgart where it was dispersed at bayonet point by Württemberg troops. In response there were uprisings in Silesia, the Rhineland, Saxony and Württemberg, all of which were speedily crushed by Prussian troops.

Kleindeutschland United Germany without Austria.

THE RADOWITZ INITIATIVE AND THE REVIVAL OF THE CONFEDERATION

The creation of a federal Germany by consent had failed [**Doc. 2, p. 120**]. Frederick William, following advice from von Radowitz the leader of the Conservatives in the Frankfurt Assembly, now attempted to impose from above a conservative *kleindeutsch* national Germany – the so-called 'Prussian

Union'. As long as Austria was still involved in counter-insurgency operations in Hungary and Italy, this gamble might have paid off. However, Austria defeated the Hungarians in August 1849 with the help of the Russians and was able to organize an increasingly effective counter-offensive against the Radowitz Plan. In September Schwarzenberg, summoned an assembly composed of the opponents of a Prussian-led *Kleindeutschland*, which included Bavaria and Württemberg. Germany was now effectively divided into two hostile blocs and unity on Prussia's terms could only be achieved by war.

Since the summer of 1849 tension had been growing between Austria and Prussia. The final crisis between the two powers was precipitated by domestic events in Hesse-Kassel. The ruler, Duke Frederick William, had replaced a Liberal ministry with an ultra-reactionary government, and then, when confronted with opposition in the *Landtag* to his government's budget, had dissolved the parliament and started to levy taxes illegally. He attempted to quell the resulting uproar by appealing to Schwarzenberg for help. Austria and its allies, diplomatically supported by Russia, were only too ready to intervene, as Hesse-Kassel (see Map 2) was a strategically important state dominating Prussia's civilian and military roads to the west, whilst also providing direct links to Hanover and thence to Schleswig-Holstein. In early November 1850 Prussian and Austrian armies, which were strengthened with units from Bavaria and Württemberg, began to mobilize and converge on Hesse-Kassel. Shots were actually exchanged between Prussian and Bavarian troops on 8 November. The Prussians, however, facing the prospect of a war against Austria, the south German alliance and Russia, backed down, and signed the treaty of Olmütz on 29 November. By this Prussia agreed to demobilize its army, abandon plans for a Prussian-led *Kleindeutschland*, and discuss plans for reforming the Confederation.

Prussia had certainly suffered a serious diplomatic and political defeat at Olmütz, but not everything was to go Austria's way. At the Dresden Conference in December 1850 Prussia was able to block Schwarzenberg's proposals for integrating Austria's non-German territories into the Confederation, and instead, the old Confederation of 1815 was revived.

AUSTRO-PRUSSIAN RELATIONS, 1853–1859

The re-establishment of the Confederation did not mark a return to an unchallenged Austrian hegemony within Germany. At Frankfurt cooperation between the two great German powers became increasingly difficult to maintain, as both, in the words of Bismarck, who was now the Prussian representative to the Confederation, were sucking 'the life blood' from each other. By this he meant that Austria needed to dominate the Confederation to protect its position as a great power, which would inevitably prevent Prussia from gaining its full potential within Germany. This fundamental clash of policies ensured that Bismarck at Frankfurt did everything he could to weaken Austria and block the development of a common policy [**Doc. 7, p. 124**].

The latent antagonism between the two states became obvious when the *Zollverein* treaty came up for renewal in 1853. The Austrians made a determined effort to join by proposing a new central European free trade zone. The prospect was attractive to the south German states and Saxony, but opposed fiercely by Prussia, which did not want to forfeit its leadership of the *Zollverein*. Rudolf von Delbrück, the key official in the Prussian ministry of commerce, managed to strengthen Prussia's position within the *Zollverein* by offering Hanover and Oldenburg entry on very favourable terms. At first, as a means of putting pressure on Berlin, the pro-Austrian states threatened to form an independent customs union with Austria, but ultimately the pull of the Prussian economy was too powerful for them to resist. The Austrians were marginalized and had no option but to sign a twelve-year trade agreement with Prussia and agreed not to raise the question of entry into the *Zollverein* until 1860.

The outbreak of the Crimean War, 1854–56, led to further friction between the two powers. Austria, fearing Russian influence in the Balkans, refused to assist the Russian Empire against Britain and France. In early 1854 Prussia reluctantly signed a defensive treaty with Austria, but rejected an Austrian proposal to mobilize the Confederation's forces under Austrian supreme command in case of a Russian invasion of the Balkans. In Frankfurt Bismarck was quick to exploit the fear of the smaller states that this would lead to war and the subsequent break-up of the Confederation to the great advantage of the French, by declaring that the Confederation would fight only to defend its own neutrality. He was thus able to imply that Prussia, unlike Austria, was a purely German state whose security interests were identical to the great majority of the states of the Confederation. The war created a lasting estrangement between Vienna and St Petersburg. The subsequent Treaty of Paris destroyed both Russia's ability and will to maintain the Vienna Settlement in Central Europe. Russian diplomacy was now directed towards abrogating the Black Sea clauses of the Treaty, which neutralized the Black Sea and closed it to all warships. That Russia was no longer interested in defending the Vienna Settlement created a more fluid international situation, which was ultimately to enable Bismarck to defeat first Austria in 1866 and then France in 1870–71 without great power intervention (see pages **25** and **56**).

When war broke out between Austria and the Franco-Piedmont alliance in April 1859 [**Doc. 5, p. 122**], Prussia again initially remained neutral, but with the defeat of Austrian forces at Magenta and Solferino, Berlin abandoned this position and prepared to drive a hard bargain with Vienna. In exchange for military assistance, Prussia now insisted on equality with Austria within the Confederation, supreme command of forces on the Rhine and military and political hegemony in northern Germany. Austria, believing that the Confederation would inevitably be drawn into the struggle anyway, was unwilling to make these concessions, but the matter was never put to the test. On 11 July France and Austria ended the war with the Armistice of Villafranca. Austria had suffered a heavy defeat in Italy and the loss of Lombardy, but had nevertheless prevented Prussia from strengthening its position within the Confederation.

THE CONSTITUTIONAL CONFLICT IN PRUSSIA

The 1848 revolts had not led to the dramatic creation of a liberal Germany, but they had revealed the strength of Nationalism and the potential for popular participation in politics, as well as confirming that a Prussian-led *Kleindeutschland* was the most likely, if not yet inevitable, formula for the united Germany of the future [**Doc. 2, p. 120**]. The revolts also led to the introduction of a parliamentary constitution into Prussia, albeit one with a **three class voting system**, that grossly distorted the political power of the property-owning classes, but as, elections later in the decade were to show, this did not rule out the possibility of liberal majorities and the potential for political change.

In October 1858 Crown Prince William was appointed regent when his brother was incapacitated by a severe stroke. Politically this was good news for the Prussian Liberals. William had supported the Radowitz Plan (see page **9**) and opposed Olmütz. He appointed a new cabinet of a moderately liberal persuasion, and, as the elections to the lower house in 1858 were no longer influenced by the government, the Liberals were able to win a majority.

By 1860 Liberalism, despite its many divisions, dominated the political debate. Liberals set the tone in the Protestant churches, the universities, local government and in business associations [**Doc. 3, p. 121**]. Throughout Germany, wherever there were free elections, they won majorities. However, these successes were deceptive. Liberalism was not a mass movement, and it failed to reach out to the peasantry, the urban lower classes and the great

Three class voting system remained in place until 1918. The voters were not divided by estate or class, but by the amount of taxes they paid. In 1849 4.7% belonged to the first category, 12.6% to the second and 82.7% to the third. Each class chose a third of the electors, who in turn chose the actual delegates. The voting system did not necessarily guarantee conservative majority. In the 1860s liberal majorities were regularly returned.

majority of the Catholics. It was led by elites, and only became the dominant force in Prussian politics at a point when the masses were not yet mobilized. The Liberals also seriously misinterpreted William's own politics. Their 'honeymoon' with him was 'based on illusory hopes and false premises' (Sheehan, 1989: 876), as was to be shown in the bitter conflict that broke out over the reform of the army.

The Liberals believed passionately in integrating the army into society and making it subject to parliament, while the main thrust of the government's army reforms went in the opposite direction, and was intended to strengthen the grip of the professional officer corps and downgrade the role of the part-time **Landwehr**, or reserve army, while at the same time doubling the size of the field army. This threatened the fundamental conception of a 'civilianized army' as represented by the *Landwehr*, which, as the historian Otto Pflanze has stressed, 'was as important to the liberals as . . . the rights of man' (Pflanze, 1990, 1: 168).

Landwehr Set up in February 1813 to comprise all men not serving in the regular army. In 1815 the *Landwehr* was reorganized to amalgamate with the regular army, but in peacetime keep its character as a militia. Increasingly the Liberals saw it in the words of General Leopold von Boyen 'the happy union of the warrior and civilian society'.

In 1860 the war minister, Albrecht von Roon, presented the *Landtag* with the Army bill which proposed the following plan for reform:

- the size of the standing army would virtually be doubled;
- the number of new recruits would be increased annually from 40,000 to 63,000;
- the period of active service would be set at three years;
- The *Landwehr* and the reserves would also be reorganized. The regular army would now be responsible for the first five years of the reserve service of the former conscripts, while the *Landwehr* would be allocated the remaining four years. The *Landwehr* would be deployed only at home and behind the front, and its officers would also gradually be replaced by professionals from the regular army.

Initially the Liberal leaders in the *Landtag* attempted to find a compromise, but von Roon, the war minister, supported by the ultra-conservative, Edwin von Manteuffel, who was hoping to persuade the Regent to abolish the constitution, and if necessary launch a conservative counter-revolution, ruthlessly exploited the Liberals' willingness to make provisional financial grants and pressed on with the military reorganization. With the foundation of the **Progressive Party** in June 1861, the left-wing Liberals were able to mount a much more effective opposition against the Crown and widened the conflict by calling for a drastic reform of the constitution. After the election of December 1861, in which the Progressives emerged as the largest group with 109 seats, the opposition began to subject the military budget to a painstaking analysis, so it could draw attention to the funds illegally being transferred to the War Ministry from other government departments.

Progressive Party The German Progressive Party was founded in 1861 in Prussia. Its programme was both liberal and national.

William retaliated by dismissing the government and appointing a Conservative administration, but the subsequent elections in March 1862 again produced an overwhelming Liberal majority. After further attempts to compromise were rejected by William, who, on the death of his brother, Frederick William IV, had now become king, the Liberals were determined not only to reject the budget but also to force the King to appoint a Liberal ministry. It was this crisis that enabled Bismarck to achieve power.

BISMARCK

Junker Prussian noble-man and landowner.

Bismarck was born in 1815 into an old *Junker* family in Brandenburg, but thanks to the influence of his mother, Wilhelmina Mencken, who descended from a distinguished but bourgeois family of civil servants and academics and whose father had been secretary of the royal cabinet, he was a frequent visitor to the Prussian royal household. Yet until 1847 he remained a brilliant misfit. After university at Göttingen he entered the Prussian civil service, but soon gave it up to farm the family estates at Schönhausen. He only began to acquire a public reputation when he became a deputy in the Prussian United Diet in 1847.

It was the revolution of 1848 and the subsequent introduction of a constitution that created the context which ultimately enabled Bismarck to become minister-president in 1862. While Bismarck in his enthusiasm to combat revolution initially emerged in the spring of 1848, to quote Lothar Gall, as 'a kind of Don Quixote of a feudal fantasy world' (Gall, 1986: 52), he did nevertheless exhibit his political skills by mobilizing popular support for the conservative cause. He was also involved in setting up the influential right-wing paper, *Die Neue Preussische Zeitung* or *Kreuzzeitung*. He was closely associated with the ultra conservative Gerlach brothers, yet, as one of his recent biographers, Katherine Anne Lerman, has stressed, he did not 'indulge in the ultra-conservative illusion that despite all that happened, the restora-tion of the past was both desirable and feasible' (Lerman, 2004: 33). He gradually emerged as a pragmatic politician who embraced different strands of conservative opinion at different times.

Bismarck served as a deputy in the Berlin National Assembly of May 1848, the parliamentary *Landtag* elected in early 1849 and the Erfurt parliament, which was convened in March 1850. His defence in December 1850 of the Olmütz Agreement was a 'landmark' (Lerman, 2004: 35) in his political career, which helped secure a year later his appointment as Prussian ambassador at Frankfurt. There he rapidly become highly critical of Austrian foreign policy. Not only did he take personal offence at the arrogance of the

Austrian delegate, but there were, as has been noted above (see page **11**), also fundamental differences between the two powers, which no shared conservative ideology could bridge. Bismarck countered Schwarzenberg's attempts to dominate the Confederation by advising his government to take every opportunity to seize the leadership of Germany. He was ready 'to consider all possible means to that end' (Pflanze, 1990, 1: 135) [**Doc. 7, p. 124**].

Bismarck played a major role in blocking Austrian membership of the *Zollverein*. When the Crimean War broke out in 1854, he urged his government to exploit Austria's rift with Russia, which was caused by her benevolent neutrality towards Britain and France. In 1856–57 he argued that Prussia occupied a 'pivotal position' between the two revisionist powers, Russia and France on the one side and Britain and Austria on the other. Consequently, he proposed that Prussia should use it to extract concessions. In March 1858 he recommended for the first time the revolutionary step of harnessing the power of German nationalism as a means of destroying Austrian influence within Germany [**Doc. 8, p. 124**]. Bismarck's Machiavellian proposals were not acted upon in Berlin. Although Frederick William appreciated his advice, the Prussian foreign office viewed his willingness to abandon the Holy Alliance of 1815 with considerable alarm. When Prince William became Regent in 1857, Bismarck's influence declined and he was sent to St. Petersburg where he was more highly regarded by the Russian government than his own. The likelihood of Bismarck achieving political office seemed by now a remote prospect.

BISMARCK'S APPOINTMENT AS PRUSSIAN MINISTER-PRESIDENT

It was, however, the escalating Prussian constitutional conflict over the Army bill that gave Bismarck his chance as a 'conservative outsider' (Lerman, 2004: 51) to become minister-president of Prussia. By September 1862 William was ready to abdicate rather than compromise with the Liberals over the military reforms, but, as a last throw, he was persuaded to turn to Bismarck, who in anticipation of this move, had been summoned to Berlin by his friend General Albrecht von Roon, the war minister. Bismarck met William on 22 September and managed to persuade him of his ability to achieve the army reforms and to defend the Crown's powers from erosion by the *Landtag*. By now Bismarck was the only alternative either to abject surrender to the Liberals or to the appointment of the military hardliner, General Edwin von Manteuffel, the Chief of the Prussian Military War Cabinet, who regarded Bismarck as an unreliable maverick and openly advocated a return to absolutism. As 'the outsider' Bismarck was 'able to slip "between the fronts"', but to survive he would, to quote Lerman, have to 'maintain a precarious balancing act, effectively holding the conflicting forces at bay' (Lerman, 2004: 60). William appointed Bismarck Prussian minister-president, but he hoped initially to find an alternative candidate to head the foreign ministry. Only when this proved to be impossible was Bismarck given this post too on 8 October.

Part 2

THE DEFEAT OF AUSTRIA

2

The Constitutional Conflict and the Liberal Opposition

CONFRONTATION WITH THE LIBERALS

Bismarck's achievements are so dazzling that historians have understandably tended to reconstruct a 'marvellous march of events, in which each stage seems to slip into its pre-appointed place' (Grant Robertson, 1918: 128). In fact Bismarck was faced with almost insuperable problems in both domestic and foreign policy during the years 1862–66 and he could only feel his way to solutions, keeping as many options as possible open. To understand these years it is wise to heed Fritz Stern's warning not 'to see his life backwards, beginning as it were with his success. For this perspective slights his years of struggle when he was groping his way to solutions' (Stern, 1977: 23).

The day after Bismarck was appointed prime minister, the *Landtag* escalated the constitutional crisis by striking out of the 1862 budget the funds which the government had already earmarked for the army. Bismarck was torn between hoping to solve the constitutional conflict before it fatally impaired his freedom of action in foreign policy, and prolonging it so that he would continue to be indispensable to the king. His initial reaction was to seek a compromise, but his room for manoeuvre was severely restricted by the king's absolute refusal to amend the Army bill. **[Doc 6, p. 123]** and by the knowledge that if he showed himself too conciliatory, he could well be replaced by General Edwin von Manteuffel.

Bismarck's initial steps were conciliatory. He established contact with the moderate wing of the Progressive Liberals, withdrew the Budget bill for 1863 and at his first session with the Budget Committee of the *Landtag* made, in the notorious 'blood and iron speech' **[Doc. 9, p. 125]**, a crudely phrased attempt to unite parliament on the basis of a revisionist foreign policy. Bismarck had intended to be conciliatory, but with his 'dangerous gift' of framing pregnant and pithy sentences (Headlam, 1899: 166) he succeeded only in polarizing opinions still further. In short, in Gall's words, he had 'completely and utterly misjudged the situation' (Gall, 1986: 201). Behind the scenes, von Roon, almost certainly with Bismarck's support, drafted a new army bill, which aimed to split the Liberal opposition by going some way towards their demand for a reduction in the length of military service. Possibly it might have won some support in the *Landtag*, but even this concession was rejected by the king despite the fact that von Roon in no way conceded parliamentary control over the army.

Bismarck skilfully avoided a direct confrontation with the *Landtag* by leaving the Upper House to reject the amendments to the 1862 Budget bill. When the Liberals protested, the *Landtag* was prorogued. To justify the unauthorized expenditure on military reorganization, Bismarck argued that the deadlock between the two houses of parliament created a 'hiatus', (Pflanze, 1990, 1: 202) which the government had a duty to fill. Bismarck's interpretation, however opportune, was legally and constitutionally defensible. Unless the Liberals were ready to take to the streets or to stage a tax strike, they were powerless to challenge it, as the constitution contained no provisions for the resolution of such a crisis.

When the *Landtag* reassembled in January 1863, relations between Bismarck and the opposition deteriorated still further. For the next six months at least Bismarck was involved in a desperate fight for political survival. Not only did the deadlock over the budget remain unbroken, but Bismarck made another serious error of judgement in negotiating the *Alvensleben* convention with Russia, which provided for common action in suppressing a revolt in Russian Poland. The convention incensed the Liberals, alienated Britain and France, and shook the king's still somewhat fragile confidence in Bismarck, so that for a time his dismissal was seriously considered. Bismarck could only effectively defend himself by convincing the king of his indispensability. Consequently, until the *Landtag* was prorogued in May, Bismarck lost no opportunity of stressing his loyalty to the crown and provoking the *Landtag* into fresh attacks on the king's government. Indeed it is arguable that he deliberately tried to complicate the domestic situation.

By late summer 1863 Bismarck had established, with the wholehearted support of the crown, a degree of governmental control in Prussia that barely stopped short of a dictatorship. The civil service was disciplined and Liberal officials were subjected to uncomfortable reprisals for their political opinions. The Press Edict of 1 June, which was based on a similar law issued by Napoleon III, effectively stopped discussion of internal political matters by the Liberal press, and a further decree banned the discussion of politically sensitive matters by municipal councils. By the standards of the time Bismarck's measures were both arbitrary and severe, but they failed to prevent another large Liberal majority in the general election of October 1863.

Like many nineteenth-century statesmen who had come into conflict with the middle classes, Bismarck was impressed by the way Napoleon III had exploited universal franchise to win mass support for an autocratic regime [**Doc. 50, p. 155**]. In the summer of 1863 informed sources were convinced that Bismarck was trying to persuade the king to agree to break the deadlock with the *Landtag* by ordering a *coup d'état*. Certainly in May Bismarck started a series of exploratory discussions with Ferdinand Lassalle, the leader of the newly created General Workers Union. Both were interested for their own reasons in destroying Liberalism. Simultaneously Bismarck also prodded his reluctant cabinet into considering schemes for social reform, so that if necessary he would be able to draw up a programme designed to attract a mass electorate.

Bismarck did, however, decide to play for time and keep his options open. Unless a sudden acute crisis occurred, his inclination was to draw out the crisis until support for the Liberals waned. In June 1865, after the *Landtag* had consistently refused funds to pay for the Danish war (see page **30**), a *coup d'état* was again discussed in the Prussian Crown Council, but Bismarck advised that a final decision should be deferred until the new year when the *Landtag* was due to meet (Pflanze, 1990, 1: 107).

The Liberal opposition was in reality a paper tiger, despite its imposing parliamentary majority. The Prussian three-class voting system (see page **12**), by discriminating against the peasantry and the working classes, effectively ensured that the majority of the Liberals' votes came from the middle classes. The opposition was also composed of an unstable coalition between the **Old Liberals**, the **Left Centre** and the Progressives. Each of these groups lacked internal cohesion and a secure extra-parliamentary base. It is thus not surprising that the Liberals frequently displayed 'the uncertainty of front-line troops thinly deployed before a determined foe and backed by no reserves' (Pflanze, 1990, 1: 189–9). The government, on the other hand, controlled the bureaucracy and was confident of the loyalty of the army. Bismarck was also fortunate to come to power during an upswing of the business cycle as this ensured he was able to collect taxes, from a population that was growing steadily richer, and which consequently paid ever greater sums in taxation.

Old Liberals In late June 1849 after the dissolution of the Frankfurt Parliament a group of moderate Liberals met in Gotha. They concluded that the unification of Germany was more important than the 'form' of its attainment. In other words they supported the use of Prussian power to secure unification. By 1861 they were known as the 'Constitutionalists'.

Left Centre Sometimes called the Bockum-Dolffs Caucus from the name of its leader. Composed of moderate Liberals, mainly from the Rhineland.

THE LIBERALS DIVIDED

While the constitutional conflict drove Bismarck and the Liberal opposition further apart, paradoxically he achieved results in his economic and foreign policy which *de facto* realized the programme of *Kleindeutsch* Liberalism.

Although he did not move nearly as quickly as many businessmen and chambers of commerce would have liked, the whole drift of his economic policy was towards creating a climate favourable to the development of *laissez-faire* capitalism. The Mining Law of 24 June 1865, for example, which established freedom of exploration and exploitation, met with universal approval from the various chambers of commerce [**Doc. 10, p. 126**]. The free-trade agreements with Belgium, England and Italy, which were modelled on the French treaty of 1862, were also popular as they integrated the *Zollverein* economy more deeply into the free-trade system of western Europe.

Bismarck did, however, skilfully exploit economic policy to divide and confuse his Liberal opponents. In 1865, for example, a series of bills were presented to the *Landtag* on state aid for railway construction, which were calculated to split the Liberal majority into warring factions. Principled opposition against what many Liberals regarded as a government ruling illegally clashed with local self-interest. Despite the bitter protests of the *laissez-faire* Progressives, the Liberal majority accepted all but one of the bills.

The growing success of Bismarck's foreign policy after 1864 also began to undermine the strength of the opposition. To many contemporaries it seemed that Bismarck was attempting to divert attention from the domestic crisis by the classic recipe of seeking adventures abroad. Publicly, Bismarck insisted on the primacy of foreign policy over domestic policy, and until the 1960s most German historians accepted this at face value. Gerhardt Ritter, for example, is emphatic that Bismarck risked war 'only in the "innermost" interests of his country' (Ritter, 1969: 246), but in many ways that judgement ignores the 'close and complex' relationship between Bismarck's domestic and foreign policy (Stern, 1977: 69).

The successful war against Denmark in 1864 (see page **30**) and the subsequent occupation of Schleswig and Holstein embarrassed the Liberals as the liberation of the local German population from Danish control had long been an aim of German nationalism. To many of their voters it seemed as if the military reorganization had been successful and that the military budget should be accepted. As it became clear in the course of the following twelve months that Bismarck was manoeuvring to annex the duchies out- right (see page **31**), the Liberals were confronted with an agonizing dilemma as to whether they should support a national policy or stand fast over the constitutional conflict. This dilemma was brutally exposed when the *Landtag* was requested to approve funds for the construction of two armed frigates and a naval base at Kiel. The majority of the Liberals refused to grant the money on the grounds that the budget was still illegal. Bismarck ironically pointed out that for the twenty years the Liberals had been dreaming of a fleet but now were rejecting the financial means for creating it. By the time parliament was prorogued in June 1865, the Liberals were both disorganized and demoralized. The liberal journalist, August Lammers, observed that 'instead of a single united party we have ten to twenty little factions' (Pflanze, 1990, 1: 275).

Many deputies were now exhausted by the struggle, and even Bismarck and von Roon in the face of the coming conflict with Austria (see page **36**) were inclined to seek a solution to the domestic crisis. In January 1865 they had tried to persuade the king to compromise, but William categorically refused to tinker with the army bill [**Doc. 6, p. 123**]. Bismarck was again forced to protect his own position by vigorously defending the crown and mounting a vehement attack on the opposition. This culminated in the prosecution of two Progressive deputies for making speeches critical of the government on the floor of the *Landtag*, and in the seizure of parliamentary papers and documents after the *Landtag* had been prorogued.

Through such tactics as these Bismarck, by the spring of 1866, had merely succeeded in reuniting the fragmented opposition at the very moment when war with Austria was imminent. By May 1866, despite his open champion-ship of German nationalism and belated attempts to win over individual Liberals, 'the predominant "movement" among the German people . . . was anti-war and anti-Bismarck' (Pflanze, 1990, 1: 326) [**Doc. 12, p. 127**].

3

The German Question, 1860–1866

PUBLIC OPINION AND GERMAN UNITY: THE *NATIONALVEREIN* AND *REFORMVEREIN*

I n the *Kleindeutsch* versions of the history of German unity public opinion and Prussian diplomatic and military action to secure German unity go hand in hand. Prussia and Bismarck are in fact portrayed as the 'instrument and ally of the national will' (Sheehan, 1989: 868). In reality this is an exaggeration. There was certainly support for a Prussian-led unification of Germany amongst the Protestant political, academic and business elites in the north, but against these stood a majority of Germans: the Catholics, the peasantry, '**junker** traditionalists', particularists and the supporters of a reformed **Grossdeutschland.** In this context it is worth remembering that under 50% of the population eligible to vote actually bothered to in the first election to the German *Reichstag* in 1871.

The Italian war of 1859 (see page **12**), which resulted in the defeat of Austria had a stimulating impact on *Kleindeutsch* nationalism. Ardent nationalists met in cities throughout Germany to consider how to follow the German example. Hundreds of articles were published in nationalist papers exploring the possibilities of unification under Prussia, and meetings and debates took place all over Germany. On 17 July a conference of left-wing Liberals met at Eisenach chaired by Hermann von Schulze-Delitzsch, and two days later a group of more moderate liberals under the chairmanship of Rudolf von Bennigsen convened in Hanover. In September these two groups amalgamated to found the **Nationalverein** [Doc. 4, p. 121]. It was inspired by the Italian National Society, which was founded in Piedmont in 1856 with the aim of raising support for a united Italy under the leadership of Piedmont. Its members wanted an 'Italian-type solution' to German unity, which would involve the creation of a united Germany under Prussian leadership and the restoration of the *Kleindeutsch* (see page **9**) constitution of 1849.

Junker Prussian nobleman and landowner.

Grossdeutschland A united Germany including the German-speaking countries of the Austrian Empire.

Nationalverein The National Association, founded in 1859.

Through agitation, propaganda and rallies it attempted to put pressure on the governments of the German states to work towards such a solution. Its task, as Johannes Miquel put it, was 'to make the fruit ripe . . . for the moment that must come'. He claimed ambitiously that 'we represent the views of the nation' (Sheehan, 1989: 866). This was hardly accurate as the mainstay of its membership was the Protestant elite: judges, professors, pastors. Although it remained a pressure group with a membership of only 25,000 people, it did much to revive the debate on the German question. The Society shrugged off arguments that its policies would lead to the Prussianization of Germany because it believed that the very process of unification would liberalize Prussia. However, once Bismarck came to power in Prussia, it became increasingly difficult for any Liberal to support Prussia as a champion of German unity, and the Society steadily lost support, with its membership declining to 17,000 in 1866.

The *kleindeutsch* policies advocated by the *Nationalverein* would inevitably lead to the division of Germany by excluding Austria. To stop this, a wide cross-section of Catholic anti-Prussians, particularists and also *grossdeutsch* liberals and democrats came together and created the **Deutscher Reformverein** in 1862. Its key attraction was really its anti-Prussianism. It failed, however, to offer a positive programme for the creation of a *Grossdeutschland*, as it was split between those who wanted only to maintain the status quo and those who wanted a genuine *grossdeutsch* parliament. As the journalist and historian Franz Herre observed, the composition of the *Reformverein* was 'like the multicoloured map of the Confederation that it wanted to transform' (Sheehan, 1989: 867).

Deutsche Reformverein (German Reform Society) Founded in reaction to the *Nationalverein* on 26 October 1862 to campaign for the creation of a *Grossdeutschland*. It had a membership of about 1500.

AUSTRO-PRUSSIAN RIVALRY AND THE REFORM OF THE CONFEDERATION, 1860–1862

By the early 1860s Austria's position, both internationally and economically, had significantly deteriorated. As a result of the Crimean war (see page **11**) the Austro-Russian axis, which had been of decisive importance in restoring Austria's position in Germany in 1850 (see page **10**), had collapsed. Austria had been seriously weakened by her loss of Lombardy in 1859 (see page **12**) and any chance of a Franco-Austrian **rapprochement** was ruled out by Napoleon's backing for Italian claims to her Venetian territory. The almost universal mistrust of Napoleon III also ensured that Europe was in a state, as Werner Mosse put it, of 'diplomatic disorientation' (Mosse, 1958: 253). Both Britain and France welcomed the prospect of German unity under Prussia as a potential check to Russia and as a possible ally against the other.

Rapprochement Establishing harmonious relations between two states.

Economically, Austria was also falling far behind Prussia. The costs of the disastrous Italian war combined with the Depression of 1857–59 ensured that the Austrian economy was severely weakened. Despite a much larger population its coal and iron ore production was under 50% of Prussia's and it produced only slightly over a fifth of the steam engines manufactured in Prussia. On the other hand Prussia's economic and strategic position within Germany had decisively strengthened over the decade. Prussia had become the strongest German power economically and dominated the *Zollverein*, and by 1860 produced a greater tonnage of steel than either France, Russia or Austria. Above all, the Ruhr – which was to develop into Europe's most dynamic region – lay within Prussian territory.

Despite defeat in Italy and growing economic weakness, Austria was not ready to recognize Prussian hegemony in northern Germany. The collapse of Schwarzenberg's **neo-absolutist regime** (see page 9) and its replacement in 1861 by a new constitution with a national parliament with full legislative rights strengthened the influence of the German Liberals within the Austrian Empire. These reforms coming at a time when Prussia was paralysed by a constitutional conflict enabled Austria to appeal more effectively to the small and middle-sized states and *Grossdeutsch* public opinion.

From 1861–63 in both Berlin and Vienna policies for the reform of the German Confederation were 'a confusion of plans, actions and counter actions, irritations and fluctuations' (Nipperdey, 1996: 627). Nevertheless broadly three main approaches can be identified:

Neo-absolutist regime
An autocratic system of government as established by Schwarzenberg in 1849.

1. Prussia hoped to achieve at the very least a dualistic hegemony with Austria. This would involve alternating the presidency of the Confederation between Vienna and Berlin and granting Prussia virtually a free hand north of the Main. In return, Prussia was ready to guarantee Austria's last possession in Italy – Venetia.

2. At times the Austrians were tempted by this guarantee, but essentially they wanted to hang on to their leading role in Germany. Their politics fluctuated between confrontation and dualistic cooperation. They did not trust Prussia and feared that such a compromise would only lead to further demands from Berlin.

3. There was opposition to both the Prussian and Austrian positions from the south German states. They wanted to strengthen the authority of the whole Confederation by standardizing its legal system and creating a parliament composed of delegates from the local *Landtage* without creating a Prussian–Austrian hegemony. In essence they saw, as Julius Froebel, one of the most influential members of the *Reformverein*, observed, that any response to the German question involved 'the three natural elements

in the German state system: Austria, Prussia and the totality of the small and medium-sized states' (Sheehan, 1989: 867).

When it became clear by the summer of 1861 that no Austro-Prussian agreement was possible the Prussian foreign minister, Albrecht von Bernstorff, revived the Radowitz Plan (see page **9**), the threat of which brought the medium-sized states, who dreaded Prussian domination, closer to Austria.

BISMARCK AND AUSTRIA, 1862–1863

Bismarck has been criticized for attempting to force European diplomacy into a preconceived mould during his first few months in power. One historian has argued that 'the most striking features of Bismarck's first year as prime minister were the irrelevance of most of his actions [and] his apparent lack of understanding of the real forces at work in Prussia, in Germany [and] in Europe' (Crankshaw, 1981: 144). Bismarck, however, inherited a situation which vindicated his longstanding suspicion of Austrian intentions. Ever since the early 1850s Bismarck had analysed European diplomacy in terms of Austro-Prussian rivalry [**Docs 7 and 8, p. 124**] and had consistently argued that Austrian domination of Germany could only be broken with French or Russian assistance (see page **15**). In the autumn of 1862 he thus lost little time in sounding out the French and bluntly warning the Austrians of his intention to establish Prussian hegemony in North Germany. His confident assumption of French support was shaken when Napoleon refused to commit himself in advance to benevolent neutrality if war between Austria and Prussia were to break out.

He then changed course and offered Austria the option of a conservative alliance which would have guaranteed Austrian interests in Italy and the Near East while conceding Prussian hegemony in North Germany. Austria, however, in an attempt to consolidate her position within Germany, persisted with her proposals for the reform of the Confederation, which were only defeated by a small majority in the Frankfurt Diet on 22 January 1863 after intense Prussian lobbying. If Bismarck had failed, he would have had little option but to appeal to *Kleindeutsch* German nationalism. Had this happened the war of 1866 might well have occurred in 1863.

Bismarck's pursuit of the French alliance was a logical and defensible policy, if rather clumsily executed, but he made a serious error when he overreacted to the revolt in Russian Poland in January 1863. He authorized General von Alvensleben to negotiate with the Russians a draft convention providing for joint military action against any Polish rebels who crossed into Prussian Poland. Traditionally the convention has been hailed as a cynical move to secure Russian support against Austria, but at the time the negative reaction it caused in London, Paris and Vienna threatened to isolate Prussia and threw Bismarck on the defensive. He immediately disowned the convention and proposed to Vienna and St Petersburg a revival of the Holy Alliance of 1815.

Austria rejected this and made one last attempt to seize the initiative in Germany by producing another plan for reform of the Confederation, which involved creating a directorate of ministers from the five largest states, an assembly of princes and a federal parliament elected from the state parliaments. The Austrians attempted to neutralize Bismarck's opposition by inviting the princes to a conference without first holding a ministerial meeting to prepare the agenda. Bismarck persuaded William to boycott the meeting and then played the nationalist card by proposing a central parliament elected by the 'entire [German] nation', which would inevitably maximize Prussian as opposed to multi-national Austrian influence within the Confederation. This effectively killed the Austrian proposals, since, when it came to the point, the *Mittelstaaten* states were not ready to act without Prussia, as they feared the consequences of unchallenged Austrian domination for their own independence almost as much as they did Prussian hegemony.

THE SCHLESWIG-HOLSTEIN CRISIS, 1863–1864

Further Austrian initiatives for Confederate reform were discouraged by Napoleon's sudden call for a European congress to revise the settlement of 1815 and by the increasingly threatening situation in Schleswig-Holstein. Ever since 1848 Schleswig-Holstein had been a '*cause célèbre* of German nationalism' (Pflanze, 1990, 1: 233). The Duchies were autonomous but under the sovereignty of the King of Denmark. Holstein was predominantly German and a member of the German Confederation, whereas Schleswig, with its mixed German and Danish population, was not, although the Germans insisted that historically the two Duchies were inseparable. In 1848 the Danish government had attempted to absorb Schleswig into Denmark, but an immediate revolt by the German population moved the Frankfurt parliament to authorize Prussian military intervention. This was, however, speedily halted by Anglo-Russian diplomatic pressure. In 1852 the Treaty of London was signed by the Great Powers, including Austria and Prussia, but it failed to solve the problem. While declaring that Denmark and the duchies should be united into 'one well-ordered whole', it also stipulated that Schleswig should never be incorporated into Denmark.

Over the next decade relations between the Germans and the Danes deteriorated, a process only accelerated by the growth in German nationalism. In March 1863 the Danish King, Frederick VII, emboldened by Swedish support and growing Austro-Prussian tension, announced a unitary constitution for Schleswig and Denmark. The German Confederation reacted slowly and cumbersomely but, urged on by both *Klein-* and *Grossdeutsch* nationalists, it demanded the repeal of the new constitution. In October the Confederation voted to proceed with armed sanctions. Saxony and Hanover were deputed to carry this out, and Prussia and Austria were to provide reserve support if necessary.

The crisis was heightened by the unexpected death of Frederick, who had no direct heir, in November 1863. Foreseeing this possibility, the London Treaty had nominated the Danish Prince Christian of Glucksburg as heir to both the Danish crown and the duchies'. His accession was unpopular both in Denmark and in the duchies. This enabled the German pretender to the duchies, Frederick of Augustenburg, to proclaim himself Duke of Schleswig-Holstein, to the delight of German nationalists who rallied to his support throughout the German states.

The *Nationalverein*, whose patron, Duke Ernst of Coburg, was a close friend of Augustenburg, in cooperation with the *Reformverein* summoned the deputies of the German state parliaments to a rally in Frankfurt in December. This voted unanimously to make the cause of Augustenburg that of the German nationalists themselves and set up a permanent committee of thirty-six to act as a 'centre of legal activity'.

THE OPTIONS FACING BISMARCK

Bismarck had consistently advocated that, unless Prussia could annex the territories outright, Danish sovereignty was preferable to their independence under a German ruler who would probably oppose Prussian interests in the Confederation and *Zollverein* [**Doc. 13, p. 128**]. He was aware of their strategic importance, and in November 1862 ordered the Prussian army to draw up plans for an invasion of Schleswig-Holstein, but this was not really a practicable possibility. Not only was the status quo guaranteed in the Duchies by Britain and Russia, but increasing Confederate involvement as a result of growing demands by the German states for intervention by the German Confederation prevented independent Prussian action and threatened to lead to the creation of an independent state under Augustenburg.

As Pflanze observed, Bismarck was sure of what he wanted but 'he knew neither how, when, nor where it would be attained' (Pflanze, 190, 1: 238). Bismarck initially adopted an attitude of studied moderation in the autumn of 1863 to convince the Great Powers, especially Britain, of Prussia's essential willingness to observe the Treaty of London. He also exploited Austria's fear that support for Augustenburg was potentially revolutionary and would lead to the destruction of the Confederation and creation of a united Germany.

Consequently throughout December Austria and Prussia tried with only limited success to moderate the Confederation's enthusiasm for Augustenburg. They had agreed to the temporary occupation of Holstein by Confederate forces, which advanced unopposed up to the river Eider on 23 December. However this very lack of opposition encouraged further demands for the liberation of Schleswig, and, in anticipation of this, Augustenburg set up court unofficially at Kiel, in Holstein. On 24 January 1864 the Dual Powers had consequently little option but to act independently if they were to forestall a Confederate invasion of Schleswig and a de facto recognition of Augustenburg. On 17 January 1864 the Austro-Prussian Convention was signed and their troops crossed the Eider into Schleswig.

Bismarck's immediate concern was to isolate the battlefield in Schleswig from possible Great Power intervention until Denmark had been decisively defeated. While he may have exaggerated the dangers of intervention, he nevertheless needed to proceed with great caution. Later he compared himself to a hunter in a marsh who 'never advanced a foot until certain that the ground . . . is firm and safe' (Pflanze, 1990, 1: 243). In February, for example, he had to control the impetuosity of the aged and eccentric commander of the Prussian forces, von Wrangel, until he had gained Austrian agreement to carry the war over the Danish frontier into Jutland. Then in March, when Britain proposed an international conference in London, Bismarck skilfully delayed its meeting until the Prussian army had decisively defeated the Danes at Düppel [**Doc. 11, p. 126**], so strengthening his position at the conference table.

Bismarck had consistently made Prussian recognition of the Treaty of London dependent on Denmark's strict fulfilment of its clauses. At the London Conference the miscalculations of the King of Denmark played straight into his hands. The Danes, believing that they enjoyed international support, stubbornly refused to restore the autonomy of Schleswig and consequently enabled the Dual Powers to repudiate the Treaty and gain freedom of action. The British cabinet refused to sanction intervention, and the Danes were left isolated when the armistice expired on 26 June 1864. They were defeated within days and surrendered the Duchies to the Dual Powers. In the Preliminary Peace of 1 August the Danish king finally ceded all his rights to the Duchies. This was confirmed two months later in a final peace treaty.

FROM SCHÖNBRUNN TO BAD GASTEIN

Denmark's refusal to compromise had confronted Austria with a serious dilemma: ultimately Augustenburg's claims would have to be recognized or the Duchies ceded to Prussia. Initially unable to countenance the inevitable strengthening of Prussia that annexation would entail, Austria chose the former course even before the London conference had ended. To avoid a rupture with Austria, Bismarck had to agree, but he insisted on such substantial constitutional concessions from Augustenburg that inevitably they were declined as they were tantamount to a virtual Prussian annexation. The ultimate fate of the Duchies was left undecided and they were ruled provisionally by a fragile Austro-Prussian condominium.

During the next two years Bismarck's diplomacy was at its most complex. His simultaneous pursuit of alternative and sometimes contradictory policies makes interpretation particularly difficult. Recent detailed research has to some extent clarified the reasons for these abrupt changes of policy by showing how he would keep his alternatives open until it was clear which one offered the maximum advantage and the least risk. It has, however, been argued that too much stress on 'the strategy of alternatives' (Pflanze, 1990, 1: 241) exaggerates the element of conscious planning in Bismarck's diplomacy. Crankshaw, for example, argues that Bismarck's thoughts were 'capable of existing in a state of something very like suspension . . . with all the ingredients hovering invisibly in solution until the right temperature is reached, the right catalyst introduced, to crystallise them beautifully out' (Crankshaw, 1981: 176–7). However, while Bismarck did not have an exact blueprint for action, he did have certain basic aims of which he never lost sight. He was working towards the annexation of Schleswig-Holstein and ultimately Prussian hegemony in North Germany.

Austria was now the main hindrance to a Prussian annexation of the Duchies, but Bismarck was in no hurry to force the issue as time appeared to be on Prussia's side. Austria, practically bankrupt, was threatened with war in the south by Italy's claims to Venetia, and was both isolated in Europe and also excluded from the *Zollverein*. It therefore suited Bismarck to maintain the alliance in the hope that the logic of Austria's position would persuade the Emperor to concede Prussian demands peacefully. In August 1864 King William and Bismarck met the Austrian Emperor and Count Rechberg, his foreign minister, at Schönbrunn. At ministerial level a verbal agreement was quickly reached whereby Prussia would gain the Duchies in exchange for a guarantee of Venetia and help in the reconquest of Lombardy from Italy. However, when Rechberg produced a more precise draft of the agreement, both monarchs rejected it. Franz Joseph refused to cede the Duchies to Prussia, while William was reluctant to ignore the legality of Augustenburg's claims. Bismarck's intentions were ambiguous. It is just possible that he was 'running full tilt after the conservative alliance' (Taylor, 1955: 75) but the majority of historians are more sceptical of his motives. It is more likely that he never intended to commit Prussia to any precise obligations and was in fact trying to ensure the advantages of continued Austrian cooperation by 'dangl[ing] once more, as so often in the past, the enticing possibility of such a bargain' (Pflanze, 1990, 1: 254).

Throughout the winter of 1864/65 the future of Schleswig-Holstein remained undecided and Austro-Prussian relations steadily deteriorated. Rechberg had resigned as a result of his failure to gain any concessions from Prussia over the *Zollverein* and was replaced by Count Mensdorff-Pouilly. The latter increasingly accepted the anti-Prussian line of his department. In the Duchies the Prussian Commissioner, Baron von Zedlitz, behaved with a provocative arrogance, while Bismarck consistently blocked any solution to their sovereignty which was not compatible with Prussian ambitions. In November Mensdorff gave Bismarck a choice between either recognizing an independent Schleswig-Holstein under Augustenburg, or buying Austrian consent to Prussian annexation with territorial concessions in Silesia and the Hohenzollern enclaves of Württemberg. An answer was delayed until February 1865, when Prussian recognition of Augustenburg was again coupled with unacceptable conditions which would have entailed a de facto Prussian annexation.

By April war seemed likely. Mensdorff encouraged Bavaria to submit to the Diet of the Confederation a motion recommending that the Dual Powers hand over Holstein to Augustenburg. Prussia was unable to prevent it passing, but signalled that she would ultimately go to war to prevent such an outcome by announcing the transfer of her main naval base from Danzig to Kiel. Yet in reality Bismarck was still reluctant to risk war [**Doc. 14, p. 128**]. At the Prussian Crown Council of 29 May 1865 he was virtually alone in advising concessions to Austria, which were rejected by William.

Bismarck's 'moderation' can partly be explained by financial considerations. The quarrel with the Liberals over the Army bill prevented Bismarck from appealing to the *Landtag* for money. Consequently he needed time to raise money elsewhere and to convince bankers that a loan to Austria would be a poor investment. On the advice of the banker Gerson von Bleichröder, the government renounced in return for compensation from the company its option to purchase the stock of the Cologne–Minden railway. By July Bleichröder had procured the necessary funds for the government and was able to inform Bismarck that 'the financial means for complete mobilisation and for a one-year military campaign [were] available' (Stern, 1977: 63) [**Doc. 15, p. 129**].

Nevertheless Bismarck still hesitated to go to war. Essentially he was only ready to fight 'for the higher aim' of creating a new relationship between

Prussia and the German medium-sized and small states. He still believed that he could extract further concessions from Austria, and in this he proved right in the short term. In August, responding to Austrian peace-feelers, a compromise, essentially inspired by Bismarck, was agreed to at the spa town of Bad Gastein, where King William had gone for a cure. Lauenburg was purchased outright by Prussia and the administration of the Duchies was divided: Schleswig was to be governed from Berlin and Holstein from Vienna. The Austrians, however, insisted that joint sovereignty over the two duchies should remain intact [**Doc. 16, p. 129**]. Bismarck's reluctance to be stampeded into war was motivated by a desire to buy time both for further diplomatic, financial and military preparations and for his already considerable achievements in foreign affairs and in the *Zollverein* renegotiations to mollify political opposition at home [**Doc. 11, p. 126**]. Arguably Bismarck hoped that the Treaty, which by its very nature was only provisional, would lead to further Austrian concessions.

AUSTRIA'S 'ECONOMIC KÖNIGGRATZ'

Parallel yet integral to the twists and turns of the Austro-Prussian diplomatic struggle ran the battle for the economic control of the *Zollverein*. In 1853 further discussions on Austria's entry had been postponed for a seven-year period (see page **11**), but by 1860 it was already clear that any attempts by Austria to enter the *Zollverein* would once again meet with implacable Prussian hostility. The following year Berlin began negotiations for a free trade treaty with France. Such an agreement would certainly be economically beneficial, but it would also serve an important political purpose, as it would effectively block Austria from joining the *Zollverein* because her industry was too weak to compete without protection against French imports. Despite intense pro-Austrian lobbying from the 'third Germany' Prussia and France signed the treaty in 1862.

Bismarck rapidly saw the potential of the treaty for undermining Austria's position in the German Confederation and tightening Prussia's grip on the smaller states. In a ruthless attempt to exploit the economic dependence of these states on Prussia he first tried to persuade Napoleon to agree that any negotiations on the extension of the Franco-Prussian Free Trade Treaty to the lesser German states should be conducted solely through the medium of Berlin. He calculated that this would give him sufficient leverage not only to force them to accept the treaty, but also to enable him in 1865 when the *Zollverein* was due to be renewed, to compel them to agree to the removal of their veto rights on economic policy and the creation of a

Prussian-dominated *Zollverein* parliament. When the French refused to concede such a key position to Prussia, Bismarck on the advice of the Prussian Economic Counsellor, Rudolf Delbrück, abandoned his more ambitious plans for the reorganization of the *Zollverein* and concentrated instead on persuading the lesser states to ratify the Franco-Prussian Free Trade Treaty, as this alone would deliver Austria a heavy blow and cut her off economically from her allies in Germany.

Throughout the member states, businessmen and industrialists opted to support the Free Trade Treaty because they feared that disagreement with Prussia might lead to the disintegration of the *Zollverein* and subsequent disruption of inter-German trade [**Doc. 3, p. 121**]. The governments of the southern states stubbornly insisted, however, that the concessions granted to Austria in 1853, which enabled her to pay minimal duties on a whole range of exports to the *Zollverein* should be preserved when the union was renegotiated. They also tenaciously opposed at both the 15th General Conference of the *Zollverein* in the spring of 1863 in Munich and at a subsequent conference in Berlin in November the Prussian proposal to make the renegotiation of the *Zollverein* dependent on the recognition of the Franco-Prussian Free Trade Treaty. Essentially while there was little opposition in principle to Prussia's free trade policy, the political implications for Austria of the free trade treaty with France were unacceptable to the governments of Bavaria, Württemberg, Hanover, Hesse-Darmstadt, Nassau and Frankfurt. Together they were able to block the unanimous ratification of the Franco-Prussian Treaty by the member states.

Bismarck promptly retaliated by announcing that he would dissolve the *Zollverein* in 1865 and make its renegotiation with the individual states dependent on their acceptance of the Franco-Prussian Treaty. He took this gamble as he was convinced that they had no realistic alternative to the *Zollverein*. He also exploited the brief new phase of Austro-Prussian cooperation made possible by military cooperation in the Danish war to attempt to detach, at least temporarily, Austria from her German allies. Negotiations on plans for an Austro-German customs union began in Prague in March 1864, but it was clear that the very different economic and administrative systems in the two areas made it, in Bismarck's words, 'an unrealisable utopia' (Hahn, 1984: 177). For Bismarck, the main value of these abortive negotiations was that it threatened the recalcitrant German states with the prospect of isolation.

After the talks broke down, Austria belatedly attempted to cobble together a united economic front with the German *Mittelstaaten*, but the time was long past when the *Zollverein* could easily be unravelled. The individual governments of the German states, under intense pressure from their local chambers of commerce and frequently too from Liberals in their *Landtage*, realized only too well that the *Zollverein* constituted, as Gall has put it, 'so solid a network of interests that breaking out of it or dissolving it in favour of further combinations scarcely seemed a serious possibility any more' (Gall, 1986, 1: 258). Not surprisingly then by midsummer of 1864 the northern and central states of Saxony, Baden, Brunswick, Thüringen and Frankfurt had all agreed to its renewal on the basis of the Franco-Prussian Trade Treaty. Bismarck then ensured the adhesion of the strategically important Hesse-Kassel, which formed a crucial link between Prussia's western and eastern provinces, simply by bribing its ruler. This effectively isolated Hanover and Oldenburg, which in July had little option but to accept the new treaty.

The remaining states were presented with an ultimatum to sign up by 1 October. Again, as in the spring of 1864, Austria provided them with little backing since Rechberg was pursuing the will-o'-the-wisp of a comprehensive settlement with Bismarck at Schönbrunn (see page **31**) and thus did not want to run the risk of alienating Prussia. The new Bavarian king, Ludwig II, signalled his surrender when he observed in August 1864 that his kingdom had no option but to renew the treaty as the South 'would be compelled through powerful interests sooner or later to join up with the rest of Germany' (Hahn, 1984: 179). On 12 October Bavaria, Württemberg, Hesse-Darmstadt and Nassau all capitulated and accepted Prussia's conditions for renewal.

It was a major economic victory for Prussia. Nevertheless, Bismarck did attempt to mitigate its impact on Austro-Prussian relations by holding out the prospect of further Austro-Prussian talks on the possibility of Austrian participation in the *Zollverein* sometime before 1872, but this was firmly vetoed by Delbrück in the Prussian finance ministry. On 16 May 1865, the *Zollverein* was formally renewed for a further twelve years. Austria's attempts to prise it apart or influence it from within had been defeated and the 'economic wall' between herself and her German allies had been strengthened.

Had Prussia now won the decisive battle for German unity? She had certainly kept intact the common German market which was dominated by herself, but as Pflanze has stressed, 'economic preponderance did not lead necessarily to political domination' (Pflanze, 1990, 1: 258). Indeed, Prussia's economic victory paradoxically strengthened the determination of Austria and her allies to defend their position within the German Confederation even more tenaciously.

ON THE BRINK OF WAR

Cooperation between Prussia and Austria was only possible on the basis of a complete Austrian acknowledgement of Prussian hegemony north of the Main, but Emperor Francis Joseph was unwilling to make that concession.

Bismarck recognized the crude logic of the situation when he offered the Austrian ambassador in October 1865 either 'a genuine alliance or war to the knife' (Taylor, 1955: 81). Bad Gastein failed to improve Austro-Prussian relations and consequently Bismarck continued to work towards isolating Austria and preparing for war without irrevocably committing himself to it. Early in October he took advantage of a visit to Biarritz to allay Napoleon's fears of a Prusso-Austrian rapprochement. Throughout the winter of 1865/66 friction continued unabated in the Duchies. In Schleswig the Prussians tried to stamp out popular support for Augustenburg, while the Austrians pursued the opposite course in Holstein. When the Austrians permitted a pro-Augustenburg rally in Altona in January 1866, Bismarck dispatched what amounted to an ultimatum. This in effect was rejected. It appeared that Bismarck had now reached 'the line of hard resistance' (Pflanze, 1990, 1: 261). Not surprisingly, at the Prussian Crown Council of 28 February 1866 it was agreed that war with Austria was inevitable and Bismarck, conscious that the real issue at stake was the future control of Germany rather than Schleswig-Holstein, urged that Prussia should proclaim herself the leader of German nationalism.

Definite preparations for war were now made. On 8 April Bismarck concluded an offensive alliance with Italy for a period of three months. On the following day an attempt was made to woo nationalist opinion when the Prussian representative at Frankfurt proposed the calling of a German parliament based on universal franchise and direct elections. Liberals throughout Germany reacted with disbelief and incredulity, and the Confederation in a delaying action referred the proposals to committee.

Throughout April and May the armies of Austria, Prussia and Italy began to mobilize, but even at this stage Bismarck kept his options open. The most serious attempt at mediation was a proposal made by the Gablenz brothers, one of whom, Ludwig, was the governor of Holstein, the other, Anton, a Prussian landowner, to divide Germany along the Main line into Austrian and Prussian spheres of influence. There is considerable disagreement as to why Bismarck appeared to accept the Gablenz plan as a basis for a settlement. It has been seen as essentially a tactical manoeuvre to head off the threat of French intervention, but it has also been strongly argued that Bismarck wanted to avoid a German civil war and genuinely desired an organic solution to German unification. Bismarck was never averse to a diplomatic settlement which conceded the substance of his demands. He detailed an official to draft a secret memorandum in an attempt to square the circle of Austro-Prussian dual control and a national German parliament. In practice this would have enabled Prussia to control North Germany and be a dominant influence in the new parliament. Not surprisingly, Austria rejected the Gablenz initiative at the end of May 1866.

The maverick policies of Napoleon III were a constant threat to Bismarck. Not only was Napoleon anxious to detach Venetia from Austria, but he also hoped to gain Luxemburg, the Saar and the Bavarian Rhineland by playing off Prussia against Austria. Despite attempts by a later generation of patriotic German historians to argue to the contrary, Bismarck did contemplate offering France limited territorial concessions since French neutrality was of paramount importance. In April he foresaw that Prussia might have to cede the Saar to Napoleon and he even drew up plans for selling the state-owned coal mines to private investors to minimize the financial loss to the government, should the Saar have to be given to France. As Pflanze has observed, 'in an extremity it is probable that he would have surrendered even more. Unlike his historians, Bismarck was never one to dogmatize political possibilities' (Pflanze, 1990, 1: 295).

THE AUSTRO-PRUSSIAN WAR

On 1 June 1866 Vienna unilaterally broke the Gastein Convention and appealed to the Confederation to solve the future of the duchies. Prussia retaliated by occupying Holstein, which the Austrians evacuated without a shot being fired, and by proposing a revolutionary plan for a *Kleindeutsch* union. The Austrians then took the final steps to war. On 11 June they called upon the lesser states to mobilize on their behalf. The fear of Prussian domination rallied the majority of the lesser states to Austria. Only the Thuringian states, Oldenburg, the two Mecklenburgs and the cities of Hamburg, Bremen and Lübeck supported Berlin. Three decades of economic and political cooperation had not sufficed to stop the states of the *Zollverein* from waging war against each other. Austria also managed to secure French neutrality by promising to cede Venetia to Italy and to agree a French satellite state on the Rhine.

Prussia replied by declaring the Confederation dissolved and sent ultimatums to the neighbouring states of Saxony, Hanover and Hesse-Kassel demanding that they demobilize their armies and join the new *Kleindeutsch* state that Bismarck proposed to form. When they refused, Prussian troops on 17 June began to occupy all three states. Hesse-Kassel then requested the Confederation for military assistance. Austria's reply that she was ready to help any member state invaded by Prussia, was interpreted by Berlin as a declaration of war. Italy declared war on Austria on 20 June. Bismarck was ready to use any weapon to achieve victory. He attempted, for instance, 'to uncoil the springs of nationalistic discontent' (Pflanze, 1990, 1: 302) within the Austrian empire by encouraging separatist movements. He approved the formation of a Slavic corps in Serbia and explored the possibility of a Hungarian–Rumanian uprising.

However, rapid victory on the battlefield rendered these plans academic. The speedy defeat of Saxony opened the way up for the Prussian invasion of Austria. Implementing the tactics of Helmuth von Moltke, three Prussian armies advanced into Bohemia. On 3 July they converged on the Austrian forces at Königgratz and inflicted a major defeat on them. A number of factors helped explain this success. Moltke, with his efficient planning and use of railways, was able to move the Prussian troops to the front with great rapidity. The breech-loading needle gun also gave the Prussian infantryman a decisive superiority over the Austrians who were still using the old muzzle-loading rifles. Nevertheless the Austrian army was not destroyed at Königgratz. Effective use of cavalry and artillery by the Austrians managed to hold up the Prussians and enable the bulk of their troops to withdraw across the Danube.

After the victory at Königgratz, Bismarck sought to terminate hostilities before Austrian forces could regroup and other powers were tempted to intervene. Indeed, on the day before Königgratz, Vienna had already requested French mediation. Bismarck struggled to restrain both the generals and the king, who desired further military operations, and finally persuaded them to accept French proposals for a short truce. He then induced William, Napoleon and Francis Joseph to accept a realistic peace, while simultaneously preparing for the possibility that Napoleon might suddenly be tempted into armed intervention against Prussia. Von der Goltz, the Prussian ambassador in Paris, cleverly won over Napoleon by appealing to his vanity as mediator and by stressing that Prussia intended to respect the independence of the south German states. He also hinted unofficially that Bismarck might be willing to make some minor territorial concessions. Bismarck had immense difficulty in persuading the king to agree to the terms [**Doc. 17, p. 130**], but on 26 July 1866 the Preliminary Peace of Nikolsburg was signed.

In early August, belatedly responding to von der Goltz's veiled offers, the French suddenly claimed the whole of the left bank of the Rhine up to Mainz. The sheer scale of these demands destroyed French credibility as protector of South German independence. It enabled Bismarck to threaten to unite the whole of Germany against Napoleon, and made it easier to negotiate, as part of the individual peace treaties with Hesse-Darmstadt, Baden, Württemberg and Bavaria, military alliances ensuring Prussian control of their armies and railways in wartime. Napoleon gave way and on 23 August the Peace was confirmed at Prague.

Although Austria lost no territory, except Venetia to Italy, Franz Joseph conceded Prussia a free hand in Germany and the replacement of the German Confederation by two new potential federations, north and south of the Main; in neither was Austria to be represented. Bismarck had hoped to include provision for their eventual union, but the French vetoed it. On 20 September 1866 Prussia annexed Schleswig-Holstein, Hanover, Hesse-Kassel, Nassau and the City of Frankfurt, all of which had been allies of Austria. Due to French pressure, Saxony escaped absorption, although she was compelled to join the North German Confederation. The southern states remained independent, but as well as having to accept the military alliance with Prussia, they were charged indemnities and had to agree to renegotiate the *Zollverein* on Prussian terms.

THE HOME FRONT

Bismarck gambled on mobilizing public opinion in Prussia to support a national war against Austria. The initial signs were not encouraging. In March there was a wave of anti-war demonstrations throughout Prussia, and Bismarck's apparent conversion to a democratic national Germany (see page **36**) was met with cynicism by the Liberals. Even the *Nationalverein* was lukewarm. Its central committee, meeting in Berlin, condemned the imminent conflict as 'a cabinet war serving only domestic interests' [**Doc. 12, p. 127**].

Once the war started, however, the traditional alchemy of patriotism began to work and public opinion rapidly veered round to supporting Bismarck. The elections for the *Landtag*, which had been dissolved on 9 May 1866, were held while Prussian troops were advancing into Bohemia. The Liberals suffered a severe defeat, losing 142 seats to the Conservatives. The decisive victory of Königgratz, as we shall see in the next chapter, finally secured Bismarck's position. It enabled him subsequently to settle the constitutional conflict and reconstruct the political and diplomatic map of North Germany. In retrospect 'the marvellous march of events' (Grant Robertson, 1918: 128) assumes an air of inevitability. Yet had Austria won the war or even forced a prolonged conflict, which would have given time for war-weariness to affect Prussia, Bismarck might have been forced to resign or even have been impeached.

Part 3

THE NORTH GERMAN CONFEDERATION

4

The Creation of the North German Confederation, 1866–1867

The Austrian defeat and the subsequent creation of the North German Confederation mark a major turning-point in modern German history. Not only were the constitutional and economic foundations of the future German **Reich** laid in the years 1866–67 but also, in the process, the party political mould of the early 1860s in Prussia was permanently shattered.

Reich The Empire or German state after 1871.

THE PRUSSIAN INDEMNITY BILL

When the first session of the newly elected Prussian *Landtag* opened in August 1866, the constitutional conflict was still unresolved. In the teeth of cabinet opposition Bismarck persuaded the king to agree to an indemnity bill by which the government would seek the *Landtag's* retrospective approval for the expenditure of the last four years. The Liberals were as surprised by his evident desire to compromise as the ultra-Conservatives were infuriated by his refusal to exploit Königgratz to establish a neo-absolutist regime. The right-wing liberals and the moderates in both the Progressive Party and the Centre Left argued for its acceptance, believing that by cooperating with Bismarck, they would be able to influence his policies. Their colleagues on the Left, however, stressed that the bill would merely legalize four years' unconstitutional rule and would set a dangerous precedent for the future. The bill was passed by an overwhelming majority of 230 to 75 on 3 September 1866. The agonizing debates it caused among the ranks of both the Progressives and the Conservatives led to a secession of moderates, which in the course of the winter of 1866/67 crystallized into the **National Liberal Party** and the **Free Conservative Party**.

In retrospect liberal historians, such as Erich Eyck, have criticized the moderate Liberals for agreeing to the indemnity bill, but at the time any other

National Liberal Party Founded in 1867, its membership was drawn from the propertied and educated elite of German society. It's most influential period was 1867–79 when it cooperated with Bismarck as his chief parliamentary ally.

choice was virtually impossible (Eyck, 1950). They were in agreement with Bismarck's economic and foreign policy, and the successful outcome of the Austrian war had made them all too aware of the impotence of the parliamentary opposition. Realistically they accepted the need for cooperating with Bismarck in shaping the North German Confederation, as the attitude of the south Germans – at least temporarily – rendered national unification impossible [**Doc. 19, p. 132**]. In other words, 'three-quarters of a loaf appeared better than none' (Windell, 1969: 295).

Bismarck also had compelling reasons for ending the constitutional conflict. His diplomatic training had equipped him to view politics in terms of a balance of forces. He appreciated that the Liberals were still a force to be reckoned with and that he would need their support to neutralize the considerable pockets of hostility in the newly annexed territories and to counter the particularism of the remaining independent states when it came to drafting the constitution of the North German Confederation.

THE SPOILS OF WAR

The outright annexation of Hanover, Nassau, Hesse-Kassel, Schleswig-Holstein and Frankfurt contrasted starkly with Bismarck's willingness to compromise with the Prussian *Landtag*. This was an arbitrary act reminiscent of Napoleon I, and, as Golo Mann put it, clear confirmation that Prussia 'had no intention of merging into Germany' (Mann, 1968: 182). The provinces were initially occupied and somewhat brutally absorbed into the Prussian administrative system. Frankfurt was forced to pay a punitive indemnity and the ruling houses of Hanover, Hesse-Kassel and Nassau were deposed.

Annexation was supported by the majority of Liberals in the defeated states as they appreciated the material advantages of union with Prussia and realized that only armed intervention could have overcome stubborn local patriotism. Nevertheless, the initial experience of occupation, particularly in Hanover, was oppressive. The press was censored, disloyal civil servants were suspended, and former Hanoverian soldiers with **Guelph** or loyalist sympathies were imprisoned. Up to the summer of 1867 a policy of crude Prussianization was carried out, but when in August Crown Prince Frederick sharply warned of the mounting hostility towards Berlin in Hanover, Bismarck intervened and conceded a tolerable degree of local autonomy, which was later extended to Hesse-Kassel and Nassau. Bismarck could not afford to ignore the fact that aggressive Prussianization would only stiffen the opposition of the south German states to eventual German unification.

THE CONSTITUTION OF THE NORTH GERMAN CONFEDERATION

Bismarck lost little time in drafting the constitution of the North German Confederation. In early August 1866 the rulers of the remaining independent states north of the Main – Saxony, Hesse-Darmstadt, Brunswick, Oldenburg, Saxe-Weimar and Coburg, Thuringia and Meiningen, as well as the Free cities of Hamburg, Bremen and Lubeck (see map on page 00) – were invited to Berlin to attend what Grant Robertson aptly called a 'congress of roaches presided over by a benevolent pike' (Grant Robertson, 1918: 225). They had little option but to accept a draft federal constitution which would be submitted for approval to a constituent assembly elected by direct universal manhood suffrage, and agree that their armed forces would now come under the supreme command of the King of Prussia in his role as President of the North German Confederation, although the administration of routine military affairs would still be left to the individual state governments.

Although Pflanze has argued that 'seldom in history has a constitution been so clearly the product of the thought and will of a single individual' (Pflanze, 1990, 1: 341) the political situation in 1867 imposed considerable restraints on Bismarck. He had to ensure the hegemony of Prussia, but at the same time needed to create 'an acceptable Prussian image south of the Main' (Windell, 1969: 296), so that it would eventually be possible to draw the southern states into union with the North German Confederation.

While recuperating from his exertions of the summer as a guest of Prince Putbus on the Baltic island of Rügen, he drew up two key documents, the so-called 'Putbus Dictates', which outlined the main points of the new constitution. The first draft of the constitution was ready by December. To make possible the eventual accession of the southern states it was 'designed to exact the minimum surrender of state sovereignty compatible with creating a viable framework within which a national state could evolve' (Windell, 1969: 298). The Confederation consequently became responsible for defence and foreign policy and could legislate on such matters as customs, commerce, banking and civil and commercial law.

In essence the constitution was to consist of the Presidency (*Praesidium*), a post to be occupied by the King of Prussia, the Federal Council (**Bundesrat**) and the Chamber of Deputies (**Reichstag**). Responsibility for foreign affairs, for the declaration of war and for the dismissal of Confederate officials was invested in the President, that is the King of Prussia, who was also Supreme Commander of the armed forces. The *Bundesrat* was composed of representatives nominated by the member states of the Confederation and was created specifically to demonstrate a continuity with the former German Confederation. Voting procedure remained unchanged, as the states' representatives

Bundesrat Federal Council or upper house of the German parliament in which the German states were represented according to their size and power.

Reichstag The lower house of the North German Confederation (1867–1970) and of the German *Reich*, 1867–1945.

voted en bloc according to the instructions of their governments. Bismarck avoided stressing the massive preponderance of Prussia's power in North Germany by allotting her a modest but adequate total of seventeen seats out of forty-three in the *Bundesrat*; that was the number reached by adding together the votes Prussia and the states which she had annexed had commanded in the former Frankfurt Diet. The *Bundesrat* had both legislative and executive functions. It could be convened independently of the *Reichstag*, initiate legislation and veto bills from the lower house. While bills had to be approved both by the *Bundesrat* and *Reichstag*, constitutional amendments required a two-thirds majority in the *Bundesrat*, which was impossible to secure without Prussian consent. The executive functions of the *Bundesrat* were to be carried out through committees dealing with particular areas of responsibility, which Bismarck assumed, but did not specifically state, would gradually evolve into Confederate departments.

Faithful to the model of the former German Confederation, the draft also initially envisaged that the chancellor, the only federal minister to be created by the constitution, would merely preside over the *Bundesrat*. He would be appointed by Berlin and receive instructions from Bismarck acting in his role of Prussian foreign minister. Originally the chancellorship was to have gone to the former Prussian delegate at Frankfurt, but Bismarck filled the post himself when its potential importance became clear. By remaining Prussian minister-president he secured himself a pivotal position within the constitution.

The role of the *Reichstag*, as Pflanze has stressed, emphasized 'the fundamental dilemma of [Bismarck's] constitutional thinking' (Pflanze, 1990, 1: 345). He wanted to use it as a potential check on the Crown, the federal states, the bureaucracy and the liberals without creating parliamentary government. He therefore took the key decision to introduce universal male franchise. Potentially this would enable him, like Napoleon III, to appeal over the heads of parliament to the people, but to discourage the formation of popular workers' and peasants' parties, there was to be no payment of parliamentary deputies. Initially in the Putbus drafts there was to be no provision for the rights of interpellation which would ensure that ministers would be subject to parliamentary questions.

Matricular contribution
Fixed contribution paid by the German states to the central government. The term comes originally from the Holy Roman Empire where member states were given a list of money and troops to be supplied annually.

The articles on taxation also 'made a mockery of parliamentary budget rights' (Pflanze, 1990, 1: 344). There was to be no annual budget or provision for parliamentary control of military expenditure. The Confederation was permitted to levy indirect taxation, but this ensured that once initial parliamentary approval had been gained, taxation would become automatic and increase as the economy expanded. The Confederation's income was to be supplemented by annual '**matricular contributions**' or fixed financial grants from the states.

From 15 December 1866 to 7 February 1867 a conference of plenipotentiaries from the state governments met in Berlin to discuss the constitution in detail. The majority of the states, intent on increasing their own power, rallied behind a proposal put forward by the representatives of Oldenburg to create a proper Confederate cabinet and an upper house of princes, designed both to weaken Prussian influence and be a check on the *Reichstag*. Bismarck countered with his familiar stick and carrot technique. He mollified the opposition by granting the individual states minor concessions, but he also threatened to harness the democratic forces of the *Reichstag* against the residual powers of the states if he failed to secure consent for the constitution of the North German Federation.

The **Constituent Reichstag** was elected on 12 February 1867. Out of a possible 297 seats the National Liberals won 79, the Free Conservatives 39 and the Progressives a mere 19, while the Conservatives gained 59. The remainder went to the small particularist and nationalist splinter parties – the Poles, Danes, Guelphs and **Ultramontanes**. When discussions began on the draft constitution, Bismarck reverted to his familiar tactics and played off the *Reichstag* against the state governments. He raised the spectre of Liberal opposition to browbeat the state governments into accepting the constitution. He then secured their agreement to a secret treaty to dissolve the *Reichstag* and arbitrarily to impose a constitution should the Liberal opposition threaten ratification.

Constituent Reichstag Parliament elected to draw up and approve a constitution.

Ultramontane Political party in favour of the absolute spiritual authority of the pope. In other words a Catholic party.

Nevertheless the Liberals did win considerable concessions which went some way to removing the basic deficiencies of the Bismarck draft and to giving the *Reichstag* many of the essential powers of a modern parliament. Bismarck conceded legal immunity to members of the *Reichstag* during parliamentary sessions, the right to interpellate and voting by secret ballot in general elections, although this did not really become effective until proper ballot envelopes and voting booths were introduced in 1902. He also agreed to the commitment to hold elections sixty days after the dissolution of the *Reichstag*. He still refused, however, to permit the payment of deputies.

The National Liberals sought to make both the chancellor and the heads of the administrative committees set up by the *Bundesrat* legally responsible to the *Reichstag*. This did not entail parliamentary government in the British sense but rather the guarantee that the chancellor and his leading officials would be legally responsible for the decisions they took. Bismarck feared that this could undermine his own power by recreating in the North German Confederation the Prussian tradition of collegial or joint ministerial responsibility. He consequently insisted that only the chancellor, together with the President, or in other words the King of Prussia, should sign all laws and ordinances.

The Liberals also subjected the financial clauses to a searching examination. They were able to force Bismarck to concede parliamentary control over an annual budget, but this by no means gave the *Reichstag* a complete grip on the Confederation's finances. Most of the Confederation's expenditure was earmarked for the military or '**iron budget**', which Bismarck refused to surrender to annual parliamentary control. After a deadlock which in early April placed the whole constitutional settlement in doubt, Bismarck negotiated a compromise with the National Liberals that was facilitated by the war scare over Luxemburg (see page **50**). The size of the army was now fixed until 31 December 1871. Thereafter any expansion and consequent increase in the budget was to be subject to approval by the *Reichstag*.

Iron budget The military budget for Prussia's and, after 1871 Germany's, armed forces.

On 16 April 1867 the *Reichstag* finally ratified the amended constitution, by 230 to 53. The constitution has never ceased to be the subject of controversy. Opinions have varied as to whether it was 'the Königgratz of liberalism in Germany' (Grant Robertson, 1918: 26, 234), or whether in fact it made Germany 'a constitutional country' with a parliament that 'possessed every essential function' (Taylor, 1955: 98). It is certainly true that the National Liberals had extracted from Bismarck greater concessions than he intended to make. On the other hand the executive was never successfully subjected to parliamentary control until 1919.

Although Bismarck had protected both the Crown's and Prussia's power within the Confederation, whilst ensuring that his own position was almost impregnable, in many ways the constitution reflected the realities of German politics in 1867 and was a compromise between the forces of liberal-nationalism, democracy and Prussian conservatism. Lothar Gall has argued that it was 'much more a consumption of something for which the time was ripe than the manipulative creation of an individual' (Gall, 1986, 1: 314–15).

5

Bismarck, Napoleon and the Southern States

Although the Treaty of Prague confirmed Prussian hegemony north of the Main and, by dissolving the old German Confederation, finally destroyed the basis of Habsburg influence in Germany, no permanent solution to the German problem had yet been found and so the situation remained unstable and potentially dangerous. The southern states were weak and divided and their close economic and military ties with the North German Confederation seemed to indicate that their absorption was only a matter of time, but it was also clear that any breach of the Main line would be bitterly opposed by the French. Napoleon, whose political position essentially depended on the international prestige of his regime, could not afford to tolerate any further Prussian aggrandizement unless accompanied by substantial concessions from Berlin. Bismarck, however, was coming under increasing pressure from the National Liberals and Free Conservatives to complete unification without sacrificing an inch of German territory. He was fortunate that there was still little danger of a hostile European alliance forming. The powers were distracted by the **Eastern question**, which had re-emerged with the Cretan revolt against Turkish rule in the summer of 1866 and remained in a state of 'diplomatic disorientation' (see page **25**) from each other.

Bismarck's own attitude towards south Germany was ambiguous [**Doc. 21, p. 133**]. Although French pressure was the real reason why he had halted at the Main, he considered the Catholic south as an essentially alien society, which would not integrate easily with the Protestant north. On the other hand he was aware of the dangers of a power vacuum in the south and of the impatient desire of the nationalists to complete unification. Taylor has argued that 'Bismarck had no clear aim after the victories of 1866 . . . he asked only to be left alone' (Taylor, 1955: 102). In fact, Bismarck developed a whole range of policies for accomplishing the gradual integration of the south by enmeshing it in a series of military, economic and constitutional links, which without overtly disturbing the status quo would eventually set up an irresistible momentum towards national unity.

Eastern Question The diplomatic and political problems caused by the decay of the Turkish Empire.

THE LUXEMBURG CRISIS

After failing to gain the Palatinate in August 1866, Napoleon redoubled his efforts to win territorial concessions elsewhere from Prussia. Increasingly he focused on Luxemburg, which he was willing to purchase from the King of Holland, but, as it had formed part of the German Confederation since 1814, it was garrisoned by Prussian troops. Bismarck's reaction to the French initiative was complex and opportunist. It is almost impossible to know whether he genuinely wanted a settlement with Napoleon or whether he deliberately provoked a major crisis in order to appeal to nationalist sentiment in the new *Reichstag* and to strengthen his hold over the southern states by conjuring up the threat of an aggressive France. Retrospectively, the French were convinced that Bismarck had set a trap for them but there is some evidence to suggest that initially Bismarck was not opposed to their purchase of the Duchy. He certainly gave Napoleon careful advice on how to proceed, and, when the news of Napoleon's negotiations with the Dutch became public in March 1867, the first reaction of the papers closest to the government was to play down the importance of Prussia's involvement in Luxemburg. It has been argued that Bismarck hoped to appease Napoleon, so that he could concentrate on consolidating the North German Confederation without fear of French intervention (Taylor, 1955). However, a crisis with France would also stimulate German nationalism and deflect Liberal criticism of the new constitution. Bismarck himself was scarcely a free agent. Once the *Reichstag* with its strong Nationalist representation met, he could not be seen to be encouraging Napoleon to purchase land which could be regarded as German.

Napoleon's best hope of success lay in acting quickly, but he missed the chance of achieving a quick settlement in September 1866 before Bismarck fell ill and retreated to Rügen (see page **45**). When Bismarck returned to Berlin in December, he increasingly had serious doubts about the purchase, but nevertheless kept his options open. By February he seemed to want to spin out the affair for a further six months before risking a rupture with France, so that he would have time to consolidate north Germany and tighten the links with the south.

Napoleon opened negotiations with the Dutch king on 16 March 1867. He also began a crude pro-French propaganda campaign in the duchy. This played into Bismarck's hands by enflaming German nationalism just when the *Reichstag* was debating the contentious issues of ministerial responsibility and parliamentary control of the 'iron budget'. On 1 April Bismarck faced an interpellation in the *Reichstag*, which he had very probably inspired, deploring the rumoured French purchase of Luxemburg. The subsequent explosion of nationalist wrath left little room for diplomatic manoeuvre. Under pressure from Berlin, the Dutch king refused to sell the duchy.

Nevertheless, despite exploiting the crisis over the next three weeks for domestic purposes, Bismarck pulled back from war and indicated to the British that he would be ready to accept the mediation of the Great Powers [Doc. 20, p. 132]. At the subsequent London Conference, a compromise was arranged whereby the Prussian garrison was withdrawn and the duchy was neutralized under a Great Power guarantee. Although Napoleon had gained a significant military concession, it was outweighed by the scale of the diplomatic defeat he had again suffered. The Luxemburg affair had emphasized the growing tension between Prussia and France and can be seen as 'the dress rehearsal for the crisis of 1870' (Mosse, 1958: 263). In retrospect the crisis appears to be a triumph of timing, yet it is more likely that Bismarck pursued his familiar 'strategy of alternatives' until his hand was finally forced in April 1867.

THE SOUTHERN STATES AND GERMAN INTEGRATION

The Luxemburg crisis provided Bismarck with an opportunity to attempt to tighten the links between north and south Germany. He tried unsuccessfully to draw Bavaria into a special or 'constitutional' alliance with the north and also failed to breach the Main line, being unable to persuade southern Hesse to join the North German Confederation.

In the short term it was only economic pressure that secured Berlin an important but far from final victory over southern particularism. In the autumn of 1866 the south had agreed to negotiate a new customs union with the North German Confederation. As an interim measure, the existing *Zollverein* remained in force but could be dissolved by Prussia at six months notice. In June 1867 the ministers of the southern states were summoned to Berlin where, under threat of a dissolution of the *Zollverein*, they agreed to a radical revision of its constitution. Despite Bavarian opposition it was accepted that the existing General Congress and **liberum veto** should be replaced by a new council under the presidency of Prussia, and a customs union parliament, in which members of the North German *Reichstag* and specially democratically elected south German representatives would sit together.

Liberum veto The right to veto.

Bismarck had, perhaps rather naively, assumed that the self-evident material advantages of the *Zollverein* would quickly overcome southern particularism and lead the way to political union. He had expected that the German nationalist parties would win big majorities when the elections for the *Zollverein* parliament were held in the southern states in February 1868. However, he overestimated the influence of the businessmen, chambers of commerce and trade associations in the less industrialized south, and the elections resulted in a decided rebuff for Prussia. Forty-nine out of a possible eighty-five southern deputies were hostile to any attempt to widen the economic union into a political one. In Bavaria a strongly Catholic and particularist patriot party had emerged, while in Württemberg the People's Party, warning that any political union with Prussia would entail excessive taxation, conscription and 'keep[ing] your mouth shut' (Craig, 1978: 19), won every seat.

When the deputies assembled in Berlin in April 1868 it was therefore clear that there would be no quick evolution from an economic into a political union. Nevertheless it can be argued that the *Zollverein* parliament was of some psychological value to the cause of German unity as it brought southern and northern deputies who were both elected by universal suffrage into direct contact with each other. Even particularists were now forced to stress their German rather than regional loyalties, although they still clung fiercely to the status quo and opposed any move towards unity.

During the next two years Bismarck appeared to accept that no immediate progress in German unity could be reached [**Doc. 21, p. 133**], but in practice he continued to exploit any chance as it arose and thus subtly and persistently undermined the Prague settlement. In the spring of 1868, for example, he welcomed a proposal by Hohenlohe, the Bavarian minister-president, for creating a southern federation because he perceived that it would weaken the strong particularist traditions of the individual states. His train of thought was clearly revealed when he observed that 'the most difficult part of the task of national reconstruction is the removal of the existing. If what exists is breached, even though it be through a south German confederation, a healthy national life will grow by itself out of the ruins' (Pflanze, 1990, 1: 400). It is not surprising therefore that both Württemberg and Bavaria eventually rejected the scheme.

Bismarck was more successful with plans for military integration. In February 1867 the southern states reluctantly agreed to reorganize their armed forces along Prussian lines and a year later decided on a joint mobilization scheme in the event of war. In 1869 Prussia also managed to gain representation on the south German military committee administering the former confederate fortresses, which Bismarck optimistically believed would evolve into a German war cabinet.

By early 1870 the evolutionary approach to German unity seemed to have failed. Southern particularism showed no signs of weakening [**Doc. 21, p. 133**]. The Patriot Party had won a decisive victory in the Bavarian elections in November 1869, while a wave of anti-Prussian feeling swept Württemberg, culminating in a popular petition demanding the repeal of the Conscription Act of 1868. Simultaneously, Bismarck was coming under pressure from the National Liberals in the *Reichstag* to complete unification. He was also increasingly aware that he would require parliamentary approval for renewing the 'iron budget' at the end of 1871 and that the more convincingly he could pose as the successful champion of German unity, the easier its passage would be. He therefore attempted to persuade the southern states to approve King William's adoption of the title Emperor of Germany, but it was clear by early 1870 that this would be rejected. To achieve unification, Bismarck needed above all 'to give Germany a new "dose" of national enthusiasm' (Taylor, 1955: 115). A major diplomatic success would probably have sufficed but victorious war was by no means excluded.

6

The Franco-Prussian War and the Unification of Germany, 1870–1871

THE HOHENZOLLERN CANDIDATURE

The extent and motivation of Bismarck's involvement in the candidacy of Prince Leopold of Hohenzollern-Sigmaringen for the Spanish throne, which was the immediate cause of the Franco-Prussian war, remains a controversial question. Despite the emergence of some information in the 1890s, only in 1945 did it become possible to analyse Bismarck's involvement in detail when the relevant files, which had hitherto been denied to historians by the German government, fell into the hands of the Allies and were published in 1957 (Bonnin, 1957). However, even this material, while confirming beyond doubt Bismarck's complicity, failed to show conclusively that he was aiming at war. After all, as Pflanze has observed, his 'favourite garment was never the straitjacket but the reversible overcoat' (Pflanze, 1990, 1: 45). Eberhard Kolb (1970) has argued that Bismarck underestimated the hostile reaction the candidature would unleash in France. Other historians stress that Bismarck exploited it either to weaken Napoleon by precipitating an internal political crisis, or to isolate the hawks within the French cabinet, thereby strengthening those who were inclined to tolerate the unification of Germany (Craig, 1978; Dittrich, 1970). However, it is more likely that Bismarck knowingly risked war, even though he probably hoped to avoid it, as there appeared no other way of accelerating the unification of Germany [**Doc. 21, p. 133**].

Bismarck's opportunity to intervene in Spanish politics occurred following the coup in Madrid in September 1868. Queen Isabella abdicated, and the provisional government decided to replace the Bourbons with a new ruling dynasty, a decision welcomed by Bismarck as it removed a traditionally Francophile dynasty from power. After unsuccessful attempts to find Portuguese and Italian candidates, Marshal Prim, the Spanish minister-president, sounded out Prince Leopold Hohenzollern-Sigmaringen, a member of the south German and Catholic branch of the Prussian royal family, who was married to a Portuguese princess. In February 1870 a formal offer was made, and Leopold finally accepted in early June after considerable pressure from Bismarck, who refused to be deterred by King William's scepticism and subtly played upon Leopold's sense of duty and ambition as a Prussian officer.

Bismarck, to quote Otto Pflanze, had by now 'deliberately set sail on a collision course with the intent of provoking either war or a French internal collapse' (Pflanze, 1990, 1: 462). He had already received several veiled warnings from the French ambassador, and an informed article in an influential Viennese newspaper in April reported that Napoleon had warned the Spanish ambassador in Paris that Leopold's accession would lead to war. Bismarck was also aware of the hawkish and mercurial nature of Gramont, the new French foreign minister. It is therefore significant that on 6 June 1870 Bismarck informed Major Max von Versen, his agent in Madrid, that 'complications' with France were exactly what he was 'looking for' (Halperin, 1973: 85).

Bismarck had hoped that Leopold's candidature would be quickly ratified by the **Cortes,** thereby presenting the French with a *fait accompli.* A muddle over dates by a cypher clerk in the Prussian embassy, however, led to an unexpected delay, during which the secret reached Paris. It was, to quote Denis Showalter 'one of those historical ball-bearings on which great events so often turn' (Showalter, 2004: 233). King William, alarmed at the bellicose reaction in Paris, persuaded Leopold to stand down.

Cortes The Spanish Parliament.

Bismarck was only saved from the greatest reverse in his career by Gramont's failure to perceive the extent of his own success. Gramont rashly insisted on the provision of guarantees against a renewal of the candidacy, but when William was confronted by the French ambassador at Ems, his summer palace, on 13 July he refused and promptly sent an account of the interview to his chancellor [**Doc. 22a, p. 134**]. Bismarck was probably more intent on warding off defeat than on precipitating war, and published in the German and European press an edited version of the Ems telegram which emphasised the rebuff delivered to the ambassador [**Doc. 22b, p. 134**]. Eyck has argued that its publication was tantamount to a declaration of war (Eyck, 1950). On 13 July the French cabinet had in fact already agreed to compromise on the guarantees, but the Ems telegram so infuriated the war party at court, the nationalist deputies and public opinion that a diplomatic settlement was impossible and Napoleon was driven to declare war on 15 July. On the other hand, the telegram was a 'clear statement of the facts' (Taylor, 1955: 121). Bismarck did not invent William's refusal and it can be said with some justice that responsibility for the war 'rests not on one side or the other but squarely on both' (Halperin, 1973: 91).

THE OUTBREAK OF WAR

Once war was declared, Bismarck had three priorities. He had to ensure that it could be fought and won in diplomatic isolation, while simultaneously exploiting the outburst of patriotism to complete German unity. Then he had to devise a peace treaty that would quickly terminate hostilities while providing Germany with a secure western frontier.

As in 1864 and 1866, the international situation continued to favour Prussia. Napoleon was unable to create a triple alliance with Italy and Austria despite the conclusion of a draft agreement in May 1869. Once hostilities had broken out both Austria and Italy remained neutral. Francis-Joseph kept his options open by partially mobilizing, but the Italian cabinet insisted on neutrality, even when Napoleon belatedly in August evacuated the French garrison from Rome, which had been guaranteeing the independence of the Papacy since 1849. Bismarck had little to fear in the short term from either Russia or Britain. The Tsar reaffirmed his 1869 commitment to occupy Galicia in the event of Austrian intervention, and Britain, suspicious of Napoleon's ambitions in Belgium, was reassured by Prussian promises to respect Belgian neutrality.

Had the Prussians suffered any serious military reverse the dangers of the war escalating into a European conflict involving the Great Powers would have increased. However, luck, the skill of the Prussian General Staff, the effectiveness of the new Krupp field batteries and the superior morale of the Prussian troops ensured a rapid series of French defeats. A swift victory was by no means a foregone conclusion. The French army was potentially a formidable force armed with the highly effective chasse-pot rifle and a small number of **mitrailleuses**. Yet the initial French mobilization was so chaotic that plans for an immediate offensive across the Rhine had to be dropped. Instead, the French had to hold a defensive line from Metz to Strasburg.

Mitrailleuse First machine-gun to be used in major combat, during the Franco-Prussian War of 1870–71.

Von Moltke responded by sending three armies into Lorraine. He hoped to encircle the French north of the Saar and repeat the great victory of Königgrätz but the French failed to fall into the trap and the German Third Army also moved too slowly. Von Moltke did, however, manage to lay siege to the French army of the Rhine in Metz. When the Army of Chalons attempted to come to its rescue, it was destroyed at the decisive battle of Sedan on 1 September, where Napoleon and over 104,000 French soldiers were taken prisoner.

Sedan destroyed the Bonarpartist regime. Napoleon became a prisoner of war and the Empress Eugenie fled to England. The war did not, however end. The Government of National Defence was set up in Paris with the avowed aim of continuing the fight. Metz fell in October and Paris itself was put under siege at the end of September. With all its attendant uncertainties and dangers, the war dragged on until the fall of Paris in January 1871. While two Prussian armies were tied up around Paris, their communications were harassed by partisans [**Doc. 23, p. 134**] and, ominously, the Government of National Defence began to prepare for a people's war. By December 'the prestige of Sedan was dribbling away and with it all hope of securing a peace as cheap and successful as that which followed Sadowa' [Königgratz] (Howard, 1962: 388).

This situation was potentially dangerous for Prussia. The longer the conflict lasted, the greater the danger of it spreading and of France acquiring allies. Consequently Bismarck, despite the opposition of von Moltke and the generals, who refused to cooperate because they desired first to complete the annihilation of the French armies [**Doc. 24, p. 135**], lost little opportunity to conduct unofficial peace talks with both Napoleon and representatives of the Government of National Defence.

It was not, however, primarily the army which prevented an early peace but rather Bismarck's demand for Alsace-Lorraine, the annexation of which was to fuel French desire for revanche over the next half-century. Historians are divided on whether Bismarck was forced by popular nationalism and military pressure into annexation or whether he himself manipulated the press and public opinion into voicing this demand. Gordon Craig has attempted to synthesize the debate by observing 'an objective view of the evidence would seem to indicate that neither public opinion nor Bismarck needed inducement' (Craig, 1978: p. 29). There is little doubt that annexation was popular. At the start of the war, nationalist journals in both north and south Germany began to call for the liberation of these two predominantly German-speaking provinces which had been annexed by France in the seventeenth and eighteenth centuries. Although not completely immune to nationalist argument, Bismarck primarily regarded Alsace and northern Lorraine as a vital strategic barrier against future French attacks. He showed surprisingly little interest in the Lorraine iron ore deposits (Silverman, 1972; Showalter, 2004).

THE UNIFICATION OF *KLEINDEUTSCHLAND*

It has been argued that the final unification of Germany was a consequence of these growing diplomatic and military uncertainties rather than the main object of the war (Taylor, 1955). The creation of the German *Reich* would, of course, ensure the continued participation of the southern states, should the war be prolonged. However, the evidence suggests rather that Bismarck exploited the war as 'a sudden blessed opportunity to complete the work of national unification which he had feared would remain unfinished for years' (Hamerow, 1972: 417). Although the war was initially accompanied by an upsurge of nationalist feeling throughout the south, unification was not the result of sustained popular pressure but ultimately the recognition by the two major southern states, Bavaria and Württemberg, that in an era of Franco-German hostility 'the price of independence was political isolation, economic decline and military insecurity' (Hamerow, 1972: 421). After Sedan, Bavaria agreed to join the North German Confederation, but only in return for concessions which would seriously have weakened its cohesion. Although Bismarck recognized that the south had to be persuaded rather than conquered, he did not hesitate behind the scenes to threaten Bavaria with economic and political isolation. By hinting at a unilateral termination of the *Zollverein* treaty with Bavaria, and by inviting the other southern states to Versailles in October to discuss unity, he forced the Bavarian cabinet to adopt a more flexible attitude. Bismarck exploited the differences between the individual states and negotiated separately with them. In practice he made considerable concessions, which strengthened the federal element in the constitution of 1867 (see page **46**), although they fell far short of Bavaria's original demands..

At the end of November the southern states had agreed to union, and King Ludwig of Bavaria was bribed to invite William to accept the title of Emperor. By January 1871 the necessary legislation had passed both the southern parliaments and the North German *Reichstag* where, despite initial demands by the Progressives for a more liberal constitution and reservations by the National Liberals on the concessions to southern particularism, the government gained a large majority. William's reluctance to make such a radical break with tradition was finally overcome, and on 18 January 1871 the Empire was proclaimed in the Hall of Mirrors at Versailles.

THE ARMISTICE AND THE TREATY OF FRANKFURT

During these complex constitutional negotiations tension continued to grow between Bismarck and the generals [**Doc. 24, p. 135**]. Bismarck was determined to start peace talks once Paris had fallen, whereas the 'politically illiterate' (Crankshaw, 1981: 290) von Moltke resented diplomatic considerations which hampered plans for the further vigorous prosecution of the war. In mid-January, when the fall of Paris was imminent, von Moltke drew up a draft surrender document which was so draconian that it would have strengthened the French will to resist. Bismarck, appalled at von Moltke's lack of diplomatic finesse, successfully persuaded William to grant him full responsibility for the armistice negotiations. Bismarck, who had consistently kept in contact with Napoleon and the Empress, was then able to exert pressure on the French Government of National Defence at Bordeaux to agree to an immediate armistice in return for recognition as the lawful government of France. On 25 January 1871 a three-week armistice was signed to enable elections to be held for a National Assembly. When it met it voted overwhelmingly for peace.

When the Preliminary Peace was signed on 26 February 1871 the Germans extracted stiff terms. Alsace and northern Lorraine – including the key fortress of Metz, which was added for strategic reasons – were annexed. An indemnity of five billion francs was also to be paid over four years, after which the army of occupation in the eastern provinces would be withdrawn. The peace was confirmed by the Treaty of Frankfurt in May. Unlike the Prague Treaty of 1866 it was no triumph for moderation. Bismarck had insisted on arbitrary annexation of Alsace and Lorraine unlegitimized by referenda, which, as Fritz Stern has observed, only 'cemented the enmity it was supposed to be the consequence of' (Stern, 1977: 146). Bismarck, fearing future French aggression, observed that 'an enemy whose honest friendship can never be won, must at least be rendered somewhat less harmful' (Pflanze, 1990, 1: 489). In retrospect, few would disagree with Lothar Gall (1970: 367) that the annexation was 'a miscalculation of great consequence' [**Doc. 25, p. 136**].

Part 4

THE ECONOMIC AND CONSTITUTIONAL CONTEXT, 1871–1890

7

The Second *Reich*: a Hybrid State

The new German *Reich* formally created on 4 May 1871 was modelled on the former North German Confederation. It consisted of a 'perpetual union' of twenty-two sovereign states and three Free Hanseatic cities. It possessed neither a national flag until 1892 nor a national anthem until 1919. Not surprisingly the new *Reich* initially presented its citizens with a considerable 'identity problem' as 'it was neither a new creation nor a product of the past' (Craig, 1978: 55). The word *Reich* invoked historic memories of the old Holy Roman Empire while, particularly for the south German states and Saxony which retained many of the outward trappings of independence, there seemed to be a certain superficial continuity with the German Confederation of 1815. On the other hand, although the new *Reich* had a democratically elected national parliament, its founder, Bismarck, went out of his way to repudiate any similarities with the Frankfurt Assembly of 1848–49. Karl Marx characterized this paradoxical structure that Bismarck had created as 'a thoroughly self-contradictory and self-nullifying hermaphrodite' (Wehler, 1985: 55), yet for all its contradictions it did lay the foundations for a new national Germany.

THE ADMINISTRATIVE AND LEGISLATIVE INFRASTRUCTURE

Initially the *Reich's* competencies covered only economic, diplomatic and military matters. The vast bulk of domestic policy still remained in the hands of the individual states, and only gradually did the *Reich* acquire the administrative apparatus of a government (Green, 2001). By the mid-1870s the commercial, financial and legal infrastructure of the new *Reich* was in place. There was a uniform commercial code with a special court to enforce it, a national currency, the *Reichsmark*, which was based on the gold standard,

Reichsbank The German
Central Bank, 1875–
1945, responsible for
the issue of currency.

and the **Reichsbank**, set up in 1875, served as the German central bank. Equally important for ultimate national unity was the drafting of the national criminal and civil law codes and the insistence on uniform legal procedure in courts throughout the *Reich*. These reforms played a decisive role in welding together the German states into a national entity, but nevertheless the old particularism of the states with their individual monarchies and parliaments (*Landtage*) lived on, at least until the 1890s.

The symbol of German unity was the *Reichstag*, the 397 members of which were elected by universal manhood suffrage. It possessed formidable constitutional powers but ultimately these were insufficient to turn the Second *Reich* into a parliamentary democracy. It was part of Bismarck's complex system of checks and balances. Although it had the crucial right to withhold its assent to legislation (including the budget) and could initiate debates, it could not dissolve itself, propose legislation or enforce the resignation of

Kaiser Emperor of
Germany.

the chancellor, who was responsible solely to the **Kaiser**. *Reichstag* elections never led to a change of government. To Bismarck, the *Reichstag* was a body which should react to events rather than initiate them. In 1884 he observed that 'it should be able to prevent bad laws from being passed . . . and the waste of public money; but it cannot govern' (Pflanze, 1990, 2: 155). Its grip on the *Reich's* finances was, however, weak. The constitution gave it the power to enforce the collection of tolls and sales taxes on certain articles such as sugar, tobacco and beer. Direct taxes, while determined by the central government, could only be collected by the individual states. Its control over the military budget was also tenuous. In 1874 the *Reichstag* agreed to the Septennial Law whereby it approved the size of the army and the military budget for a set period of seven years.

The upper house, the *Bundesrat,* was not directly elected. It was composed of delegations from the eighteen German states. The *Bundesrat* had to give its approval before war could be declared or action taken against a rebellious member state. A vote of fourteen, rather than two-thirds, as originally in 1867 (see page 46), could now block any constitutional amendment, putting a veto within reach of the southern states if they could form a common front. Bavaria, Württemberg and Baden alone could command fourteen votes between themselves. Special concessions to these three states also authorized local taxation and administration of the postal and telegraph systems, while Bavaria and Württemberg were allowed to maintain their own armies in peacetime.

Although these concessions 'helped preserve a climate in which particularism would remain respectable' (Windell, 1969: 300), the *Bundesrat* nevertheless remained, as Pinson put it, a 'camouflage for Prussian supremacy' (Pinson, 1954: 159). As Prussia commanded seventeen out of a total fifty-eight votes, she could effectively veto any constitutional change. Prussian and *Reich* institutions were closely enmeshed at executive level: the Emperor was the King of Prussia, and the chancellor was the prime minister, foreign minister and head of the Prussian delegation to the *Bundesrat*.

Initially Bismarck had no clearly thought-out plan for creating an efficient and rational administrative structure for the new *Reich*. In August 1867 he set up a chancellor's office where, as he expressed it, 'the different administrative branches' could come together and find 'their focal point' (Pflanze, 1990, 2: 133). Over the next seven years the need to draft legislation on a national scale which had to be approved by the *Reichstag* forced Bismarck dramatically to expand the scope of his office, until by 1878 there were eight separate *Reich* departments: the foreign office, the treasury, the interior office, the admiralty, posts and telegraphs, and the departments for Alsace-Lorraine, the railways and judicial affairs. To coordinate the work, a *Reich* chancellery was set up under Delbrück, through which Bismarck communicated his instructions to heads of all the departments except the foreign office whose state secretary reported directly to him. Bismarck abhorred the idea of a cabinet government and thus there were no cabinet discussions and collective responsibility on the lines of the British model and only twice did he call a meeting of state secretaries to discuss policy.

THE PROBLEM OF PRUSSIA

Germany was a federal empire, but the position of the individual states was far from equal. Although Prussia controlled only seventeen out of the fifty-eight seats in the *Bundesrat* and could theoretically be outvoted by a combination of the southern states, its size, wealth and military power placed it in a category of its own. In many important respects the *Reich* appeared to be but an extension of its powers. Prussia supplied the great majority of officials who worked in the new central agencies. The *Reich* was also dependent on Prussia financially. As the central government had very limited powers of taxation, its income was supplemented by grants paid by the individual states on the basis of the size of the population. Inevitably, then, Prussia's financial contribution was crucial for the national budget which could not be planned without close cooperation with the Prussian minister of finance. It was, however, in military affairs that Prussian hegemony within Germany was most clearly expressed. The Prussian army, despite the 'decorative' (Pflanze, 1990, 1: 497) concessions to Bavaria and Württemberg, was in reality the German army. The Prussian General Staff took over the role of strategic planning for all the German land forces and the Prussian minister of war doubled as the *Reich* minister of war.

The new *Reich* could only function smoothly if there was close coopera-tion between the Prussian and *Reich* administrations. In 1872 Bismarck rashly resigned his post as Prussian minister-president, but he rapidly discovered that this led to such friction between the *Reich* and Prussia that within five months he resumed it. His presence in those two pivotal posts was also to some extent a reassurance to the south Germans that in the final analysis, Prussian power could be restrained in the interests of the constitu-tional compromise that Bismarck himself had brokered in 1867 and 1870. As the role of the *Reich* chancellor's office expanded, friction between the *Reich* and Prussia grew. Prussian ministers particularly resented not being consulted by Delbrück on the drafting of the new *Reich* laws, when their cooperation would later be crucial to their execution. So in 1878 Bismarck attempted radically to improve *Reich*–Prussian relations by proposing in the Deputy bill the abolition of the *Reich* Chancellery and its replacement with new departments which would be jointly run by both the *Reich* and Prussia. He intended to extend the existing union between the Prussian king and German emperor and Prussian minister-president and chancellor to the whole Imperial bureaucracy. Arguably this would lessen and perhaps eventu-ally eliminate the tension between the national government and Prussia. However, there was vigorous opposition from the non-Prussian-state delega-tions in the *Bundesrat* and the federalist parties in the *Reichstag* which effectively defeated the measure. Bismarck therefore had to ensure Prussian cooperation by the cruder method of dismissing recalcitrant ministers and replacing them with his own nominees.

Bismarck failed to find a long-term solution for effectively controlling the centrifugal tendencies within the *Reich*. By force of personality and influence he was able to hold the federal structure together, but the danger remained, as John Röhl observed 'that under a different monarch and a different chan-cellor the old disunity would reassert itself' (Röhl, 1967: 23) and that a future German government would be confronted by the conflicting pressures of a conservative Prussia where the continued existence of the three-class voting system (see page **12**) ensured after 1878 a large Conservative majority in the *Landtag*, and a more left-wing *Reichstag* voted in on universal franchise.

8

Economic Developments, 1871–1890

The unification of Germany triggered a short-term speculative boom. The *Gründerjahre* of 1871–73 witnessed an annual productivity increase of nearly 5%. Because of the growth in railway construction, as many iron and steel works were built between 1870 and 1875 as had been over the preceding seventy years. Expansion was helped both by the generous credit policies of the banks and by the liquid capital injected into the economy by the punctual payment of the French indemnity. This was used to finance public works and military projects and to pay off war loans. The currency reform of 1871 also added some 762,000,000 marks to the amount of free capital in the economy.

Gründerjahre The years when the Second *Reich* was established, circa 1871–73. These were characterized by rapid economic and a stock boom and subsequent crash.

Unlike the banks in Britain, the German banks invested much of their capital in trade and industry. In 1872, taking just Prussia alone, forty-nine new banks were formed, amongst which were two giants of the future, the *Dresdner Bank* and the *Deutsche Bank*. These poured money into the new **joint stock companies**, the formation of which had been made easier by the law passed by the *Reichstag* in June 1870, but many of these lacked adequate financial backing and gambled on amassing short-term profits that would in time help them to build up adequate capital reserves. By exaggerating their commercial prospects in the general financial euphoria of the times they had little difficulty in selling their shares at inflated rates [**Doc. 27, p. 137**]. Consequently a large number of unsound limited companies were set up.

Joint stock company A corporation or business partnership involving two or more legal persons. Certificates of part ownership (shares) are issued by the company in return for each financial contribution, which the shareholders are free to sell.

As in 1929, there followed a spectacular crash. Confidence was first shaken by revelations in the *Reichstag* of the fraudulent practices of the successful speculator, Bethel Strousberg – the fact that he was Jewish was to fuel anti-Semitism – but it was the collapse of the Viennese stock market in April 1873 and the financial crisis in America that finally touched off a whole string of bankruptcies in Germany in the autumn.

THE IMPACT ON THE ECONOMY OF THE 'GREAT DEPRESSION'

The collapse of the European capital market led to a slowing up of economic growth and a decline in business confidence that did not fully recover until the mid-1890s. Although the severity of the slump has been exaggerated, it was the first serious check to growth since 1857–59. At first a backlog of railway projects kept the economy afloat, but by 1876 falling demand hit both the textile and engineering industries. The engineering firm Borsig, for instance, produced 166 locomotives in 1875, but only 80 in 1876. Inevitably this led to wage cuts and unemployment. In Berlin in 1879, 25% of the industrial work force were unemployed. There followed a long period of retarded, or at best intermittent growth. In 1880 production achieved the levels of 1872–73, and for the rest of the decade the average growth rate of the economy was 2.5% per annum. Given these figures, it can indeed be argued that 'there is no way in which the term "Great Depression" can have any meaning when applied to Germany after 1880' (Milward and Saul, 1977: 22–3).

STRUCTURAL CHANGES IN THE GERMAN ECONOMY

It was during this period of relative economic stagnation in the 1880s that the foundations of Germany's later technological supremacy were laid. In contrast to the rest of Europe, large sums were invested in such pioneering inventions as the Thomas-Gilchrist steelmaking process, which enabled German industrialists to exploit local low-grade iron-ore to undercut foreign competition. Due to increased mechanization and rationalization, there were impressive increases in productivity during this decade in the textile, coal, iron and steel industries.

The 1880s was the decade in which industry for the first time began to employ more workers than agriculture. Between 1880 and 1890 the number of cities with a population of over one hundred thousand increased from fifteen to twenty-six, and by 1910 Germany had nearly as many large cities as the whole of the rest of the continent [Doc. 28c, p. 138]. Migration of the population in the rural **east Elbian** provinces to Berlin and the Ruhr was accelerated by the introduction on the *Junkers'* estates of modern machinery, and the planting of potatoes and sugar beet which were more effectively harvested by cheap immigrant Polish labour employed on a seasonal basis [Docs 28, 29, pp. 138–39]. Although the new towns were brash and ugly

East Elbian Germany east of the Elbe: a predominantly rural area dominated by the great estates owned by the *Junkers*.

and the workers lived in expensive and crowded tenements [**Doc. 33, p. 142**], the availability of work (at least in the 1880s), static or even sinking food prices [**Doc. 35, p. 144**] and the growing awareness of both the government and big business that socialism could only be contained by a state welfare policy, created conditions far removed from early nineteenth-century Manchester.

While before the onset of the depression entrepreneurs were broadly in favour of *laissez-faire*, the slump made them more than ready to seek protection from vicious competition in contracting markets (see below). In order to streamline production and counter the effect of sinking prices, large engineering and steel firms like Borsig and Krupp began to expand vertically by acquiring coal and iron-ore mines, while many other industries such as cement, textiles and chemicals formed **kartells** which helped to stabilize prices and production. Between 1875 and 1890 over two hundred *kartells* were set up, setting a trend that was to continue into the Third *Reich*. The increasing concentration of German industry into large units produced an elite of powerful industrialists and bankers who were to form a close alliance with the aristocratic Prussian ruling class.

Kartell Cartel or manufacturers' association to control and regulate production. Also an alliance of political parties.

THE POLITICAL CONSEQUENCES OF THE 'GREAT DEPRESSION'

Politically, as the historian Hans Rosenberg argued, the economic crisis in combination with new global economic trends helped to shift 'the centre of gravity of political agitation . . . from issues of political policies, from national unification and constitutional reconstruction . . . to a crude emphasis on economic objectives' (Rosenberg, 1943: 64). Pressure from the industrialists and the east Elbian *Junkers*, who were both anxious to preserve their share of the home market, was an important factor in Bismarck's decision to abandon free trade in 1879 and break with the National Liberals (see page **81**).

The campaign against free trade was initiated in 1871 by the League for the Protection of the Economic Interests of Rhineland and Westphalia – the so-called 'Long-name Society' – and the Southern Union of German Textile Industrialists. It was powerfully reinforced in November 1873 by the League of German Iron and Steel Industrialists, which quickly built up a national network of committees representing some 214 firms. In 1876 a still more formidable pressure group emerged when leading industrialists founded the Central Association of German Industrialists. By appealing to both commercial and nationalist sentiments with the argument that Germany should be as self-sufficient as possible, the protectionists gradually won over the local chambers of commerce. In September 1875 they even convinced the Congress of German Economists, which had hitherto been a 'citadel of free-traders' (Böhme, 1966: 371).

The protectionists were unable to exert effective pressure on the government until they had won the support of the powerful east Elbian farming lobby. Initially the *Junkers* had welcomed the fall in the price of industrial goods, but by 1875 German farmers were experiencing keen competition from imported American and Russian grain and even wool from Australia. This had been made possible by the construction of railways in the prairies and southern Russia and vastly improved shipping services. In 1876 Germany became a net importer of grain and east Elbian agriculture faced the prospect of cut-throat competition and ultimate bankruptcy [**Doc. 30, p. 140**]. The political consequences of the agrarian crisis were highly explosive, as the traditional Prussian ruling elite was directly threatened. The first step in the campaign to protect agriculture was taken when a group of predominantly east Elbian landowners set up the Association for the Reform of Taxation and Economy in 1876 [**Doc. 31, p. 140**]. Initial cooperation with the industrial pressure groups was impeded by the League's conviction that only those with large estates could effectively regenerate Germany and its essentially anti-business ethos, which desired the repeal of most of Bismarck's commercial legislation since 1862. Nevertheless ever-increasing foreign competition rapidly brought about an effective working partnership between the agrarians and the industrialists. In February 1877 industrialists and farmers in Westphalia drew up a general declaration in favour of protective tariffs [**Doc. 32, p. 141**], and in October the Central Association and the League agreed on a detailed tariff scale for industrial and agricultural imports which not only ensured a successful assault on free trade, but also laid the foundations of the alliance between the *Junkers* and heavy industrialists which was to dominate late Wilhelmine politics.

The perceived failure of liberal *laissez-faire* economics helped weaken political Liberalism, which became associated by its critics with the

Manchesterism General term for the political, economic and social movements of the nineteenth century that originated in Manchester, such as free trade and liberalism.

excesses of free trade and '**Manchesterism**'. The crash of 1873 also provided 'a golden opportunity for prophets of disaster', such as Paul de Lagarde (Rosenberg, 1943: 60) as it discredited both economic and political Liberalism and enabled the Conservatives and survivors of the pre-capitalist era successfully to attack the Liberal ethos. Owing to their prominence in banking and on the stock exchange the Jews became the scapegoats for the crash and the symbol of all that was destroying the familiar pattern of the pre-industrial lifestyle. Anti-Semitism developed into an economic and political mass-movement, and in 1890 five deputies campaigning on a specifically anti-Semitic programme were elected to the *Reichstag* [**Doc. 34, p. 144**].

Measured in economic terms the depression may indeed have been mild, but it irreparably damaged Liberalism and rallied behind the Conservatives potentially strong anti-modernist forces, which equated Liberalism and democracy with a Jewish conspiracy.

The depression also played a part in bringing together the forces of the left. Although as early as 1867 the Elberfeld and Barmen Chamber of Commerce reported that 'the working class is awaking from its dull apathy' (Hamerow, 1972: 359), initially the patriotic fervour aroused by Sedan and the benign effects of full employment militated against left-wing politics. In the years immediately after 1873, however, the fear of redundancies, wage cuts and a constant feeling of insecurity created ever-growing support for a mass working-class movement. The two leading working-class parties, the General German Workers Association and the Social Democratic Workers' Party (SDAP) cooperated in the election of 1874, and a year later united to form the **Social Democratic Party** (SPD). In the 1877 election the party polled nearly 10% of the popular vote, and won twelve seats in the *Reichstag* [Doc. 34, p. 143].

SPD (Sozialdemokratische Partei Deutschlands) The German Social Democratic Party was formed through the amalgamation of Ferdinand Lassalle's General German Workers' Association and Bebel's Social Democratic Workers' Party at the unity congress at Gotha in 1875. Despite Bismarck's Anti-Socialist Law, the SPD survived to become the largest party in the *Reichstag* in 1912.

Part 5

DOMESTIC POLITICS, 1871–1890

9

The *Kulturkampf* and the Decline of the National Liberals

A BISMARCK–LIBERAL AXIS?

I n 1871 the National Liberals, and to a lesser extent the Progressives, were still the natural parliamentary allies of Bismarck and cooperated closely in creating the administrative and legal infrastructure of the new *Reich* by supporting bills for a national coinage, a new commercial code, the setting up of a central bank and the introduction of a uniform legal procedure. The Conservatives were uncertain and divided in their reaction to the formation of a modern secular state and suspicious that Bismarck had become 'the lackey of Liberalism' (Gall, 1986, 2: 11). The **Zentrum**, which was founded in December 1870, attracted the south German Catholics, the Poles and the other nationalist minorities, and was inevitably particularist in sympathy and a strong defender of the rights of the German states.

Zentrum (Centre Party) Founded by Ludwig Windhorst to defend Catholic interests in a united and predominantly Protestant country. It survived the *Kulturkampf* strengthened.

Taylor has argued that it was difficult to say between 1871 and 1877 whether 'Bismarck or the National Liberals determined the character of German policy' (Taylor, 1955: 160). Bismarck's government was certainly drawn in a liberal direction in the early 1870s, but the limits of the Liberals' influence were revealed whenever Bismarck's intentions diverged from their own. Bismarck, for example, pointedly refused to force a constitution on the reactionary state of Mecklenburg. Even the Prussian local government reforms of 1872 and 1875, which were bitterly opposed by the Prussian aristocracy, in fact reflected Bismarck's genius for granting concessions 'in form but not in substance' (Berdahl, 1972: 10), as the *Junkers* were still able to retain much of their power in the county and provincial diets. The Liberals' ideological struggle with the *Zentrum* and their desire to support a national policy weakened their will to oppose the government even on the most fundamental issues. Refusing to contemplate a temporary alliance with the *Zentrum*, which was worse than 'the kiss of death' (Anderson, 1981: 190) they failed in 1874 to defeat an authoritarian press law, which empowered the government to imprison newspaper editors for publishing sensitive information, and they weakly agreed to a septennial rather than annual military budget.

THE *KULTURKAMPF*

The fanaticism with which the Liberals persecuted the Catholics is only explicable if viewed within the context of the struggle between the Liberal and Catholic movements to shape the cultural and social framework of German society. In the 1860s the south German Liberals were strongly anti-clerical. In Baden, for example, the Church Law of 1860 and the Elementary School Law of 1868 curtailed the freedom of the Roman Catholic Church within the state. The tradition of German Liberalism was anti-Catholic. Many of the leading Liberals were the sons of Protestant pastors and 'the historiography they learned at their mothers' knees depicted Luther as a national and liberal as well as a religious hero' (Anderson, 1981: 197). Their inherent distrust of Catholicism was fuelled by the uncompromising nature of the contemporary Papacy under the leadership of Pius IX. In 1864 the *Syllabus Errorum* sweepingly condemned the doctrines which Liberals all over Europe believed formed the essential basis of a free society, and in 1870 the Vatican Council further offended Protestant opinion by promulgating the dogma of Papal Infallibility, which was even opposed by the majority of Catholic bishops in Germany.

Kulturkampf Struggle between cultures. A term used to describe Bismarck's conflict with the Catholic Church, 1872–87.

Superficially it seems puzzling that Bismarck should have launched so divisive a campaign as the **Kulturkampf** instead of attempting to integrate the large Catholic minority peacefully into the new *Reich*. His attitude towards the Catholics had been essentially pragmatic. In 1870, when Italian troops occupied Rome, he even considered the diplomatic advantages of offering the Pope asylum in Germany. Theoretically, at least, the Prussian-dominated *Zentrum*, according to Margaret Anderson, 'could have been an excellent engine for integrating discontented foreign and German particularists into the new Empire' (Anderson, 1981: 145).

Bielefeld school of historiography Based at Bielefeld University, where H.J. Wehler was Professor of History, 1971–96. This is one of the leading structuralist centres in Germany.

Hans-Ulrich Wehler and the **Bielefeld school of historiography** sees the *Kulturkampf* as a classic example of Bismarck's technique of 'negative integration' whereby he attempted to unite the Protestant majority in the *Reichstag* against 'the Roman menace' and deflect the Liberals from pursuing awkward constitutional questions (Wehler, 1985) [**Doc. 50, p. 154**]. There is little doubt that Bismarck did exploit the political advantages afforded by the *Kulturkampf*, but this interpretation underestimates his genuine fear that the *Zentrum*, which was led by Ludwig Windthorst, who was already an effective spokesman of popular particularism, was the natural rallying point for the enemies of *Kleindeutschland* – the Poles, the Bavarian Patriots and the inhabitants of Alsace-Lorraine [**Doc. 36, p. 145**].

Since the key areas of education and religion were state rather than *Reich* responsibilities, the *Kulturkampf* was waged principally by the Prussian government, with parallel struggles in Baden and other states. In 1871 the Catholic division of the Prussian ministry of culture was abolished and in January its Conservative minister was replaced by Adalbert Falk. The most important element of Prussia's *Kulturkampf* legislation was contained in the May Laws of 1873, which extended state control over the education of the clergy, undermined the authority of the Papacy by setting up a Royal Tribunal for Ecclesiastical Affairs, and empowered provincial governors to veto the appointments of parish priests. In 1874 further laws provided for the confiscation of the endowments of dissident parish priests and the deposition and ultimate imprisonment of recusant bishops. For the Catholics Prussia became a police state. In the first four months of 1875, for example, 241 clergy and 136 editors were fined or imprisoned and over a thousand parishes were left without incumbents. The isolation of the Catholic population from the rest of the community became particularly apparent on such occasions as the *Kaiser's* birthday or Sedan Day, which were celebrated overwhelmingly by the Protestants.

Relations with the Polish and Alsace-Lorraine minorities also worsened as a result of the *Kulturkampf*. The Prussian government viewed the Poles in the eastern provinces with a new intolerance, which merely strengthened Polish nationalism. The attempt to introduce German into Polish primary schools in 1873 led to the growth of local peasant organizations, which sought both to protect Polish culture and prevent the ejection of Polish peasants from their farms by Germans (see page **87**). Similarly in Alsace-Lorraine the resentment caused by the clumsy attempts to Germanize the population was exacerbated by the *Kulturkampf*.

Although there were isolated riots in the Rhineland and the eastern provinces, Windthorst discouraged extra-parliamentary opposition on the grounds that it would only afford the government fresh opportunities for attack. Consequently he did not support Felix von Loë's attempt to emulate Daniel O'Connell's successful campaign in Ireland in the 1820s to achieve Catholic emancipation, by setting up the Association of German Catholics, as he feared that Bismarck would use it as an excuse to crack down even harder on the Catholics. Windthorst's reservations were confirmed when the executive committee of the Association was arrested and its rallies broken up by the police. Windthorst's policy of urging Catholic voters to make the elections 'a great plebiscite' (Anderson, 1981: 182) against Bismarck's policies was impressively rewarded in the *Reichstag* elections of 1874 when the *Zentrum*, in alliance with the Danes, Poles and Alsatians, won ninety-one seats

[Doc. 34, p. 34]. Within the *Reichstag* and the Prussian *Landtag* his tactics were less successful, as he failed to exploit effectively Conservative suspicions of Bismarck or to prod the Liberals into opposing the government on constitutional issues. Nevertheless, it was clear that Bismarck had visibly failed to defeat the *Zentrum* as a major force in German politics and had 'suffered the first significant defeat of his political career' (Pflanze, 1990, 2: 179).

PROTECTIONISM AND THE END OF THE LIBERAL ERA

In the early 1870s the *Kulturkampf* cemented the unity of the National Liberals and tightened the party's links with Bismarck. However, the crash of 1873 and the subsequent lengthy depression gradually began to create a new political and economic climate, which was eventually to transform domestic politics (see page **69**). As the champions of *laissez-faire*, the Liberals were made 'to bear responsibility for what various groups did not like about the contemporary world' (Sheehan, 1982: 144). They were thrown on the defensive by demands for a change in the government's economic policy. A potential Conservative–*Zentrum* economic consensus was beginning to emerge by 1876. The agrarian crisis reunited the Conservative Party and transformed it into a protectionist party with a natural reservoir of support amongst the Protestant peasantry. The *Zentrum* was also forced to abandon free trade under pressure from its voters, many of whom were small farmers and craftsmen who were particularly severely hit by the depression [Doc. 31, p. 140].

The collapse of the economic consensus and the emergence of parties based on sectional interests accelerated the decline of German Liberalism. Fundamentally both the National Liberal and the Progressives lacked the necessary constituency organization and electoral base to compete successfully in a democratic franchise. They had at first profited from the low turnout in national and state elections, but their percentage of the vote steadily declined as the *Zentrum*, the Conservatives and later the SPD began to mobilize the hitherto apathetic masses. The impact of these external challenges was increased by the growing divisions within Liberalism. After Eugen Richter, who was a 'Progressive first and a Liberal second' (Sheehan, 1982: 138), became leader of his party in 1874, the differences between the two Liberal parties grew and by 1877 cooperation between them had virtually broken down. Simultaneously disagreements between the left and right wings of the National Liberal Party began to intensify.

The depression caused an acute crisis in the *Reich's* finances, as the decline in industrial activity led to a fall in the tax receipts of the individual states.

This in turn undermined their ability to pay their regular matricular contributions to central government and was ultimately to check the expansion of the Imperial government's power at the expense of the states. The background of the threatening international crisis in the Balkans (see page **99**) made a solution to the financial problem even more urgent.

Between 1875 and 1878 Bismarck considered ways of strengthening the *Reich's* finances, making them independent of both the *Reichstag* and the individual states and in the process became aware of the potential for fresh political alignments, which would free him from his dependence on the Liberals. Initially Bismarck had no overall plan and 'as so often in the critical moments of his career, he experimented with several alternatives before settling on a definite course' (Stern, 1977: 194). He had hoped to tap new sources of revenue by nationalizing the lucrative German railway companies, but he drew back in the face of opposition from Bavaria, Saxony and Württemberg. The simplest solution was to increase indirect taxation on such articles as tobacco, sugar and brandy. However, indirect taxation entailed a lessening of parliamentary control over the executive, since its payment became automatic once initial consent was granted, and both Liberal parties opposed it.

It is difficult to determine when Bismarck was converted to tariffs. In 1876 he discreetly began to encourage the protectionist campaign, but carefully avoided any commitment. It has been argued that he needed time to manoeuvre entrenched free-traders like Delbrück and Camphausen, the Prussian finance minister, out of their posts, but it is more likely that he was still keeping his options open (Windell, 1969) [**Doc. 37, p. 145**]. Nevertheless, both domestic and foreign pressures were nudging Bismarck into a decision against free trade. The protectionist campaign was gaining momentum and privately the banker, Bleichröder, informed Bismarck of the adverse effects of foreign competition on the Ruhr industries. Growing economic friction with Russia (see page **99**) predisposed the government to protect German agriculture from Russian imports and made desirable closer diplomatic and commercial relations with protectionist Austria. This would be easier to achieve if Germany raised her tariffs to the Austrian level.

In late 1877 Bismarck attempted to win over the National Liberals to a programme of financial and constitutional reforms by offering their leader, von Bennigsen, a seat in both the Prussian and *Reich* cabinets. However, they attempted to exploit the offer to secure a further advance in parliamentary government and insisted that two further colleagues, the Mayor of Breslau, Max von Forckenbeck, and the Munich *Reichstag* deputy, Baron von Stauffenberg, who belonged to the left wing of the party, should also join the cabinet. Their terms proved unacceptably high both to the *Kaiser* and Bismarck.

These negotiations came to an end when Bismarck signalled his change of course by announcing in the *Reichstag* on 22 February 1878 the first stage of a comprehensive financial reform that would almost certainly involve the introduction of tariffs. It is possible that Bismarck was finally prompted into this decision by the election of Pope Leo XIII, who had indicated his desire for better relations with the *Reich*. Nevertheless, although the prospects of gaining limited *Zentrum* support for tariffs may have been improved, it would hardly be realistic to argue that Bismarck was about to convert the *Zentrum* to a permanent ally. The wounds of the *Kulturkampf* were still too deep for that.

Having broken with the National Liberals, Bismarck had lost control of the *Reichstag*. In the spring of 1878, a majority for his finance legislation was uncertain. The first draft of the deputy bill was also so emasculated that its main purpose of coordinating the *Reich* and Prussian governments was defeated. Ideally, the solution to Bismarck's problems lay in an early dissolution of the *Reichstag* and the election of a more manageable parliament in which a malleable National Liberal Party purged of its left wing would cooperate with a greatly strengthened Conservative Party [**Doc. 38, p. 146**].

On 11 May an attempted assassination of the *Kaiser*, by a 21-year-old plumber which was at first erroneously thought to be a socialist plot, provided Bismarck with a chance to draft an anti-Socialist bill, that would not only strike at the fledgling SPD but, arguably more importantly in Bismarck's eyes, also drive a further wedge between the moderate and radical wings of the National Liberal Party. The bill was overwhelmingly defeated in the *Reichstag* by 251 to 57 votes. What in Bismarck's eyes was a marvellously opportune second attempt on William's life in June by a psychopath, Karl Nobiling, enabled him to call a crisis election, in which the main thrust of his campaign was directed against the Progressives and left-wing National Liberals. Both Liberal parties were weakened and the Conservatives correspondingly strengthened, but the *Zentrum*, supported by the minor Nationalist groups, now held the balance in the *Reichstag*.

If Bismarck had been calculating that electoral defeat would bring the National Liberals to heel, their support for the second anti-Socialist bill appeared to justify his tactics. In return for a concession which limited the law to an initial two-and-a-half-year period, the National Liberals joined the Conservatives and Free Conservatives in voting for the bill. It banned socialist meetings and publications and empowered the government to expel agitators from their homes (see page **85**) [**Doc. 39, p. 146**]. The passage of the bill, however, subjected the National Liberal Party to intense internal strain. The left wing, led by Lasker, was appalled by the right wing's delight in cooperating with the Conservatives. The right for its part was contemptuous of the left's reservations. Lothar Gall has observed that 'in the end the issue smashed the National Liberal Party, for in voting as it did the party destroyed the basis of shared convictions on which its internal cohesion rested (Gall, 1986, 2: 100–101).

THE TARIFF ACT OF 1879

In the spring of 1879 Bismarck introduced legislation for levying tariffs on iron, iron goods and grain [**Doc. 40, p. 147**] and for increasing indirect taxation on selected luxury goods. In a *Reichstag* of 397 members the support of the *Zentrum* bloc of 94 deputies was essential if the tariff bill was to pass. Windthorst supported protectionism for economic reasons but opposed indirect taxation if it enabled the government to evade financial control of the *Reichstag* and to weaken the power of the individual states. Bismarck sought to compel Windthorst's cooperation by negotiating directly with the Papacy on alleviating the *Kulturkampf*, and to appease him by making minor concessions such as supporting the election of the *Zentrum* deputy, Baron Georg von Franckenstein, as vice-president of the *Reichstag* and president of the tariff committee. Windthorst was, however, under considerable pressure from the *Zentrum* voters to demonstrate that support for protection did not entail general backing for Bismarck, who was still seen as the hated perpetrator of the *Kulturkampf*.

It soon became clear that Bismarck would have to choose between concessions to the *Zentrum* and to the National Liberals. Bennigsen, in a desperate attempt to preserve the unity of his party, agreed to support the bill provided the *Reichstag* could determine the salt tax and coffee duties annually, as well as two-thirds of the tariff income. Bismarck had no intention of strengthening parliament and probably only negotiated with Bennigsen to exert pressure on Windthorst. The bill's passage was finally assured when Bismarck accepted a *Zentrum* amendment proposed by Franckenstein. This strengthened the federal nature of the constitution by ensuring that only a fixed percentage of the income from the new duties and taxes would go directly to the central government and that the rest would be allocated annually to the states, which would continue to make their annual matricular contribution to the *Reich*. On 12 July 1879 a Conservative, Free Conservative and *Zentrum* majority, joined by fifteen right-wing National Liberal rebels, approved the bill.

The *Zentrum* had indeed made itself, as Windthorst was to observe, the liquidator of the 'bankruptcy of the Liberal economy' (Anderson, 1981: 233) and enabled Bismarck to abandon free trade. The unity of the National Liberal Party was irreparably damaged. The fifteen tariff rebels resigned, and the party became prey to bitter internal conflicts. These resulted in the secession of the left a year later. A foreign observer remarked that Bismarck had scored 'one of the most substantial triumphs of his political career' (Stern, 1977: 207), but, as the following decade was to show, Bismarck had in reality failed to solve any of the fundamental problems facing the *Reich*.

10

The Conservative Empire

THE 'SECOND FOUNDATION OF THE *REICH*'

To historians of the Bielefeld school, who have reinterpreted Bismarck's politics 'through the lens of economic interest' (Eley, 1992: 3), 1879 is a more important date than 1871. By securing the *Reichstag's* assent to the protective tariffs of 1879, Bismarck won the support of a formidable alliance of industrial and agrarian capital and interest groups. This immensely strengthened the Conservative-Prussian German establishment and made any challenges to its power unlikely to succeed. This, they argue, constituted the virtual refounding of the *Reich* in a more authoritarian form (Wehler, 1985; Böhme, 1966). Lothar Gall, too, sees the years 1878–79 as a *Wende* or turning point. He argues that Bismarck renounced his role as a mediator of compromise between the Conservatives and Liberals, trade and agriculture and instead threw in his lot with the traditional classes (Gall, 1986, 2: 110).

Certainly 1878–79 was an important turning point and Bismarck's break with the Liberals made the peaceful evolution towards a constitutional monarchy much more difficult. However, the transformation of German politics was not as comprehensive as is often depicted. Bismarck neither succeeded in making the *Reich* financially independent of the individual German states nor in persuading the *Zentrum* to join an anti-democratic *Sammlung*. Despite the dramatic events of 1878–79, Bismarck lost control of the *Reichstag* until 1887 and his basic aim of adapting an essentially auto-cratic political structure to new socioeconomic realities without any further concessions to democracy could only be fleetingly achieved by employing one expedient after another. To defend the fragile structure of the Empire from revolutionary change became, to quote Wehler, a 'labour of Sisyphus' (Wehler, 1970: 147) which increasingly involved resorts to the Bonapartist tactics of plebiscitary elections and imperialist diversions in Africa [**Docs 37**

Sammlung A concentration or coalition of forces and groups.

and 50, pp. 145 and 155]. Arguably, as one of Bismarck's recent biographers has pointed out, in reality nothing much changed: The *Reich* had been conservative and authoritarian from the start and the crisis merely highlighted the 'weaknesses within the national liberalism'. Little changed at just the point when the *Reich* should have begun to evolve into a parliamentary state (Lerman, 2004: 197).

BISMARCK'S LOSS OF CONTROL OVER THE *REICHSTAG*

For the National Liberals the upheavals of 1878–79 marked a traumatic turning point. Bismarck's assumption that the party would split and that the rump would rally behind the government proved correct, but the divide fell nearer to the centre of the party than he had hoped. This delayed until 1887 the formation of an effective government bloc in the *Reichstag*. The National Liberals were barely able to fight the Prussian elections in 1879 as a united party, and in 1880 Lasker's resignation precipitated the **secession** of a further twenty-seven deputies. In the *Reichstag* elections a year later secessionist candidates won almost as many seats as the National Liberal Party itself [**Doc. 34, p. 143**]. The character of the National Liberal Party changed as the traditional professional element was gradually replaced by businessmen and industrialists who favoured tariffs and cooperation with the Conservatives. The drift rightwards was accelerated when the National Liberals in south Germany endorsed the Heidelberg Declaration in 1884. This unequivocally supported protection, approved of Bismarck's social insurance scheme (see page **86**) and acknowledged the importance of agriculture in Germany's economic life.

Seccession The breakaway of twenty-seven *Reichstag* deputies led by Lasker in 1880 from the National Liberals. Later known as the 'Liberal Union'.

The political realignments of 1878–80 greatly strengthened the position of the *Zentrum* in the *Reichstag*. Its vote for the tariff legislation of 1879 had demonstrated the value of its support for the government. In an attempt to ensure further cooperation, and thus a manageable parliament, Bismarck was ready to end the *Kulturkampf*, not by a premature capitulation to the *Zentrum* but on the basis of the new status quo created by the May Laws. He was prepared to make some limited concessions provided the essence of the Laws was preserved. Bismarck's initiatives for contrary reasons were consequently viewed with suspicion by both the Catholics and the National Liberals. In July 1880 the Discretionary Relief bill, which would have empowered the government to suspend the May Laws on a selective basis, was amended when the Conservatives, prompted by the National Liberals, deleted a key provision enabling the Prussian government to pardon exiled prelates.

Sacraments The core
of Catholic teaching is
the seven sacraments:
Baptism, Confirmation,
Eucharist, Penance, An-
ointing of the Sick, Holy
Orders, and Matrimony.

Bismarck also tried to split the *Zentrum* by wooing its right wing. However, Windthorst skilfully blocked any 'seepage on the right' (Anderson, 1981: 301) by annually submitting to the *Landtag* a motion calling for the exemption of the administration of **sacraments** from criminal prosecution, which would have rendered the May Laws unenforceable. Its inevitable defeat by both the National Liberals and Conservatives enabled Windthorst to rally his party behind him and cooperate with the Progressives, who with the *Zentrum* had voted against the amended relief bill. The rejection of this bill showed with brutal clarity that Catholic priests celebrating the Eucharist, or indeed any of the other Christian sacraments could legally still be arrested.

Bismarck suffered a serious setback in the election of 1881 [**Doc. 34, p. 143**]. Over three-quarters of the *Reichstag* was now hostile to the government. Arguably the voters were not so much rejecting Bismarck's reactionary politics as protesting against a sharp rise in retail prices and the financial effects of the tobacco monopoly. The Progressives and the Liberal Union (the former Secessionists) won 106 seats between them. Even the SPD increased its number by three despite the anti-Socialist law and Stoecker's new Christian Social Party, which exploited anti-Semitism and promised a state welfare system.

Confronted by an unruly *Reichstag*, Bismarck openly talked of the possibility of a *coup d'état* [**Doc. 41, p. 148**], as he had done in the early 1860s. He purged the Prussian cabinet and civil service [**Doc. 42, p. 142**] and the *Reich* chancellor's office of Liberally inclined officials. He erected a further barrier against parliamentary control of the army by persuading William to allow the military cabinet and general staff to report directly to the Emperor rather than to the war minister. In 1880 Bismarck took the first step in a plan, which drew its inspiration from Bonapartist France, for eventually neutralizing parliament by setting up a Prussian Council on Political Economy in which representatives of 'the productive classes' of commerce, industry and agriculture would sit. Bismarck viewed it as a prototype for a *Reich* Council and informed William candidly that he eventually intended to 'bypass' the *Reichstag* with it. When the scheme was debated it was overwhelmingly defeated by a *Zentrum* and Liberal majority. Bismarck's attempt to engineer a decrease in the number of parliamentary sittings by replacing annual with biennial budgets was also defeated in April 1881. So too in 1886 was the project for an Imperial Liquor Monopoly, which by tapping a new and uncontrolled source of revenue for the *Reich* would have gravely weakened the *Reichstag's* power to set the budget. For all his bluster and threats nothing could disguise the fact that he had lost control of the *Reichstag*. At this stage of his career Bismarck's predicament reminded one American historian in 1990 'less of an Iron Age Chancellor than George Bush, facing a Democratic Congress on the defense budget' (Pflanze, 1990, 2: 376).

BISMARCK AND THE SPD

While the *Kulturkampf* effectively ran into a dead end in the early 1880s, Bismarck intensified the attack against the SPD and the socialist trade unions. Initially the SPD was severely affected by the anti-Socialist law. Although its deputies were not expelled from the *Reichstag*, its constituency organizations were broken up, the Labour press was virtually eliminated and socialist trade unions and working-class clubs were dissolved. By the time the law lapsed, some 1500 party members had been imprisoned and many others exiled.

At a conference at Schloss Wyden in Switzerland in 1880 the party over-whelmingly decided to oppose the government by constitutional means and expelled the two principal exponents of political terrorism. The party adopted an organizational pattern that was 'informal, diffuse and often transitory' (Lidtke, 1966: 97). A new party paper, the *Sozialdemokrat*, was printed in Zürich and smuggled over the frontier by the 'red postmaster', Julius Motteler. Financial contributions were secretly collected, and an intelligence system was devised to counter the work of police informers.

In the end, as with the *Kulturkampf*, the anti-Socialist law proved counter-productive. In the legalistic German culture of the *Kaiserreich* the Social Democrats managed to mitigate its impact. As one Breslau member observed, 'every law and every ordinance has a back door' (Anderson, 2000: 287). New electoral organizations, masquerading under the bland but legal name of 'societies for municipal elections', were created in the large cities, which enabled the SPD to rebuild its grassroots organization. Above all, the SPD could exploit the fact that the Bismarckian constitution did not recognize parties as a legal entity. By Article 29 a parliamentary deputy was a representative of the 'whole people'. Consequently, as Margaret Anderson has pointed out, 'any voter, even a socialist' could compete as a candidate of 'the whole people' (Anderson, 2000: 278). Once in parliament, deputies were protected by parliamentary immunity and the right to the freedom of speech. Consequently by reporting a speech delivered in the *Reichstag*, sympathetic newspapers could legally give wide coverage to even the most inflammatory SPD speech.

BISMARCK'S SOCIAL WELFARE PROGRAMME

Bismarck attempted to balance outright repression of the SPD with the introduction of a welfare programme. Although he was far from blind to the need to achieve greater social justice, the main aim of his welfare programme was to avoid revolution through timely social reform and to reconcile the working classes to the authority of the state. It was the 'carrot' to the anti-Socialist law 'stick' (Blackbourne, 1997: 346). Above all he aimed, in Pflanze's words, to 'integrate the workers into a German national consensus based on the Prussian-German establishment' (Pflanze, 1990, 3: 350). In this he failed – at least in the short term – as periodic labour unrest and the increasing number of votes cast for the SPD showed [**Doc. 34, p. 144**]. However, the scale of the programme was impressive and was unrivalled in other countries for decades. Few historians would disagree with Taylor that it alone is sufficient 'to establish his reputation as a constructive statesman even if he had done nothing else' (Taylor, 1955: 202).

The first accident insurance bill in March 1881 applied only to certain particularly dangerous industries. The employers were to pay two-thirds of the premiums, and the workers one-third, while the state was to supplement their contributions; but the National Liberals and the *Zentrum* combined to vote against the principle of state contribution, as the former suspected state socialism and the latter feared any strengthening of the central government. The bill also confronted the SPD with a dilemma. Either they had to accept economic amelioration at the hands of a suspect Bismarck or to adopt the ideological argument that genuine state socialism was only possible in a democratic society. A damaging split was avoided by the party's decision to propose amendments which the government would reject, thereby enabling the SPD to unite against the bill.

After the elections of October 1881 Bismarck returned to his welfare programme. The *Reichstag* approved a health insurance scheme in May 1883 and an amended accident insurance bill in 1884, which was expanded to cover more industries without involving any financial contributions from the state. In both schemes Bismarck introduced a novel element of **corporatism**, which was in tune with his attempts to set up a *Reich* Council on Political Economy (see page **84**). The health insurance scheme was partly based on the already existing organization of miners' and crafts' guilds and was administered by local health committees which were elected jointly by employers and workers. The accident insurance scheme was run by the employers, who were organized in groups according to industries. Bismarck confided to a leading civil servant in the Prussian ministry of commerce that he hoped that these corporative associations would ultimately form the basis for a future representative body, which would be 'a substitute for, or as a parallel body to, the *Reichstag*, even if it must be raised to this status by means of a *coup d'état*' (Pflanze, 1990, 3: 156).

Bismarck completed his welfare legislation with the introduction of the old age pension in 1889. This was administered by the traditional bureaucracy both in Prussia and the other German states.

Corporatism The attempt to defuse class hatred and unify society by giving both employers and workers a joint role in the running of welfare agencies, industry, etc. In the 1930s Mussolini attempted to create a corporate state in Italy.

JEWS AND POLES AND THE POLICY OF GERMANIZATION

Bismarck was not an anti-Semite. Indeed he was annoyed by attacks on wealthy Jews like Bleichröder, but nevertheless he was ready to exploit anti-Semitism politically. In June 1880, for instance, he criticized the *Kaiser's* chaplain, Adolf Stoecker, who had formed the Christian Social Workers' Party not because it was anti-Semitic, but because it was too left-wing. When Stoecker moved to the right, Bismarck's tolerance of him grew as he perceived him to be 'an extraordinary, militant and useful ally' (Pflanze, 1990, 3: 51).

For Bismarck the Poles were a major threat to the unity of the *Reich*. As Catholics they were staunch allies of Windthorst and also with their own language and cultural traditions represented what Bismarck considered to be 'a state within a state'. In 1881 he responded to demands from the Conservatives to control illegal Polish and Jewish immigration, which had dramatically increased after the start of the **pogroms** in Russia, by strengthening border controls along the eastern frontiers of the *Reich*. When it was seen that this had relatively little impact on stemming the flow, the local authorities were suddenly ordered four years later to expel within two weeks all illegal aliens. During the winter of 1885/86 some 16,000 Poles and Jews with Russian citizenship were herded across the frontier in often appalling conditions. By January 1888 over 32,000 aliens, some 10,000 of whom were Jews, had been expelled. Officially the expellees were described as Russian 'conscription dodgers', although in fact many had lived in the eastern provinces of Prussia for generations.

Pogrom Organized attacks on Jewish settlements in Russia.

When the Polish deputies in the *Reichstag* in November 1885 backed by the other ethnic parties, the *Zentrum* and the Liberals sought to question the government about it, Bismarck argued that it was a Prussian rather than a *Reich* matter and refused to answer the interpellation. Nevertheless, in January 1886 the *Reichstag* insisted on debating the issue and a majority censured the Imperial government for sanctioning 'unjustified' expulsions. Bismarck responded rapidly to this defeat by introducing a bill for the Protection of German National Interests in the Eastern Provinces', which appealed successfully to the Nationalism of the National Liberals and was approved by the *Reichstag*. It was an ambitious plan for Germanizing the Polish-speaking areas of Posen, West Prussia and Silesia where some 2,300,000 Poles lived. It created the Prussian Colonization Commission to buy up land from bankrupt Poles and to lease it to German peasants. Over the next two years there were further measures, such as the abolition of Polish language teaching in all elementary schools and the obligatory requirement that all Prussian officials and conscripts of Polish origin should be posted to western Germany where they would 'learn the blessings of German civilization' (Pflanze, 1990, 3: 206).

Even when Bismarck ended the *Kulturkampf* in 1887 (see page **90**), he excluded the Polish dioceses of Gnesen-Posen and Kulm from concessions permitting the reopening of seminaries for the education of Catholic priests. Indeed it can be argued that Bismarck was making peace with the Catholics in order, as Professor Mosler, a senior member of the *Zentrum*, remarked 'to be able to trample down the Poles to his heart's content' (Anderson, 1981: 328).

As with the *Kulturkampf*, Bismarck miscalculated the effectiveness of force which merely strengthened Polish patriotism and determination to stay put on the land. The Poles set up a land bank in 1889 to assist Polish farmers to buy land and pay their debts. By 1914 it was clear that Bismarck's measure had failed to change the ethnic character of the border populations in the east. The Poles and Germans were 'deadlocked in their competition for landowning primacy, neither one clearly winning or losing' (Panayi, 2000: 101).

Bismarck's Germanization policies also affected the Danes in northern Schleswig and the French speakers in Alsace-Lorraine. In Schleswig the Danish minority emulated the Poles by setting up their own cultural organizations, while in Alsace a considerable number of French speakers emigrated across the boarder into France.

THE FORMATION OF THE *KARTELL* AND A BRIEF PERIOD OF STABILIZATION

Besides attempting to tame the *Reichstag* through threatened coups, procedural reforms and the embryonic organization of a corporate state, Bismarck continued to encourage a Conservative–National Liberal *Sammlung*, and to woo the right wing of the *Zentrum*. In 1884 he attempted to split both the *Zentrum* and the new **Deutsche Freisinnige Partei (Freisinn)**, which had been formed out of the two left-wing Liberal parties the Progressives and the Liberal Union, by ostensibly seeking a renewal of the anti-Socialist law, but in reality hoping for its defeat so that he could prematurely dissolve parliament and fight the ensuing election on a programme which would expose their internal divisions. In light of the possibly imminent accession of the pro-Liberal Crown Prince Frederick, Bismarck's great fear was the emergence of a strong reunited Liberal Party. Although this tactic to divide the *Freisinn* was thwarted by a combination of right-wing *Zentrum* deputies and former Liberal Union members, whose vote just had enabled the bill to pass, it did nevertheless show the potential divisions in left-wing Liberalism. When the regular triennial *Reichstag* elections were held in the autumn, the *Freisinn*, penalized by middle-class voters for its official opposition to the bill and by working-class voters for the support which contrary to the party line,

Deutsche Freisinnige Partei (Freisinn) The German Free Thought Party formed from the Progressives and Liberal Union, 1884 (the former Seccessionists).

some of its members gave to the measure, lost nearly forty seats. Although the Conservatives won twenty-eight, the National Liberals made only modest gains [**Doc. 34, p. 144**]. The SPD increased its seats to twenty-four, which entitled it to regular representation on the *Reichstag* committees.

The underlying trend of the election results was distinctly encouraging for Bismarck. The 'nightmare' (Gall, 1986, 2: 172) of a large left-wing Liberal Party receded and the dramatic rise in the Socialist vote paradoxically facilitated the creation of a pro-government *Sammlung* in the *Reichstag*. Bismarck's expansionary policy in Africa and South-East Asia (see Chapter 12) gave the National Liberals a rallying cry and led to their close cooperation with the Free Conservatives on the colonial question. An increase in agrarian tariffs [**Doc. 40, p. 147**] and the bill of 1886 aimed at buying out Polish farmers in the eastern provinces appeased the Conservatives. Nevertheless he was still confronted with an unmanageable *Reichstag* and was ready to exploit any further opportunity to dissolve at a favourable moment. He privately hoped for another assassination attempt on the *kaiser*, but the SPD stubbornly pursued a pragmatic and constitutional approach and, as Margaret Anderson has remarked, no 'socialist gunmen' (Anderson, 1981: 336) presented themselves as they had so conveniently in 1878.

It was the conjunction of the Bulgarian crisis with the rise of Boulanger in France in 1886 (see page **102**) that finally gave Bismarck the chance to call an election under crisis conditions. Bismarck insisted on a 10% increase in the size of the army and demanded a new **Septennat**, while the current one still had over a year to run. His intentions became clear when the *Reichstag* was dissolved in January 1887. This was in spite of a *Freisinn* motion for an immediate grant of the necessary funds for an initial period of three years, which the *Zentrum* was even willing to extend to five years, on the grounds that the issue at stake was not the length of the budget, but 'whether the Empire is to be protected by an imperial army or a parliamentary one' (Anderson, 1981: 341). It was clear Bismarck was by now not interested in a compromise but wanted a clear-cut electoral victory.

Septennat Septennial military or iron budget.

He went into the election with the backing of the Conservatives, Free Conservatives and the National Liberals, who were convinced that the gravity of the international situation was such that there was little option but to approve the *Septennat*. The election was fought in an atmosphere of artificially contrived crisis. The police vigorously enforced the anti-Socialist law and reservists were called up for manoeuvres in Alsace-Lorraine. The *Freisinn* and SPD each lost over half their strength, while the electoral *Kartell*, composed of the Conservatives, Free Conservatives and National Liberals, won 220 seats [**Doc. 34, p. 144**].

Bismarck had at last engineered a majority, which passed the *Septennat* and enabled him, in March 1888, to meet with equanimity the accession of the pro-liberal Frederick III, who died three months later of cancer. However, the *Kartell* was not an entirely reliable or subservient majority. There were tensions between the National Liberals and Conservatives which erupted in 1888 when the former voted against further protective duties on wood and grain. Bismarck's reservations about the residual liberalism of the National Liberals were confirmed when Bennigsen demanded in 1889 the appointment of a *Reich* finance minister responsible to parliament.

Bismarck did not exclude the possibility of eventual cooperation with the *Zentrum*. In 1885 he secured Papal support for the first 'Peace bill', which, despite some important concessions to the Catholics, still compelled the Church to register ecclesiastical appointments in Prussia with the provincial governors. Further concessions except to the Poles (see above) were made in the second 'Peace bill' in April 1887, which effectively ended the *Kulturkampf*. The right wing of the *Zentrum* greeted it 'as the end of an unnatural 15 years of domestic exile' (Anderson, 1981: 370) and welcomed the opportunity to work with the Conservatives. The first indication of a possible rapprochement between Bismarck and the *Zentrum* came in mid-July 1889 when Bismarck raised no objection to the return of the Catholic Order of the Redemptionists to Bavaria.

BISMARCK'S FALL

The accession to the throne of the 29-year-old William II introduced a new political factor, which Bismarck consistently underestimated. William, flattered and encouraged by Field-Marshal von Waldersee and the new leader of the National Liberals, Johannes Miquel, was determined not to be a mere figurehead. The court became a magnet for those officials and politicians who opposed Bismarck. On several key issues William found himself at loggerheads with his chancellor. He agreed with Bismarck's critics in the foreign office on the allegedly dire consequences of ending the *Kulturkampf*, so far as internal developments in Bavaria and the future of the alliance with the anti-clerical government of Italy were concerned. William was also critical of Bismarck's unrelenting hostility towards the SPD and consented to receive a delegation of miners during the strike in the Ruhr coalfields in 1889. He was also a keen supporter of the *Kartell* at a time when Bismarck was considering breaking with the National Liberals.

The events leading to Bismarck's resignation on 20 March 1890 have been obscured, partly by the nostalgia of German historians of the Weimar period who saw 1890 as the end of a golden age, and partly by Bismarck himself, who in retirement championed the cause of the *Kartell* parties, particularly the National Liberals, and therefore hid his earlier disagreements with them. By the autumn of 1889 it seems likely that Bismarck had decided not to support the *Kartell* in the coming elections and instead to encourage a *Zentrum*–Conservative alliance since he increasingly disagreed with the National Liberals over a whole range of domestic and foreign issues. John Röhl argued that this sudden U-turn was intended to create 'a situation of such chaos . . . at home and abroad' that Bismarck, in the words of Friedrich von Holstein, a senior foreign office official, 'would have [had] the Kaiser in the palm of his hand' (Röhl, 1966: 77). This is possibly an exaggerated view of his intentions, which reflects more accurately the strongly anti-Catholic views of the *Kaiser's* advisers. It is significant, for example, that when Bismarck started negotiations with Windthorst in March 1890, he took care to ensure that it would not endanger Germany's relations with the anti-clerical Italian government. However it would be misleading to cast Bismarck in a moderate role in 1890. He was ready to risk confrontation with the SPD and to use the familiar scare of the 'red peril' as an election issue. This would also provide an excuse for a coup against the *Reichstag* if he failed to secure a *Zentrum*–Conservative bloc.

In October Bismarck prepared a new anti-Socialist bill which was not only intended to operate permanently once it became law but also contained a draconian clause for the expulsion of Socialist agitators. At the Crown Council meeting of 24 January 1890 Bismarck refused to modify the bill [**Doc. 43, p. 149**], and it was defeated in the *Reichstag* two days later. The *Kartell* broke up, and the subsequent election in February led to a strengthening of the *Zentrum*, the *Freisinn* and the SPD [**Doc. 34, p. 144**]. Having already broken with the *Kartell*, Bismarck's only options were to turn to the Conservatives and the *Zentrum* or to recommend a coup.

Bismarck and the *Kaiser* were set on mutually opposing courses. The *Kaiser* already had General von Caprivi waiting in the wings as the new chancellor. Bismarck's former political expertise appeared to desert him when he clumsily tried to prevent William hosting an international Labour conference in Berlin and insisted that his Prussian ministerial colleagues paid absolute obedience to himself by resurrecting the cabinet order of 1852, which restricted free access to the crown to the minister-president. He also had contingency plans drawn up to deal with civil unrest, which seemed to be more provocative than preventative. On 12 March 1890 Bismarck made his last serious attempt to stay in power when he approached Windthorst, but any hopes of a Conservative–*Zentrum* alliance were dashed when the leader of the Conservatives in the *Reichstag*, von Helldorf-Bedra, refused to cooperate and informed the *Kaiser*. On 17 March William finally demanded that Bismarck should either withdraw the cabinet order of 1852 or resign. Isolated and defeated, Bismarck had little option but to resign the following day and on 29 March he left Berlin as a private citizen for his estate in Friedrichsruh. Ultimately, as the contemporary novelist Fontane observed, 'the power of the Hohenzollern monarchy . . . was stronger than [Bismarck's] genius and his falsehoods' (Craig, 1978: 371).

Part 6

GERMAN FOREIGN AND COLONIAL POLICY

11

Germany and Europe, 1871–1890

A s long as William I lived, German foreign policy was conducted by Bismarck alone. Although the quality of German diplomats was of the highest calibre, Bismarck's autocratic temperament in the long run served only to destroy their initiative and consequently his diplomatic system remained, as one of his biographers remarked, 'a one-man band' (Palmer, 1976: 219). Occasionally his views were challenged but invariably he overcame any opposition and his diplomats had little option but to 'fall into rank like soldiers' (Lerman, 2004: 205).

In retrospect, the year 1871 marks a natural turning point in his foreign policy: after three wars in a mere eight years there followed nearly twenty years of unbroken peace. Between 1862 and 1871 Bismarck had created a new Europe and now, like Metternich before him in 1815, he needed peace to preserve it. The implications of France's defeat in 1871 were far-reaching. Disraeli only slightly exaggerated contemporary fears when he observed that 'the war represents the German revolution . . . a greater event than the French Revolution of the last century' (Röhl, 1970: 23). The military and diplomatic balance had shifted from Paris to Berlin and it was uncertain whether Bismarck would be able to contain the momentum of German nationalism within the frontiers of 1871. Yet the new Germany was still a 'delicate compromise' (Geiss, 1976: 12), which could be destroyed by a hostile European coalition. Bismarck had therefore to reassure the European Great Powers, especially Austro-Hungary and Russia that Germany was 'satiated' and had no desire to create a *Grossdeutsch Reich* which would include the millions of Germans still outside the Germany of 1871 [**Doc. 44, p. 150**]. Relations with Austro-Hungary improved significantly when the Prussophobe Friedrich Beust was replaced as foreign secretary by Count Gyula Andrassy in November 1871.

THE LEAGUE OF THE THREE EMPERORS

In the immediate post-war years Bismarck was primarily concerned to ensure French isolation. Both the severe terms of the Treaty of Frankfurt and the instability of internal French politics appeared to rule out an immediate military and economic revival. In the longer term, however, a French recovery was inevitable. The League of the Three Emperors of Germany, Austria-Hungary and Russia in 1873 is sometimes seen as a premeditated attempt to isolate France, but initially it was more the product of mutual Austro-Russian distrust. Anxious to ensure that Vienna did not exploit her increasingly cordial relations with Berlin to Russia's disadvantage in the Balkans, Tsar Alexander II 'gate-crashed' (Palmer, 1976: 172) on Francis Joseph's visit to Germany in September 1872. In the subsequent hastily arranged tripartite talks Bismarck allayed Russia's suspicions and encouraged discussions on the maintenance of the status quo in the Balkans.

It was not until the following year, when a series of summits between the three Emperors produced the Agreements of 6 June and 22 October, that the League was finally created. Bismarck rejected plans for a Russo-German military pact and consequently the League remained essentially no more than an 'empty frame' (Geiss, 1976: 30) in which the three powers stressed their desire for peace and agreed on mutual consultation before taking unilateral action in the event of war. Its conservative and anti-revolutionary bias led the historian William Langer to describe it as 'a new Holy Alliance against revolution in all its forms' (Langer, 1931: 25), but it is more likely that Bismarck valued it chiefly as a means for isolating the French and enabling Germany to avoid making a choice between Russia and Austria. It initiated a policy which in varying degrees he attempted to follow until his resignation.

The League's limitations were first revealed by a sudden crisis with France in 1875. The speed with which the French managed to pay their indemnity and rebuild their army alarmed the German government and persuaded Bismarck to resort to some crude sabre-rattling and to inspire a series of threatening articles in the German press. Among these was the notorious leader in the *Berliner Post* entitled 'Is War in Sight?' that suggested that Bismarck was about to launch a pre-emptive strike against France. Conscious that both Britain and Italy were equally alarmed, the Tsar visited William to express his concern, while Gorchakov, his chancellor, was authorized to demand from Bismarck explicit assurances of peace. Although the crisis soon abated, Bismarck's miscalculations had enabled France, at least temporarily, to escape isolation and exposed the essential hollowness of the League of the Three Emperors. The crisis, as Katherine Lerman reminds us, also shows that Bismarck did not change overnight in 1871 from being a bold and sometimes impetuous foreign policy gambler to a conservative statesman' (Lerman, 2004: 207).

THE EASTERN CRISIS, 1875–1878

Bismarck's diplomacy was subjected to a more testing challenge when the very existence of the Turkish Empire in Europe was threatened by a chain of events, beginning in July 1875 with uprisings in Bosnia and Herzegovina. The possible collapse of Turkish power in the Balkans threatened to create a vacuum which both Austria and Russia would compete to fill. At worst this might lead to Austro-Russian conflict in which the rival powers would each seek a German alliance. At best a conference would be held where again the two powers would compete for German diplomatic support. In both situations Bismarck would be placed in essentially the same dilemma: he would be forced to chose between Vienna and St Petersburg, with the consequence that the unsuccessful power would attribute its defeat to German intervention and so look towards France. Initially Bismarck attempted to reduce the growing tension between Russia and Austria-Hungary, while he avoided giving the Tsar the decisive backing he desired. Despite the brutal crushing of the Bulgarian revolt by Turkish forces and the declaration of war on Turkey by Serbia and Montenegro, Russia and Austria-Hungary were still able to cooperate throughout the summer of 1876. At *Reichstadt* in July they drew up provisional plans for a peaceful partition of the Balkans. However, when Turkey, contrary to expectations, defeated both Serbia and Montenegro, Alexander came under increasing **Pan Slav** pressure to intervene. In October he asked the German government bluntly whether it would remain neutral in the event of war with Austria. Bismarck's reply was evasive and infuriated Gorchakov. He reiterated his hope for an Austro-Russian accord and stressed that Germany could ill afford to see either empire permanently weakened. The immediate threat of war abated when the Great Powers accepted a British proposal in November for an international conference to impose internal reforms on Turkey. When these were rejected by the Turkish Sultan, Abdul Hamid II, in January 1877, Turkey was effectively isolated and, after talks in Budapest, Austria at last agreed in March to Russian intervention at the price of acquiring Bosnia and Herzegovina.

Pan Slav Initially a programme based on the brotherhood of Slav nations, and then increasingly synonymous with Greater Russian nationalism.

These developments did not prevent Russo-German relations during the winter of 1876/77 deteriorating to a point where the Prussian General Staff professed alarm at Russian troop movements in Poland. Bismarck, concerned by reports of a Russian diplomatic initiative in Paris, attempted both to exploit British suspicion of Russia's Balkan policy by proposing an Anglo-German alliance and to draw closer to Vienna. In November 1876 he told the Austro-Hungarian ambassador that any weakening of the Dual Monarchy 'would be contrary to German interests', and in February 1877, when London rejected an alliance, he added that he was considering a 'permanent organic link' between the two empires (Böhme, 1966: 495, 443).

Although the coolness between Berlin and St Petersburg partly reflected the personal animosity between Bismarck and Gorchakov and the Tsar's irritation that Germany had not proved a more reliable friend, it was also a result of fundamental changes in the social, economic and political structures of the two states. These were causing a growing friction that steadily exacerbated diplomatic differences. As a consequence of the prolonged European depression, Russian industrialists, supported by Pan Slavs amongst the intelligentsia and in the government, were becoming increasingly resentful of German economic penetration. They attempted to counter growing Russian dependence on German finance by urging their government to raise loans in Paris and to protect the Russian home market with high tariffs. The government responded, and in 1877 the German export trade was severely damaged when Russian tariffs were abruptly raised by 50%. This was followed by further increases of 10% in both 1881 and 1884 (Kennan, 1979).

Russia invaded Turkey in April 1877, but the Turkish force held out unexpectedly at Plevna and it was not until January 1878 that the Russians at last reached Constantinople. They then proceeded to negotiate a settlement that ignored the Budapest agreements and was consequently repudiated by both London and Vienna. To avoid a European war Bismarck had little option but to propose a congress in Berlin. Bismarck had hoped to deflect Russian hostility away from Austria and Germany towards Britain, but he failed, as his very neutrality and refusal to put pressure on Vienna was 'in essence a decisively anti-Russian act' (Taylor, 1954: 248). This forced Russia to come to terms with Britain even before the congress met. Although Russia made some very real gains at the congress, the partitioning of Bulgaria, which was interpreted as an attempt to hinder the spread of Russian influence in the Balkans, and the occupation of Cyprus and Bosnia and Herzegovina by Britain and Austria-Hungary respectively, gave rise to the bitter complaint in Russia that the congress had been 'a European coalition against Russia under the leadership of Prince Bismarck' (Craig, 1978: 113).

THE DUAL ALLIANCE AND THE THREE EMPERORS' ALLIANCE

The 'War in Sight' crisis of 1875 followed by the steadily intensifying eastern crisis led Bismarck to reformulate his thinking on German foreign policy, which he summed up in the Kissinger Diktat of 15 June 1877. It outlined his fears of an anti-German coalition of the Great Powers and pronounced the key Bismarckian doctrine that in a Europe dominated by five great powers, Germany should always seek to be one of a grouping of three. Bismarck's overall aim was to achieve a 'political situation in which all the great powers except France have need of us by their relations with one another' (Lerman, 2004: 211). These ideas were to lead to the formation of a complex web of alliances over the next decade.

In the immediate aftermath of the congress Bismarck tried to revive the League of the Three Emperors, but by November it was clear that this was no longer possible. In the winter of 1878/79 he began to work towards an alliance with Austria-Hungary. Historians disagree about his motives. Some argue that Bismarck hoped to pacify Austria-Hungary and to compel 'Russia to adopt a more peaceful policy' (Waller, 1974: 250) and that consequently his emphasis on the organic character of the alliance was merely, to quote A.J.P. Taylor, 'an emotional coating' for home consumption (Taylor, 1955: 209). On the other hand, Langer, who described the alliance as 'the logical completion of German unification begun in the 1860s' (Langer, 1931: 196), and more recent German historians credit Bismarck with the much more fundamental aim of creating a Central European *bloc* or *Mitteleuropa*. This would both provide 'a sphere of influence for the commercial and political dynamism of the new Reich' (Böhme: 1966: 591) and hold the balance between the emerging giants of Russia in the east and the British Empire in the west (Gall, 1986, 2). The alliance was potentially popular within Germany as it appealed to Catholics, National Liberals, Conservatives and the army. At a time of intense political divisions over tariffs, therefore, it can also be seen as a means for creating an internal consensus [**Doc. 45, p. 150**].

Emperor William remained stubbornly loyal to the Tsar and opposed to the Austrian alliance, but Bismarck's policy was facilitated by the increasing hostility of the Russian government. This was heightened by close Austro-German cooperation on the various technical commissions supervising the execution of the Berlin Treaty and then further by the German tariff of July 1879 (see page **81**) which discriminated against Russian grain imports. The German grain tariffs [**Doc. 40, p. 147**] were a particularly severe blow against the Russian economy. Over the next decade they did much to strengthen anti-German feeling at St Petersburg. Three-quarters of all Russian exports were in corn, most of which went to Germany, and the profits had played an important part in financing the industrialization of Russia.

In August the Tsar crudely attempted to bring Germany to heel by writing directly to William the so-called 'Box on the Ears Letter' in which he bluntly warned him of the consequences for Russo-German relations of Bismarck's policy. Chancellor and Emperor disagreed profoundly in their reaction. For Bismarck, acutely conscious that the pro-German Austrian foreign minister, Count Andrassy, was about to resign, it was the signal to accelerate negotiations with Austria. William, on the other hand, visited the Tsar in an attempt to lessen the tension. Fearful that William would surrender abjectly and commit Germany to an alliance with an unstable Russia, Bismarck, in a series of lengthy memoranda at the beginning of September, argued strongly that only an Austrian alliance could stabilize the Balkans, prevent the isolation of Germany, and compel Russia to agree to the recreation of the Three Emperors' League. In the end it was Bismarck's threatened resignation that finally persuaded William to sign the Austrian treaty on 7 October [**Doc. 45, p. 150**]. The Dual Alliance was a 'landmark in European history' (Craig, 1978: 114), but it fell far short of Bismarck's original *bloc* concept and even failed to secure Austro-Hungarian support in the event of war with France. For an initial period of five years it provided that if either power were attacked by Russia, its ally would come to its assistance, but that if either partner were attacked by any other power, then its ally would observe benevolent neutrality. Konrad Canis, an Austrian historian, has recently argued that Bismarck had failed to grasp that Austria was now a 'multinational rather than a German power' (Lerman, 2004: 213; Canis, 1996).

Even while Bismarck was concluding this alliance with Austria, he began to restore Germany's relations with Russia. Alexander, having failed to call Bismarck's bluff, indicated in late September 1879, when he sent the pro-German Petr Saburov to Berlin, that he desired a rapprochement with Germany and would even consider a new tripartite agreement involving Austria. The Saburov mission was a diplomatic victory for Bismarck as it vindicated his belief that Russian policy would become more flexible in response to a definite Austro-German alliance. Little progress could be made, however, until Austria was ready to give up the prospect of a British alliance. When Gladstone won the general election in April 1880 and abandoned Disraeli's hawkish policy in the Balkans, the Austrians agreed to tripartite talks in Berlin in August 1880. Having guaranteed her empire against Russia, Bismarck could now afford to exert pressure on Austria to respond to Russian demands less negatively. In his desire to square the circle he had to mislead the Russians into believing that the Dual Alliance did not entail the automatic defence of Austria-Hungary by Germany in the event of a Russian attack. The Three Emperors' Alliance was concluded initially for three years on 18 June 1881 [**Doc. 46, p. 151**]. Although it was 'a hard-headed practical agreement' (Taylor, 1955: 209), it was in many ways 'little more than an armistice' (Medlicott and Coveney, 1971: 110) as it did not remove the long-term causes of Austro-Russian rivalry in the Balkans. Austria conceded the eventual reunification of Bulgaria in exchange for the recognition of her right at some future date to annex outright Bosnia and Herzegovina. Russian security was strengthened by the reaffirmation of the closure of the Straits to warships, which effectively put the Black Sea beyond the range of the British navy. Bismarck was, at least temporarily, freed from the fear of a Franco-Russian treaty by the declaration that in the event of war with a fourth great power, the signatory powers would be bound to benevolent neutrality.

The Alliance of the Three Emperors did not lead to a stable Russo-German *détente*. The humiliation of Russia at the Berlin Congress had, according to George F. Kennan the effect of 'unbalancing psychologically the designing of Russian foreign policy' (Kennan, 1979: 417) and of strengthening Pan Slav influence. The young and inexperienced Alexander III, who succeeded his father in 1881, received conflicting advice from his pro-German foreign minister, Giers, and his Pan Slav advisers. He reacted to this by attempting to implement both viewpoints simultaneously. Giers was encouraged to seek close diplomatic cooperation with Berlin, while behind his back the Pan Slavs in the foreign office and the military high command were permitted to intrigue in the Balkans and mastermind anti-German press campaigns. The increasing anti-German bias to Russian policy became apparent in December 1881 when the ardent Pan Slav Nikolai Obruchev was appointed to the General Staff of the Russian Army and the construction of strategic military railways was begun in Russian Poland. In January 1882 Bismarck was particularly annoyed when the popular and charismatic General Skobelev addressed a meeting of Serbian students in Paris and described the Germans as the natural enemies of the Slavs.

To preserve the alliance Bismarck had both to deter Pan Slav hostility and encourage Giers at the Russian foreign office. Consequently when Italy, annoyed by the French occupation of Tunis, proposed an alliance with Austria, Bismarck seized on the chance to create a Triple Alliance which indirectly strengthened Austria. Superficially the terms favoured Italy, in that the Central Powers would assist her in the event of a French attack, while in return she would support them militarily only if they were attacked by two other Great Powers. The real gain for Bismarck, however, was that Austria was freed from the fear of an Italian attack, should war break out with Russia. Austria's position was further consolidated by an alliance with Serbia in June 1882 and with Rumania in 1883, to which Germany also acceded, thereby forming 'a clear defensive alliance against Russia' (Taylor, 1954: 277). Simultaneously, Bismarck also attempted to mitigate the growing economic tension between Russia and Germany by refusing demands from both *Junkers* and industrialists for further tariff increases. Despite this there were large increases in 1885 and 1887 [**Doc. 40, p. 147**]. He also used Russian dependence on German capital as an inducement to secure a more cooperative policy and he facilitated the renewal of the Three Emperors' Alliance in March 1884 by persuading Bleichröder and other German financiers to subscribe to Russian loans floated on the Berlin capital market.

The Triple Alliance certainly ensured that Germany had achieved Bismarck's aim of being 'one of three in a Europe of five great powers'. It was 'the cornerstone of a complex web of alliances that Bismarck built up in the 1880s'. It was not however a rigid 'system' but rather 'a series of relationships intermeshed with one another' (Lerman, 2004: 214). Bismarck intended to make each member of the alliance dependent on German support, and so tied firmly to Berlin.

THE FRANCO-GERMAN ENTENTE

The emergence of a moderate and peaceful bourgeois republic in France by 1877 had enabled Bismarck, contrary to his earlier fears, to concentrate on the 'Eastern Question' without any real danger from French revisionism. Bismarck had every interest in keeping France pacific and as early as 1878 he began to prepare the ground for a Franco-German *entente*. He supported French interests in Rumania, the Near East and North Africa and made no secret of his motives when he told the French ambassador in 1880, 'I want you to turn your eyes from Metz and Strasburg by helping you to find satisfaction elsewhere' (Taylor, 1954: 272). Bismarck was delighted to see the French 'scatter their energies in new areas while picking up new enemies on the way' (Stern, 1977: 330). He encouraged them to take Tunis and exploited their resentment of the British occupation of Egypt in 1882.

Entente Friendly understanding between two states.

Taylor argued trenchantly in one of his early books that the German seizure of African colonies in 1884 was an attempt 'to make herself presentable to France [by] provok[ing] a quarrel with England so that Franco-German friendship should have the solid basis of anglophobia' (Taylor, 1938: 18). Although Bismarck's brief foray into colonial policy was motivated by a number of factors (see page **106**), it did, of course, provide him with opportunities to draw closer to France. In August 1884 he negotiated a Franco-German colonial *entente* and then cooperated closely with Paris in preparing the agenda for the Berlin Congo Conference. He surprised the French premier, Jules Ferry, with a proposal for an 'Association' of continental powers as a 'counterweight to English colonial supremacy' (Wehler, 1969: 385). He may, as Lothar Gall suggests, have been momentarily reverting to his concept of a continental *bloc* as a balance to the growing strength of the British Empire and Russia (Gall, 1986).

The rapprochement, with France, however, did not survive the fall of the Ferry government in March 1885. The defeat of the moderate Republicans in the subsequent French elections effectively terminated Franco-German cooperation and led to the appointment as war minister of the strongly anti-German General Boulanger in January 1886.

THE BULGARIAN CRISIS AND ITS CONSEQUENCES

In September 1885 the Eastern Crisis again erupted when Bulgaria united under Prince Alexander of Battenberg. The Tsar now opposed unification as he feared the pro-British and German tendencies of the prince who had married Princess Victoria, the granddaughter of both Kaiser Wilhelm I and Queen Victoria. Initially the unity of the Three Emperors' Alliance was not threatened as Austria and Russia agreed on the necessity of restoring the status quo. Then in November 1885 Serbia attacked Bulgaria in an attempt to enforce a new partition, but was decisively beaten at Slivnitza. Russia reacted by exerting renewed pressure on Prince Alexander, which led first to his kidnapping and then to his resignation. This in turn alarmed Austria who announced in November 1886 that a Russian occupation of Bulgaria would be unacceptable [**Doc. 47, p. 152**]. On the other hand Bismarck, ready in the final resort to tolerate a Russian occupation of Bulgaria, tried to restrain both his allies whom he compared to 'two savage dogs' (Pflanze, 3: 225).

Although Bismarck exploited the rise of General Boulanger to fight a general election at a favourable moment, the conjunction of the Bulgarian crisis with the renewed threat from France was potentially dangerous. Bismarck was particularly concerned that this might lead ultimately to a Franco-Russian alliance. He manoeuvred desperately, therefore, to preserve a link with Russia whilst simultaneously strengthening Austria-Hungary. He encouraged Britain, Italy and Austria-Hungary to conclude the first Mediterranean Agreement in February 1887 to contain Russia in the Balkans and at the Straits.

The Tsar refused to renew the Three Emperors' Alliance but agreed to negotiate with Germany alone what became known as the 'Reinsurance Treaty' of 18 June 1887. Bismarck made considerable concessions, secretly acknowledging Russia's right to exert a dominant influence in Bulgaria and agreeing to the closure of the Straits to warships of all foreign powers. However, to maintain the Dual Alliance with Austria-Hungary, he had to consent to a Russian proposal binding both signatories of the Reinsurance Treaty to neutrality in a war fought by the other with a third power, except in the situation where Germany attacked France or Russia attacked Austria. Bismarck had at least lessened the danger of a Franco-Russian alliance, but he had committed Germany to support Russia in Bulgaria in contradiction to Austria-Hungary's wishes, and consequently he ran the risk of encouraging the very war in the Balkans he wished to avert.

The pressure on Bismarck eased when Boulanger was dropped from the French cabinet in May 1887, but the Reinsurance Treaty did not immediately

lessen the tension in the Balkans. Russia viewed the election in July of Prince
Ferdinand of Coburg to the Bulgarian throne as an Austrian conspiracy.
Throughout the autumn the familiar manifestations of Russian displeasure
with Germany were exhibited: there were fresh troop movements on the
Polish frontier and constant attacks on Bismarck in the press. Bismarck had
initially been sympathetic to Russian protests, but he did not hesitate to use
financial pressure to avert a Russian occupation of Bulgaria, even though
in the longer term this would strengthen Russian financial ties with France.
In November the German government effectively vetoed a loan to Russia
when it ordered the *Reichsbank* not to accept Russian bonds as collateral
security for loans. This led to a sudden collapse of confidence in Russian
credit and a dramatic decline in the value of Russian securities held in
Germany. In December Bismarck created a further bulwark against Russia
when he successfully persuaded Britain, Austria and Italy to conclude the
second Mediterranean Agreement, which aimed to preserve the status quo
in the Near East.

Bismarck's complex financial and diplomatic moves restrained the Tsar
from overt military action, but for the next two years Russia consistently
attempted to undermine Ferdinand and to isolate Bulgaria. Russia also turned
to the French money market where, in March 1890, a loan was so over-
subscribed that she was able to finance large-scale and threatening military
manoeuvres on the German, Austro-Hungarian and Rumanian frontiers.
Paradoxically the accession of William II, who listened to the anti-Russian
counsels of General Waldersee and the diplomat von Holstein, and showed
a marked preference for a British alliance, made the Tsar more appreciative
of Bismarck and anxious to renew the Reinsurance Treaty. Bismarck was ready
to extend the treaty indefinitely, but he was dismissed in March 1890 before
negotiations could begin. Convinced by General von Caprivi, Bismarck's
successor, that a renewal would alienate Britain and contradict the spirit of
the Triple Alliance, William allowed it to lapse in June and 'one of the pivotal
agreements' (Langer, 1931: 503) of Bismarck's alliance system collapsed.

Reacting against Langer's famous encomium that 'no other statesman of
[Bismarck's] standing had ever before shown the same great moderation and
sound political sense of the possible and the desirable' (Langer, 1931: 503–4),
more sceptical historians have described his complex and contradictory
alliance system as a 'conjuring trick' (Taylor, 1954: 278), castigated it for
'expediency rather than creativity' (Craig, 1978: 102) and argued that the
preservation of peace was in fact more a result of 'the good sense and
moderation of others' (Waller, 1974: 254) than the inherent consequence of
Bismarck's genius. Ultimately Bismarck's alliance system failed because it did
not remove the basic causes of international instability. Bismarck aimed both
to prevent an Austro-Russian war and discourage either power from allying

with France against Germany. However, as this involved an assumption of permanent French isolation and of close cooperation between Vienna, St Petersburg and Berlin, it was unsustainable in the long term. There was no guarantee that the multiracial and multilingual Austria-Hungary would not fragment and that Russian expansionism could indefinitely be kept in check. Bismarck therefore had little option but to pursue a 'system of stopgaps' (Hildebrand, 1990). Bismarck's diplomacy was also becoming unpopular within Germany where economic differences with Russia and a hostile reaction against the anti-German bias of Pan Slav opinion made the doctrine of preventive war against Russia and cooperation with Austria-Hungary increasingly attractive.

12

The Creation of the German Colonial Empire

BISMARCK'S MOTIVES

The haste with which Bismarck in 1884–85 created a colonial empire five times the size of the German *Reich* is one of the most controversial aspects of his chancellorship (see map 3). Up to that point he had always apparently dismissed colonial acquisitions as an expensive luxury comparable to 'a poverty stricken Polish nobleman providing himself with silks and sables when he needed shirts' (Townsend, 1930: 160).

There have been attempts to resolve this contradiction, as Taylor does, by arguing that German colonies were 'the accidental by-product of an abortive Franco-German *entente*' (Taylor, 1938: 6), or by casting Bismarck in the role of a crypto-imperialist, who since 1871 had patiently laid his plans for a colonial empire. Mary Townsend, for example, interprets the despatch of German consuls to Africa and the South Seas in the early 1870s as evidence of 'cautious preparation and watchful waiting' (Townsend, 1930: 62).

Other historians argue that Bismarck's imperialism was principally motivated by short-term domestic objectives and that he played the colonial card in 1884 'like a magician producing a rabbit from a hat' (Craig, 1978: 167) to strengthen the appeal of the National Liberals in the autumn elections. Thanks to the success of the **Kolonialverein**, which had been founded in 1882 to promote colonial acquisitions, and the growing consensus of opinion among leading National Liberals that imperialism would help reunite their party, the prospect of an active colonial policy was a potentially popular election cry. Economically it would also appease the free traders and the strong mercantile interests in Hamburg and Bremen which deeply resented Germany's move to protectionism. Conscious of the apparently imminent accession of the anglophile crown prince, Bismarck may also have favoured imperialism as an issue which could be exploited to produce an immediate

Kolonialverein Colonial Association founded in 1882. Its membership was roughly about 15,000 and was drawn mainly from political, financial and commercial circles.

quarrel with the British, should Frederick ever attempt to dismiss him and form a Liberal ministry.

Hans-Ulrich Wehler (Wehler, 1969 and 1970) argues that Bismarck's colonial policy was essentially 'manipulated social imperialism'. By this he means that Bismarck, in the interests of the traditional social and economic power structures of the Prussian-German state, sought through colonial adventures to create a climate of cooperation and stability within the *Reich* by diverting attention away from divisive domestic problems [**Doc. 50, p. 155**]. The very comprehensiveness of this view has led to further debate. Paul Kennedy, drawing on a series of detailed studies of Bismarck's colonial policy, argues that the concept of social imperialism, although relevant to the later Wilhelmine period, is not applicable to the 1880s. He interprets Bismarck's policy rather as a pragmatic and limited response to pressure on German trade in Africa and the South Seas, and to his determination that Germans 'should not be pushed out of tropical markets where they had been operating for years at a time when industry and trade were already in the doldrums' (Kennedy, 1972: 139).

THE ANNEXATIONS IN AFRICA AND THE FAR EAST

In the early 1880s German merchants faced increasing competition in Africa and the Pacific. In New Guinea their interests were threatened by the territorial ambitions of the British Australian colony of Queensland, and the cabinet in London had imperiously rejected a request for setting up a joint commission to review the claims of German merchants on the Fiji islands [**Doc. 48, p. 153**]. At the same time colonial trading companies in Hamburg and Bremen were pessimistic about their prospects in Africa. In the summer of 1883 Bismarck was so alarmed by reports that an Anglo-French partition of west Africa was imminent that he took the unusual step of consulting the Hamburg chamber of commerce, which confirmed his fears. Bismarck was persuaded in August to drop his lukewarm attitude towards the plans of F.L. Lüderitz, a Bremen tobacco merchant, for setting up a trading station on the south-west African coast at Angra Pequena, and not only to grant him consular protection but also to enquire whether Britain had any claims to the territory. It is possible that Bismarck had already decided on annexation, but he may have been hoping for written confirmation of British indifference so that he would be able to avoid the expense of a formal annexation.

As Fritz Stern observed, 'in their almost incredible bungling born of complacency and arrogance, Lord Granville at the Foreign Office and Lord Derby at the Colonial Office must be regarded as the patron saints of Bismarck's empire' (Stern, 1977: 410). In November Bismarck was ambiguously informed that while Britain did not exercise sovereignty over the south-west African coast, she would regard it as an infringement of her 'legitimate rights' (Turner, 1967: 62) for another power to claim it. In December, when Bismarck sought clarification, he received no answer for six months. His suspicions were further aroused by the activities of local British officials at Cape Town and on the Gold Coast, who were pressing for the annexation of south-west Africa, Togoland and the Cameroons. German traders were also alarmed at the implications for the future of German trade in Central Africa when the Anglo-Portuguese Treaty of February 1884 allotted the mouth of the river Congo to Portugal, a power seen as a British satellite in Africa.

In the spring of 1884 Bismarck decided to grant formal protection not only to Lüderitz's acquisitions but also to German trading interests in Togoland, the Cameroons and New Guinea, and he despatched plenipotentiaries to west Africa and the South Pacific to negotiate with the local chieftains. Bismarck's reservations about the cost of colonies had been overcome by a formula devised by Heinrich von Kusserow, a foreign office official, which by ceding responsibility for the internal administration of the territories to the trading companies themselves, would leave the *Reich* only with responsibility for external protection. The British were informed of the decision to protect Lüderitz in a cryptic note on 24 April, which Taylor interprets as a manoeuvre to goad Britain into opposition (Taylor, 1938 and 1954). It is more likely to have been a deliberate attempt to mislead London so as to prevent any last minute effort to pre-empt German plans in south-west Africa and elsewhere. In retrospect this secrecy was justified, as the British did in fact send out an official to annex the Cameroons, who, unaware of rival German plans, arrived five days too late.

Bismarck took the obvious step of bringing pressure to bear on the British by exploiting Anglo-French differences in Egypt. In August 1884 Germany consequently supported France at the international conference on Egyptian finances in London. He also needed French support to counter Anglo-Portuguese policy in the Congo. Bismarck's refusal to recognize the validity of the Anglo-Portuguese Treaty of February 1884, which reserved navigation rights on the Congo River to Britain alone, in exchange for British support for Portuguese control of the mouth of the river, led to the convocation of the Congo Conference in Berlin in December 1884. Bismarck, who presided over the conference, worked closely with Jules Ferry to outmanoeuvre the British. Ironically, despite his repeated threats to organize a league of neutrals against Britain, a common desire to preserve free trade in the Congo led to an unexpected Anglo-German rapprochement and a corresponding weakening of the Franco-German *entente*. Bismarck was satisfied when the powers set up the Congo Free State under Belgian administration and stipulated that its frontiers were to remain open to international commerce.

Bismarck also hoped to strengthen German access to central African markets by negotiating with the Sultan of Zanzibar, who controlled an extensive stretch of the east African coast, a commercial treaty on such favourable terms to the *Reich* that the Sultan would virtually become a client monarch of the *Kaiser*. This essentially diplomatic approach was threatened by the conquistatorial activities of Carl Peters, the eccentric founder of the Society for German Colonization. Attempting to emulate the deeds of his English heroes in India, Warren Hastings and Clive, Peters penetrated the east African interior and rapidly concluded a series of treaties with the local chiefs by which he secured some 60,000 square miles of land. Rapidly transforming his Colonial Society into a trading company, he was able to persuade Bismarck of the commercial potential of the territory and gain Imperial protection in February 1885. The Sultan's objections to Peters' activities were overcome by a naval demonstration, and finally in December a commercial treaty covering the transit of goods through the Sultan's territory was signed.

Although Britain disliked Germany's colonial policy, she was distracted by French hostility in Egypt and Russian threats in Asia, and therefore had no choice but to tolerate it. In June 1884 the British cabinet recognized the German *fait accompli* in south-west Africa and in October the protectorates in Togo and the Cameroons. In 1885 Britain abandoned her claims to north-eastern New Guinea and the adjacent islands of New Britain. By the Anglo-German agreement of October 1886 Britain finally recognized the German possessions in east Africa.

BISMARCK'S DISILLUSION WITH THE COLONIES

None of these territories was to prove profitable. Bismarck had hoped to create a colonial empire on the cheap, but having once intervened, the *Reich* was unable to extricate itself. In Togo and the Cameroons the *Reich* failed to devolve responsibility for internal administration to the local merchants and, where administrative responsibility was handed over to a chartered company, the experiment was short-lived. In 1888 the East African Company provoked the African population into rebellion, compelling Bismarck to send troops and partially to suspend its charter. Meanwhile the South-West African Company showed itself so incompetent that its powers were vested in an Imperial Commissioner, and in 1889 the New Guinea Company went bankrupt.

It is not surprising that Bismarck rapidly became disillusioned with colonies, as they proved to be a financial and administrative burden rather than a cheap means of guaranteeing a prosperous colonial trade. Apart from an unsuccessful attempt to strengthen the East African Company by acquiring the lease of some important coastal strips from Zanzibar in 1888, Bismarck sanctioned no further expansion. He showed no interest in plans for annexing Uganda and in early 1890 even favoured selling up German commercial interests in Samoa to the Americans. Increasingly he looked towards China and Latin America to provide potential export markets.

Bismarck's motives for this *volte face* are unclear. To historians like Taylor believing in the principle of the primacy of foreign policy in modern German history it is the natural consequence of the failure of the French *entente* and of Germany's need for British support during the Bulgarian crisis. The diplomatic situation certainly played some part, but it is probable that he was influenced at least as much by the financial failure of his colonial policy. Hence on pragmatic commercial grounds he became increasingly sceptical of the value of Germany's new colonies.

Plate 1 The Frankfurt Assembly was the first elected German parliament. This coloured lithograph by Gustav May shows the Assembly's delegates meeting in the Paulskirche, Frankfurt in 1848.

Photo: akg-images/ullstein bild

Plate 2 A colour print based on a popular water colour by Carl Röchling (1855–1920). It depicts Prussian troops defending Sviep Wood near Cishkoves during the Battle of Königgratz.

Photo: akg-images

Plate 3 A portrait of Field Marshal von Moltke in 1890, a year before his death, by the artist Franz von Lenbach.
Photo: Hamburger Kunsthalle, Hamburg, Germany/The Bridgeman Art Library/German/out of copyright

Plate 4 A photograph of Bismarck at the height of his political powers in 1870 just before the outbreak of the Franco-Prussian war.
Photo: German School Private Collection/The Bridgeman Art Library/German/out of copyright

Plate 5 The proclamation of William I as German Kaiser in the Hall of Mirrors on 18th January 1871. In front of him stand Bismarck (right) and von Moltke (left).

Photo: Schloss Friedrichsruhe, Germany/The Bridgeman Art Library/German/out of copyright

Plate 6 A cartoon in the German satirical magazine, *Kladderdatsch* in 1875 depicting the *Kulturkampf* as a chess match between Bismarck and Pope Pius IX, which the former is about to win.
Photo: akg-images

Plate 7 A cartoon from the English satirical magazine, *Punch*, 28 September 1878, which refers to the Anti-Socialist Law. It shows Bismarck attempting firmly to close the lid on the socialist jack-in-the-box, who is depicted as the devil.
Photo: akg-images

NEW MAP OF TURKEY

CONTENTION

SIMPLY THIS.

IT IS EVER THUS WITH ARBITRATORS.
"TURKEY, TURKEY, EVERY WHERE, AND NOT A BIT FOR US?"

Plate 8 An American cartoon from *Harper's Weekly*, 27 July 1878, commenting on Bismarck's role at the Congress of Berlin. The caption says: 'Turkey, Turkey everywhere, and not a bit for us?'
Photo: akg-images

Plate 9 A picture by Ernst Henseler showing Bismarck addressing the *Reichstag* on 6 February 1888.
Photo: Angermuseum, Erfurt, Germany/The Bridgeman Art Library/German/out of copyright

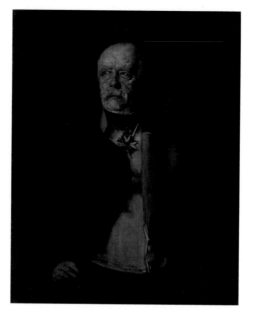

Plate 10 Bismarck in his old age. A picture by Ernst von Lenbach, c.1890.
Photo: Tucherschloss Nuernberg, Nuremberg, Germany/The Bridgeman Art Library/German/out of copyright

Plate 11 A cartoon in the Russian magazine, *Strekoza*, commenting on Bismarck's dismissal on 20 March 1890 from the *Reich* Chancellorship.
Photo: akg-images

Part 7

ASSESSMENT

13

Bismarck in Myth and Reality

BISMARCK IN RETIREMENT

Foreign observers in Berlin were surprised by the relief which greeted the news of Bismarck's resignation. The Austrian ambassador, for instance, recorded that the officials in the *Bundesrat* felt as if 'a heavy load has been taken away' (Stürmer, 1971: 310). By 1890 Bismarck appeared to have exhausted his genius for improvisation and to have 'had no other answer for the problems of his society but violence' (Craig, 1978: 179). His resignation was popular and regarded as inevitable, but within a year he became a considerable political force again when Caprivi, his successor, alienated both the Conservatives, by lowering agricultural tariffs, and the National Liberals, by the occasional tactical alliance with the *Zentrum*. Bismarck began to write scathingly critical articles for the *Hamburger Nachrichten* and was even elected as a National Liberal to the *Reichstag*, although he never took up his seat.

In sharp contrast to his attitude between 1886 and 1890, when he rejected any further colonial acquisitions on the grounds that they were too expensive to maintain, he supported the imperialist and *Grossdeutsch* **Pan-German League,** which enabled his successors to claim Bismarckian authority for a German **Weltpolitik**. He also gave his blessing to the **Agrarian League** which was set up to oppose Caprivi's tariff policy and grew into a powerful pressure group, reinforcing Conservative determination to maintain the status quo. Bismarck's estate at Friedrichsruh became a Mecca for students and representatives of various patriotic organizations, who were treated to lectures on the political blunders of his successors. By the time he died in 1898 the 'historical Bismarck' had already been eclipsed by 'the superhuman Bismarck, who from the Meuse to the Memel decorated market places and rural resorts in stone and bronze'. In retirement he had become 'an archetypal father figure and a national symbol' (Stürmer, 1971: 317), who lent his name to causes which, as chancellor, he would have treated with greater circumspection.

Pan-German League An extremist political interest organization which was officially founded in 1891. Its members believed in the unification of all Germans in Europe within one state. Consequently for the Pan-German League the unification of 1871 was just a starting point.

Weltpolitik Literally world policy; in other words, a global pursuit of German political interests and the intention to create a colonial empire.

Agrarian League Extra-parliamentary organization founded in 1893. Formed to combat the free-trade policies of Chancellor Caprivi.

BISMARCK'S ACHIEVEMENTS

Hohenzollern monarchy
Ruling dynasty of Kingdom of Prussia, and then Germany, 1701–1918.

However much the legacy left by Bismarck may tarnish his achievements in retrospect, his skill as a diplomat and politician cannot but impress the historian. In the modernizing traditions of the **Hohenzollern monarchy** and its ministers, which stretched back to the seventeenth century, Bismarck imposed a revolution from above. He steered Prussia through the Schleswig-Holstein crisis, won the wars of 1866 and 1870–71 and negotiated the constitutional settlements of 1867–71. The victory at Königgratz enabled Bismarck to end the constitutional crisis and to appease the Liberal opposition. The constitutional settlements of 1867–71 were real if fragile compromises between the Prussian crown, the German states and the Liberal movement, even though in the final analysis they preserved the power of Prussia, its king and army. For more than a decade after 1866 Bismarck enjoyed what was effectively an alliance with the National Liberals, and although he continued to pay lip-service to the past, his policies were in practice more concerned with the future. The work of creating the legal, financial and economic infrastructure of the new German nation was a fulfilment of the Liberals' agenda.

The constitution only remained viable as long as the majority of the *Reichstag* refrained from pushing for a constitutional monarchy and Bismarck could reconcile the interests of Prussia with those of the *Reich*. This was the case during the 'golden age of the politics of compromise' (Hamerow, 1972: 337) between 1867 and 1873, but the prolonged economic depression and the rapid tempo of industrialization in the 1880s [**Doc. 28, p. 138**] changed the context of German politics. The introduction of tariffs in 1879 and Bismarck's subsequent alliance with the agrarians and industrialists sharpened class tensions and encouraged the growth of a strong SPD, which the anti-Socialist law was unable to prevent. Bismarck then employed every means he could, although he was not always successful, to strengthen the executive and to secure a pliant *Reichstag* [**Doc. 50, p. 155**].

He was certainly an admirer of Louis Napoleon's manipulation of a mass electorate and was skilful in seizing chances to hold elections at favourable opportunities. It is also clear that in times of confrontation with parliament he was tempted to follow the example of Napoleon's *coup d'état* of December 1851. Yet the *Reich* was genuinely more liberal and democratic than the Second French Empire until Napoleon's new constitution of 1870. In Germany, unlike Bonapartist France, parliament was a force to be reckoned with. Perhaps, as Mitchell has suggested, Bismarck in his refusal to modernize the constitution in the 1880s could be compared more with Louis Phillipe's conservative Prime Minister, Guizot, in the 1840s than to Napoleon. Nevertheless, it is true that by 1890 Bismarck was convinced that the constitution of 1871 was unworkable. With far-reaching consequences for both Germany and

Europe, Bismarck failed to adapt it so that it could accommodate change peacefully. His only solution was to play with the idea of a counter-revolution which would at the very least have involved the abandonment of universal suffrage.

'With the egoism that accompanies greatness' (Mann, 1968: 219) Bismarck also failed to prepare any successor to take over the complicated machine he had constructed. No one, as the historian Richard Evans observed, 'neither the erratic kaiser William II' nor the chancellors who succeeded him, was capable of plugging the gap left by his departure (Evans, 1978: 17). But even the most gifted statesman would have found the legacy difficult. The accelerating industrialization of Germany created tensions which appeared insoluble within the existing constitutional framework, particularly as the Prussian generals and *Junkers*, strengthened by formidable peasant and artisan pressure groups, blocked any moves towards creating a parliamentary democracy. Although in the years immediately before the First World War the German *Reichstag* did assert itself more strongly, it was unable to conquer what Pflanze has called 'the castle keep of the Prussian-German establish-ment and its encircling battlements' (Pflanze, 1990, 3: 440). Only the threat of imminent military defeat in 1918 was able to break this deadlock.

Yet for all its internal problems the new German state under Bismarck was a stabilizing factor in central Europe. Nevertheless here too he bequeathed his successors difficult if not insoluble problems. Economic pressures and rivalry in the Balkans with Austria were driving Russia into a French alliance. However, the mistakes that plunged Germany into war in 1914 were very much the fault of his successors who abandoned the Reinsurance Treaty and then alienated Britain by building a large navy. They may well have risked war in 1914 to 'strengthen the endangered [Bismarckian] status quo' (Wehler, 1985: 196), but it is reasonable, although of course entirely hypothetical, to assume that Bismarck would have trodden more carefully and not unleashed a war at a time when the diplomatic balance no longer favoured Germany.

BISMARCK AND THE HISTORIANS

The interpretation of Bismarck's legacy remains one of the most crucial ques-tions in German historiography (Urbach, 1998) [**Doc. 49, p. 150**]. After the collapse of the Second *Reich* in 1918 only a few German historians, such as Eckart Kehr, for example, dared question the Bismarckian legacy. Later in 1933 Hitler naturally claimed to be in direct line of succession to Bismarck, although he was nevertheless critical of the Iron Chancellor for his lack of rigour in dealing with the Jewish 'problem' and the later moderation of his foreign policy (Pflanze, 1990, 1: Introduction).

The experiences of the Nazi period encouraged historians to reappraise Bismarck's achievements and to ask, like Meinecke writing in the shadow of 1945 'whether the germs of the later evil [Nazism] were not already present in the Bismarckian *Reich*' (Meinecke, 1950: 13). Yet with the notable exception of the liberal historian Eyck (1950) whose monumental biography was originally published in Switzerland during the Second World War, most German historians up to the early 1960s agreed with Kaehler that any attempt to link Bismarck with Hitler was 'legend', 'prejudice' and 'propaganda' (Pflanze, 1990, 1: Introduction). Many foreign historians on the other hand, not surprisingly perhaps, were quicker to see a direct causal link between the Bismarck era and the horrors of the Third *Reich*. The American historian, Otto Pflanze, later the author of one of the most authoritative studies of the Bismarck era, argued for instance in 1955 that 'if one line of development runs from the revolution of 1848 through Treitschke to Hitler another certainly goes from Bismarck through Ludendorff to Hitler' (Pflanze, 1955: 566).

It was Fritz Fischer's seminal study of Germany's aims in the 1914–18 war (Fischer: 1967) and the emergence of the new predominantly left-wing post-war generation of German historians in the 1960s which paved the way for a radical reappraisal of the political and social structure of the Second *Reich*. By the mid-1970s, as a result of the reprinting of the essays of Eckart Kehr (1977) and important new works by Böhme (1966), Wehler (1985 [1973]) and Mommsen (1995), the traditional interpretations of Bismarck had been replaced by what was to become a '**new orthodoxy**' (Eley, 1986: 16), arguing that the key to understanding Bismarckian Germany was the paradox that it was a politically backward and repressive state with an ultra-modern economy. It had industrialized without undergoing a 'bourgeois revolution' (Evans: 1987: 762). Bismarck's deliberate decision to stop Germany developing into a constitutional liberal state through his skilful manipulation of the political parties, plebiscitary elections and negative integration tactics [**Doc. 50, p. 155**] set Germany on a special path or *Sonderweg*, which continued until 1945. Germany was an industrial giant whose population was accustomed, as Max Weber put it, 'to expect that the great men at the top would provide their politics for them' (Pflanze, 1990, 3: 441). This, it was argued, inevitably resulted in creating major problems for the democratic Weimar Republic when it was constituted in 1919.

The 'new orthodoxy' does not, of course, go unchallenged. Detailed research into local German history, particularly by British historians, suggests that it underestimates the grassroots pressure exerted on Bismarck and the German elites. Eley, for instance, criticizes the Bielefeld school's work for being too 'statist' or Prusso-centric in its approach. While not disputing the

'New orthodoxy' Name given to historical interpretation of the Second *Reich*, which was adopted by Hans-Ulrich Wehler (see Bielefeld school) and other historians, arguing that the key to understanding Bismarckian Germany was that it had industrialized without undergoing a 'bourgeois revolution'.

Sonderweg Literally unique path or development. Scholars such as Hans-Ulrich Wehler, using Britain and France as models, have argued that industrialization in Germany was not accompanied by 'modernization or democratization'. Hence Germany took its own 'special path'. This is disputed, especially by D. Blackbourne and G. Eley.

seriousness of the political defeat of Liberalism in the *Reichstag* in 1879, he argues that a study of local politics and socio-cultural changes considerably modifies the picture of a people ruthlessly manipulated by Bismarck and the Prusso-German elites. In practice, he insists, the middle classes did seize power at local level and there was what amounted to a middle-class revolution from below. Furthermore he questions the *Sonderweg* theory by arguing that 'the very modernity' of the Bismarckian state with its universal male franchise for *Reichstag* elections and excellent welfare, administrative and educational systems made further democratization for the time being unnecessary (Eley, 1992: 26). The Bielefeld school has not been impervious to these debates. In many important aspects it has significantly modified its *Sonderweg* thesis. For instance, it now concedes that the bourgeoisie were culturally as influential in Wilhelmine Germany as in France or Britain. It was their failure to gain political power that made Germany so different from the western European liberal states (Evans, 1997).

The reunification of Germany in 1990 has also affected how the Bismarckian *Reich* is perceived by German historians. As late as 1980 Lothar Gall (1986, 2: 233) could observe that 'today we see the *Reich* of 1871 . . . as a highly unstable and short lived'. Now it is the division of Germany after 1945 that was abnormal rather than the creation in 1871 of the *Reich*. Arguably the reunification of Germany is a vindication of Bismarck's achievements of 1866–71. Christian von Krockow, for example, observed that reunification in 1990 gave 'Bismarck and his work a new almost haunting significance' (von Krockow, 1990: 8–9). Inevitably the reunification of Germany produced a change of perspective and, in the words of Arnulf Baring of the Free University of Berlin, 'very old questions about Germany's role in the middle of Europe will force themselves back on the agenda' (Berger, 1995: 203). By 1998 there were signs of what Karina Urbach (1998) calls a 'Bismarck Renaissance' complete with coffee-table books and a *Bismarcklexicon*.

Bismarck played so important a role in moulding the German state, the creation of which was to have such fateful consequences for Europe that it is unlikely that a definitive and universally accepted assessment of this great statesman will ever be agreed upon by historians. His subtle and impregnable defence of the powers of the Prussian monarchy and his refusal to revise the constitutional settlement of 1867–71 undoubtedly helped strengthen anti-democratic and anti-liberal sentiments in Germany and preserved the power of the pre-industrial elite. Paradoxically, however, he did create a German state with a very modern infrastructure. Its bureaucracy, industry and educational and state welfare systems were the envy of Edwardian Britain.

Part 8

DOCUMENTS

Document 1   ARMINIUS RIEMANN'S SPEECH AT THE WARTBURG FESTIVAL, 1817

On 18–19 October 1817 the (Burschenschaften) Fraternities student held a rally at the Wartburg, which was attended by over 500 students. Arminius Riemann had fought in the War of Liberation in 1813–14, studied theology and was a member of the fraternity in Jena. His speech is shot through with a bitter disillusionment about how the realization of German unity had been frustrated. Only Archduke Charles of Weimar had carried out his promise to grant a constitution by 1817.

Four long years have flowed by since [the battle of Leipzig]; the German people had built up lovely hopes. They have all been frustrated. Everything has turned out differently from what we expected. Much that is great and splendid, that could and should have happened, has not taken place; many holy and noble feelings have been treated with mockery and derision. Of all the Princes of Germany, only one has honoured his given word, that one in whose free land we are celebrating the festival of the Battle.

Source: H. Schulze, *The Course of German Nationalism: From Frederick the Great to Bismarck, 1763–1867*, trans. Sarah Hanbury-Tenison, Cambridge: Cambridge University Press, 1991, p. 122.

Document 2   THE HISTORIAN A.J.P. TAYLOR ON THE 1848 REVOLUTIONS

A.J.P. Taylor wrote The Course of German History *at the end of the Second World War. His negative view of the consequences of the 1848 revolutions, 'as the turning point that did not turn' reflects the period it was written in. Today historians stress rather that the revolutions laid the basis for the emergence of a new kind of politics by the end of the 1850s.*

1848 was the decisive year of German, and so European history: it recapitulated Germany's past and anticipated Germany's future. Echoes of the Holy Roman Empire merged into a prelude of the Nazi 'New Order'; the doctrines of Rousseau and the doctrines of Marx, the shade of Luther and the shadow of Hitler jostled each other in bewildering succession. Never has there been a revolution so inspired by a limitless faith; never has a revolution so discredited the power of ideas in its result. The success of the revolution discredited conservative ideas; and the failure of the revolution discredited liberal ideas. After it, nothing remained but the idea of Force, and this idea stood at the helm of German history from then on. For the first time since 1521, the German people stepped on to the centre of the German stage only to miss their cues once more. German history reached its turning point and failed to turn. This was the fateful essence of 1848.

Source: A.J.P. Taylor, *The Course of German History*, London: Methuen, 1961, p. 69.

THE ECONOMY AND NATIONAL UNITY **Document 3**

The Bremer Handelsblatt, *a leading Liberal and pro-Zollverein newspaper, was founded by Karl Andree, who participated as a student in the German national movement, in 1848. In an article on 11 July 1857, of which this document is an extract, the* Handelsblatt *stressed that the economy urgently needed political unity if it were to thrive. The newspaper's journalists were later active in the* Nationalverein.

Whoever looks at the situation without prejudice and fear will recognize immediately the intimate connection, especially in Germany, of the national economic with the national political problem, this Alpha and Omega of German politics. The commerce and transportation of a country have, in spite of the egoism among individuals, a common aspect. They demand one law, one legislation, one defence abroad. This need has been satisfied in all other countries which we may mention, but not in Germany. A common code of commercial law is now slowly struggling to life; a common legislation is a pious wish, and abroad we all enjoy the same right, defencelessness . . .

Source: from *The Social and Political Conflict in Prussia, 1858–1961*, by Eugene N. Anderson by permission of the University of Nebraska Press. Copyright 1954 by the University of Nebraska. Copyright renewed 1982 by the University of Nebraska Press.

THE *NATIONALVEREIN* PROGRAMME, 1859 **Document 4**

The Nationalverein *advocated the creation of a united Germany under Prussian leadership. It was founded in September 1859. It was inspired by the Italian National Society, which was founded in Piedmont in 1856 with the aim of raising support for a united Italy under the leadership of Piedmont. The* Nationalverein's *members wanted an 'Italia-type solution' to German unity, which would involve the creation of a united Germany under Prussian leadership and the restoration of the Kleindeutsch (see page 9) constitution of 1849.*

1 We perceive in the present political situation of the world great dangers for the independence of our German fatherland, dangers which have been increased rather than decreased by the peace concluded between Austria and France.
2 These dangers have their ultimate cause in the defective common constitution of Germany, and they can be removed only through a prompt alteration of this constitution.
3 For this purpose it is necessary that the German federal diet be replaced by a stable, strong, and permanent central government of Germany, and that a German national assembly be convoked.

4 Under present circumstances the most effective steps for the achievement of this goal can come only from Prussia. We should therefore strive to bring it about that Prussia assumes the initiative in this matter.

5 Should Germany in the immediate future once again be directly threatened from abroad, then, until the final establishment of the German central government, the command of the German military forces and the diplomatic representation of Germany abroad are to be assigned to Prussia.

6 It is the duty of every German to support the Prussian government to the best of his ability, insofar as its endeavours are based on the principle that the tasks of the Prussian state coincide essentially with the needs and tasks of Germany, and insofar as it directs its activity toward the introduction of a strong and free common constitution for Germany.

7 We expect of all German friends of the fatherland, whether they belong to the democratic or the constitutional right-wing liberal party, that they will place national independence and unity above the demands of the party, and that they will work together harmoniously and perseveringly for the achievement of a strong constitution for Germany.

Source: from HAMEROW, THEORDORE S.; *THE SOCIAL FOUNDATIONS OF GERMAN UNIFICATION, 1858–1871, IDEAS AND INSTITUTIONS* © 1969 Princeton University Press, 1997 renewed PUP reprinted by permission of Princeton University Press.

————◄●►————

Document 5   THE PRUSSIAN LIBERALS LONG FOR A GERMAN CAVOUR, 1861

By 1861 Italy was united, except for Rome and Venetia. Piedmont under the leadership of Cavour had played a key role in achieving this. Karl Twesten in a speech in the Prussian Landtag is well aware of the lessons that this had for the achievement of German unity where Prussia would play the role of Piedmont. Although he was a member of the Progressive Party he was ready to tolerate the use of Machiavellian policies to achieve German unity. Not surprisingly, despite his opposition to the Army bill, he voted in 1866 in favour of the Indemnity bill and was a founder member of the National Liberal Party.

If some day a Prussian minister would step forward in the same way and say . . . 'I have moved boundary markers, violated international law, and torn up treaties, as Count Cavour has done', gentlemen, I believe that we will then not condemn him. And if an inexorable fate should carry him off in the midst of his brilliant career, as happened to the former, before he achieved his high goal to its full extent, then we will erect a monument to him, as the history of Italy will erect one to Count Cavour, and I believe that even a soaring ambition will be content with such a monument.

Source: from HAMEROW, THEORDORE S.; *THE SOCIAL FOUNDATIONS OF GERMAN UNIFICATION, 1858–1871* © 1972 Princeton University Press, 2000 renewed PUP reprinted by permission of Princeton University Press.

————◄●►————

KING WILLIAM AND THE ARMY BILL   **Document 6**

The king contemptuously brushed aside an attempt by an old Liberal acquaintance, von Saucken-Julienfelde, to explain the position of the Landtag *on the military question. In the extract from the letter below written in August 1862, 'one can still hear the pen stab the paper and the ink explode', as E.N. Anderson so aptly observed. William was adamant that he would not compromise over the Army bill.*

War to the death against the monarch and his standing army has been vowed, and in order to reach that goal the Progressivists and democrats and ultra liberals scorn no means, and indeed with rare consequence and deep conviction . . . the shortening of the term of service is demanded so that firm, well-disciplined military training, the effects of which will hold during the long period of leave, shall not be given the soldier. The under-officers shall become officers, not as everyone could in Prussia since 1808 by passing one and the same examination, but without proving this equality of cultural level, so that a schism will develop in the officers' corps and dissatisfaction will slowly creep into them and the democrats will be able to develop an officers' caste of their own which, because they are neither trained nor steeled in their views to stand loyally by the throne, are to be won for the revolution. Since loyalty and self-sacrifice for King and throne are to be expected from the present officers and through them to be transferred to the troops, *therefore* the officers' class is slandered in every possible way, and then one wonders that the officers are angry? And even censures them for this!!

'A peoples' army [behind] Parliament.' That is the solution revealed since Frankfurt am Main [he referred to a speech by Schulze-Delitzsch] to which I counter with the watchword: 'A disciplined army that is also the people in arms, [behind] the King and war lord.'

Between these two watchwords no agreement is possible.

Source: reprinted from *The Social and Political Conflict in Prussia, 1858–61* by Eugene N. Anderson by permission of the University of Nebraska Press. Copyright 1954 by the University of Nebraska. Copyright renewed 1982 by the University of Nebraska Press.

BISMARCK FORESEES WAR WITH AUSTRIA   **Document 7**

The Crimean War marked a turning point in European diplomatic relations. Austria's refusal to help Russia against Britain and France ensured that Russia would no longer be ready to defend the Vienna settlement of 1815. Bismarck was quick to appreciate this and to urge the Prussian government to exploit Austria's isolation. In April 1856 Bismarck sent Otto von Manteuffel and Leopold von Gerlach his assessment of Austro-Prussian relations – the so called 'Prachtbericht' *or* 'Showpiece Report'.

Because of the policy of Vienna, Germany is clearly too small for us both; as long as an honourable arrangement concerning the influence of each cannot be concluded and carried out, we will both plough the same disputed acre, and Austria will remain the only state to whom we can permanently lose or from whom we can permanently gain . . . For a thousand years intermittently – and since Charles V, every century – the German dualism has regularly adjusted the reciprocal relations [of the powers] by a thorough internal war; and in this century also no other means than this can set the clock of evolution at the right hour . . . In the not too distant future we shall have to fight for our existence against Austria and . . . it is not within our power to avoid that, since the course of events in Germany has no other solution.

Source: G. Craig, *The Politics of the Prussian Army, 1640–1945*, Oxford: Oxford University Press, 1955, p. 160.

Document 8   BISMARCK AND THE GERMAN CONFEDERATION

In March 1858 Bismarck wrote a lengthy memorandum for Prince William, which became known as the Booklet. His basic argument was that Prussia should exploit the moral force of German nationalism to win over the smaller states to Prussia's plans for a Kleindeutschland.

No state has the urge and opportunity to assert its German point of view independently of the *Bund* assembly to the same extent as Prussia. . . .

Prussian interests coincide exactly with those of most of the *Bund* countries except Austria, but not with those of the *Bund* governments, and there is nothing more German than the development of Prussia's particular interests, properly understood . . .

Source: W.N. Medlicott and D.K. Coveney (eds), *Bismarck and Europe*, London: Edward Arnold, 1971, p. 21.

Document 9   'BLOOD AND IRON'

Bismarck's first major speech as minister-president was made to the Budget Commission of the Prussian Landtag *on 29 September 1862. He attempted to turn the attention of the deputies away from the constitutional deadlock caused by their rejection of the Army bill to foreign affairs. The speech was witty, forceful but at times threatening and seemed ill-judged even to many of his supporters. However it does show that he realized that only a successful foreign policy could secure both Prussia's and his own position.*

[He said] he would gladly agree to the budget for 1862, but without giving any prejudicial explanation. A misuse of constitutional powers could happen on any side, and would lead to a reaction from the other side. The crown, for example, could dissolve [parliament] a dozen times, and that would certainly be in accordance with the letter of the Constitution, but it would be a misuse. In the same way it can challenge the budget cancellations as much as it likes: but the limit is difficult to set; shall it be at 6 million or 16 million, or 60 million? – There are members of the National Union, a party respected because of the justice of its demands, highly esteemed members, who considered all standing armies superfluous. Now what if a national assembly were of this opinion! Wouldn't the government have to reject it? – People speak of the 'sobriety' of the Prussian people. Certainly the great independence of the individual makes it difficult in Prussia to rule with the constitution; in France it is different, the independence of the individual is lacking there. A constitutional crisis is not shameful, but honourable. Furthermore we are perhaps too 'educated' to put up with a constitution; we are too critical; the ability to judge government measures and bills of the National Assembly is too widespread; there are in the country too many subversive elements who have an interest in revolutionary change. This may sound paradoxical, but it goes to show how difficult it is in Prussia to carry on a constitutional existence . . . We are too ardent, we like to carry too heavy a weight of armour for our fragile bodies: but we should also make use of it. Germany doesn't look to Prussia's liberalism, but to its power: Bavaria, Wurttemberg, Baden can indulge in liberalism, but no one will expect them to undertake Prussia's role; Prussia must gather and consolidate her strength in readiness for the favourable moment, which has already been missed several times; Prussia's boundaries according to the Vienna treaties are not favourable to a healthy political life; not by means of speeches and majority verdicts will the great decisions of the time be made – that was the great mistake of 1848 and 1849 – but by iron and blood. . . .

Source: W.N. Medlicott and D.K. Coveney (eds), *Bismarck and Europe*, London: Edward Arnold, 1971, pp. 30–1.

————◄●►————

BISMARCK AND COMMERCIAL REFORM, 1865   **Document 10**

The Essen Chamber of Commerce in its annual report for 1865 approved of the new Prussian Mining Law which came into effect on 1 October 1865. Despite the bitter conflict over the Army bill there was considerable potential common ground between Bismarck and the Liberals. His Zollverein policy was popular, and the Mining Law of 24 June 1865, which established the freedom of exploration and exploitation, was welcomed by industry and the Chambers of Commerce.

Unquestionably the most important event of the past year for our district was the coming into effect on October 1 of the 'General Mining Law for the Prussian States.' The new mining law marks the conclusion of a long period of striving for reforms and of their partial introduction. It completely removes everything antiquated and constraining, and instead gives mining the free movement which alone can make it great and beneficial. While the confusion in mining legislation was immeasurably increased by the vast number of laws and legal regulations which rested on the most diverse foundations and contained the most contradictory provisions, the new law on the other hand brings in clear and precise form a common standardization of the mining code, uniformly applicable to all mines in the state, which everywhere seeks to take into account the requirements of practical operation and the general legal views of the present time.

Source: from HAMEROW, THEORDORE S.; *THE SOCIAL FOUNDATIONS OF GERMAN UNIFICATION, 1858–1871* © 1972 Princeton University Press, 2000 renewed PUP reprinted by permission of Princeton University Press.

Document 11   THE INTERNAL IMPACT OF DÜPPEL

The Battle of Düppel in April 1864 was the first Prussian military victory for half a century. It filled both soldiers and civilians with pride and for the time being softened the opposition to Bismarck. In a letter to W. Rossmann (29 April 1864), J.G. Droysen, a distinguished historian, former Liberal deputy in the Frankfurt Assembly 1848–49 and one of the leaders of the Kleindeutsch movement, confided his joy at the news of the military victory over the Danes at Düppel.

I am certainly no Bismarck enthusiast, but he has the ability to act . . . I look forward to the future with pleasure. There is something invigorating, after fifty years of peace, in a day like the battle of Düppel for the young Prussian troops. One feels as if all one's nerves had been refreshed. And what a blessing that in the face of all the manoeuvring of the princes and the grandiloquence of the true Germans, the Austrian project for reform, and the *Nationalverein*, the full force of real power and real activism should make itself felt. . . . It is time that the importance of the medium-sized and small states were kept within its real limits. . . . They will go on saying that Prussia under Bismarck is not to be trusted; they will denounce more loudly than ever Prussia's greed for annexations and use it as a pretext for dissociating themselves; they will continue to say that the real Germany is outside Prussia and menaced by Prussia. With God's help all this will not stand in the way of what has been begun . . .

Source: W. Simon (ed.), *Germany in the Age of Bismarck*, London: Allen & Unwin, 1968, p. 104.

LIBERAL OPPOSITION TO THE WAR OF 1866   **Document 12**

Despite the favourable impact on public opinion of the victory over Denmark, Bismarck was unable to persuade William to compromise over the Army bill, or to reconcile the majority of the Liberals. Indeed Bismarck's attempts to stifle free speech and prosecute deputies for speeches in the Landtag *in early 1866 united the Liberals in opposition to him. On 20 May a congress of Liberal deputies met in Frankfurt and condemned the imminent war with Austria.*

The victory of our arms [over Denmark] has restored our northern boundaries to us. Such a victory would have elevated the national spirit in every well-ordered state. But in Prussia, through the disrespect shown for the rights of the reconquered provinces, through the effort of the Prussian government to annex them by force, and through the fatal jealousy of the two great powers, it has led to a conflict that reaches far beyond the original object of the dispute.

We condemn the imminent war as a cabinet enterprise, serving merely dynastic ends. It is unworthy of a civilized nation, threatens all achievements of fifty years of peace, and adds fuel to the greed of foreign countries.

Princes and ministers who will be responsible for this unnatural war, or who increase its dangers for the sake of special interests, will be guilty of a grave crime against the nation.

The curse, and the punishment for high treason, shall strike those who will give up German territory in their negotiations with foreign powers.

Source: August Bebel, *Reminiscences*, New York: Socialist Literature Company, 1911, pp. 151–3.

BISMARCK AND SCHLESWIG-HOLSTEIN   **Document 13**

Bismarck indicated his thinking in the early stages of the Schleswig-Holstein crisis in a letter to the Prussian ambassador in Frankfurt on 22 December 1862. He was not ready to go to war with Denmark merely to see

Augustenburg installed on the throne. His ultimate goal was annexation by Prussia of the Duchies.

I am certain of this, that the whole Danish business can be settled in a way desirable for us only by war. The occasion for such a war can be found at any moment that we find favourable for waging it. Until then, much more depends on the attitude of the non-German Great Powers towards the affair than on the intrigues of the Würzburg coalition governments and their influence on German sentiment. The disadvantage of having signed the London Protocol [sic], we share with Austria and cannot free ourselves from the consequences of that signature without war. If war comes, however, the future territorial status of Denmark will depend upon its results.

It cannot be foreseen what development of German Federal relations is destined for the future; as long, however, as they remain about the same as in the past, I cannot regard it as in the interest of Prussia to wage a war in order, as the most favourable result, to install in Schleswig-Holstein a new Grand Duke, who in fear of Prussian lust for annexation, will vote against us in the Diet and whose government, in spite of the gratitude due to Prussia for its installation, will be a ready object of Austrian machination . . .

Source: from *The Schleswig-Holstein Question*, Harvard Historical Studies, Harvard University Press (Steefel, L.D. 1932) p. 52, originally from *Die Gesammelten Werke*, IV, No. 17 (Bismarck).

Document 14   BISMARCK DEFENDS THE AUSTRIAN ALLIANCE, FEBRUARY 1865

By February 1865 relations between Austria and Prussia were rapidly deteriorating. The Austrians favoured Augustenburg's claims to the Duchies, while Bismarck would only agree to hand over Schleswig-Holstein to him provided that Prussia retained effective control of them. However he was not yet ready to break with Austria as the alliance might still be useful in extracting concessions. Bismarck argued in a despatch to von der Goltz, the Prussian Ambassador in Paris, that the Austrian alliance was worth preserving until circumstances changed.

I think it more useful to continue for a while the present marriage despite small domestic quarrels, and if a divorce becomes necessary, to take the prospects as they then prevail rather than to cut the bond now, with all the disadvantages of obvious perfidy, and without now having the certainty of finding better conditions in a new relationship later.

Source: F. Stern, *Gold and Iron: Bismarck, Bleichröder and the Building of the German Empire*, London: Allen & Unwin, 1977, p. 56.

FINANCING MOBILIZATION, JULY 1865   **Document 15**

Von Roon, the Prussian minister of war, informs Bismarck's old friend, Moritz von Blanckenburg, of the government's success in raising money in a letter dated 28 July 1865. Acting on Bleichröder's advice, the Prussian government had sold its legal rights to the purchase of the stock of the Cologne–Minden railway, which had raised sufficient capital.

We have money, enough to give us a free hand in foreign policy, enough, if need be, to mobilize the whole army and to pay for an entire campaign. This gives our stance *vis à vis* Austria the necessary aplomb so that we may hope that they will give in to our reasonable demands without war, which none of us wants . . .

Whence the money? Without violating a law, primarily through an arrangement with the Cologne–Minden Railway, which I and even Bodelschwing [Prussian finance minister] consider very advantageous.

Source: F. Stern, *Gold and Iron: Bismarck, Bleichröder and the Building of the German Empire,* London: Allen & Unwin, 1977, p. 63.

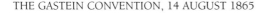

THE GASTEIN CONVENTION, 14 AUGUST 1865   **Document 16**

After prolonged tension over the situation in Schleswig-Holstein, the breach with Austria was 'papered over' by the Gastein treaty. Austria abandoned Augustenburg and agreed to the provisions for shared administration. Given Prussia's determination to seize complete control of the Duchies, this repre-sented a serious diplomatic defeat for Austria.

Article I The exercise of the Rights acquired in common by the High Contracting Parties, in virtue of Article III of the Vienna Treaty of Peace of 30th October, 1864, shall, without prejudice to the continuance of those rights of both Powers to the whole of both Duchies, pass to His Majesty the Emperor of Austria as regards the Duchy of Holstein, and to His Majesty the King of Prussia as regards the Duchy of Schleswig.

Article II The High Contracting Parties will propose to the Diet the estab-lishment of a German Fleet, and will fix upon the Harbour of Kiel as a Federal Harbour for the said Fleet. Until the resolutions of the Diet with respect to this proposal have been carried into effect, the Ships of War of both Powers shall use this Harbour, and the Command and the Police Duties within it shall be exercised by Prussia . . .

Article III The High Contracting Parties will propose in Frankfurt the eleva-tion of Rendsburg into a German Federal Fortress. Until the Diet shall have issued the regulations respecting Garrisoning the said Fortress, the Garrison shall consist of Imperial Austrian and Royal Prussian troops under a command annually alternating on the 1st July.

Article IV While the division agreed upon in Article I of the present Convention continues, the Royal Prussian Government shall retain two Military Roads through Holstein; the one from Lübeck to Kiel, the other from Hamburg to Rendsburg.

Article VI [Provision for the Duchies eventually to enter the *Zollverein*.]

Article IX His Majesty the Emperor of Austria cedes to His Majesty the King of Prussia the Rights acquired in the aforementioned Vienna Treaty of Peace with respect to the Duchy of Lauenburg; and in return the Royal Prussian Government binds itself to pay to the Austrian Government the sum of 2,500,000 Danish rixdolars, payable at Berlin in Prussian silver, 4 weeks after confirmation of the present Convention by their Majesties the Emperor of Austria and the King of Prussia.

Article X . . . The joint Command-in-Chief, hitherto existing, shall be dissolved on the complete Evacuation of Holstein by the Prussian troops and of Schleswig by the Austrian troops, by the 15th September, at the latest . . .

[L.S.] G. Blome

[L.S.] von Bismarck

Source: W.N. Medlicott and D.K. Coveney (eds), *Bismarck and Europe*, London: Edward Arnold, 1971, pp. 48–9.

Document 17   BISMARCK'S PEACE POLICY, JULY 1866

Bismarck describes in his memoirs the difficulties of convincing both the king and the generals at Nikolsburg of the advantages of a moderate peace with Austria. The Austrian army had not been destroyed at Königgratz and further fighting ran the risk of French intervention.

On 23 July, under the presidency of the King, a council of war was held, in which the question to be decided was whether we should make peace under the conditions offered or continue the war. A painful illness from which I was suffering made it necessary that the council should be held in my room. On this occasion I was the only civilian in uniform. I declared it to be my conviction that peace must be concluded on the Austrian terms, but remained alone in my opinion; the King supported the military majority. My nerves could not stand the strain which had been put upon them day and night; I got up in silence, walked into my adjoining bedchamber and was there overcome by a violent paroxysm of tears. Meanwhile, I heard the council dispersing in the next room. I thereupon set to work to commit to paper the reasons which in my opinion spoke for the conclusion of peace; and begged the King, in the event of his not accepting the advice for which I was responsible, to relieve me of my functions as minister if the war were continued. With this Document I set out on the following day to explain it by word of mouth . . .

We had to avoid wounding Austria too severely; we had to avoid leaving behind in her any unnecessary bitterness of feeling or desire for revenge; we ought rather to reserve the possibility of becoming friends again with our adversary of the moment, and in any case to regard the Austrian State as a piece on the European chessboard and the renewal of friendly relations with her as a move open to us. If Austria were severely injured, she would become the ally of France and of every other opponent of ours; she would even sacrifice her anti-Russian interests for the sake of revenge on Prussia.

Source: J.C. Röhl, (ed.) *From Bismarck to Hitler: The Problem of Continuity in German History*, London: Longman, 1970, pp. 20–1.

RUSSIAN AND BRITISH VIEWS ON PRUSSIA'S VICTORY, 1866

Document 18

a) *On 6 October 1866 Lord Loftus, the British Ambassador in Berlin, informed Lord Stanley, the foreign minister, of the opinion of his Russian colleague in Berlin, d'Oubril.*

The former sympathy for Prussia appears to have returned, no expression of disapproval of Prussian annexation is heard. 'Les faits accomplis' no longer find a murmur. The only Legation of a neutral state which illuminated (altho' very modestly) on the eve of the entry of the victorious Prussian Army [into Berlin] was that of Russia. In short, the attitude of M d'Oubril is no longer one of jealous disquietude but has become one of passive and calm satisfaction.

b) *Lord Stanley viewed the future with some pessimism in a private letter to Lord Cowley, 18 August 1866.*

I begin to suspect that the German revolution may go farther and faster than its authors intend. Bismarck wants a new German federation. Napoleon wanted an Italian federation. We know what came of that: may not the precedent be followed? In any case the southern states will not long endure exclusion: and then will be seen, whether France and Russia will tolerate a German empire. But, as I think you said in one of your letters, it is a question for '68 rather than for '66.

Source: W. Mosse, *The European Powers and the German Question, 1848–71*, Cambridge: Cambridge University Press, 1958, pp. 248–9.

Document 19   THE NATIONAL LIBERALS AND THE NORTH GERMAN CONFEDERATION

a) *This letter by the Hanoverian Rudolf von Bennigsen, who was one of the founders of the* Nationalverein, *to A. L. Rochau, 29 December 1866, reveals that the National Liberals had realistic expectations of the North German Confederation.*

According to reports from Berlin very many conservatives will be elected [to the Constituent *Reichstag*] from the eastern provinces of Prussia, on the Rhine and in Westphalia allegedly a somewhat large number of ultramontanes. The physiognomy of the parliament will be extraordinarily different from that of 1848, and will play in terms of the standards of that time, a very modest role. If there is success, for which I do not despair, in organizing all north and central Germany with the help of parliament militarily and economically, and in these areas some emergency bridges are built to south Germany, a very firm basis for further development will have been achieved. The nation cannot ask for more at this time . . .

Source: G.G. Windell, 'Bismarckian Empire; Chronicle of Failure', *Central European History* 2(4), 1969, p. 295.

b) *Bennigsen's colleague, Johannes von Miquel, was equally realistic in his electoral campaign address at Osnabrück, 1867.*

The time of ideals is past. German unity has descended from the world of dreams into the prosaic world of reality. Politicians must ask today, not as before, what is desirable, but what is achievable.

Source: G.G. Windell, 'Bismarckian Empire; Chronicle of Failure', *Central European History* 2(4), 1969, p. 295.

Document 20   BISMARCK ON WAR, MARCH 1867

The background to Bismarck's letter to Count Bethusy-Huc, a Conservative deputy in the Landtag, *was the Luxemburg crisis. On 19 March King William of Holland had agreed to sell Luxemburg to France, but Bismarck then intervened and made clear that the North German Confederation Reichstag was hostile. On 3 April he warned the Dutch King that war would result if the sale went through.*

Unhappily I believe in a war with France before long – her vanity, hurt by our victories, will drive her in that direction. Yet, since I do not know of any French or German interest requiring a resort to arms, I do not see it as certain. Only a country's most vital interests justify embarking on war – only its honour, which is not to be confused with so-called prestige. No statesman has a right to begin a war simply because, in his opinion, it is inevitable in a given period of time. If foreign ministers had followed their rulers and military commanders into the field, History would record fewer wars. On the battlefield – and, what is far worse, in the hospitals – I have seen the flower of our youth struck down by wounds and disease. From the window I can see many a cripple hobbling along the Wilhelmstrasse, looking up and thinking to himself if that man up there had not made that wicked war I would be at home strong and well. Such memories and sights would leave me without a moment's peace if I thought I had made the war from personal ambition or national vanity. . . . You may rest assured that I shall never advise His Majesty to wage war unless the most vital interests of the Fatherland require it.

Source: from BISMARCK by Alan Palmer used by permission of Campbell Thomson & McLaughlin Ltd on behalf of the author.

BISMARCK AND GERMAN UNITY IN 1869

Document 21

By early 1869 it seemed as if the momentum towards German unity had ground to a halt. Bismarck was now being accused of inactivity by his southern supporters. However in this much quoted dispatch to the Prussian envoy in Munich in February 1869 he counselled patience until the circumstances favoured more decisive action.

That German unity could be promoted by actions involving force I think is self-evident. But there is a quite different question, and that has to do with the precipitation of a powerful catastrophe and the responsibility of choosing the time for it. A voluntary intervention in the evolution of history, which is determined by purely subjective factors, results only in the shaking down of unripe fruit, and that German unity is no ripe fruit at this time leaps, in my opinion, to the eye. If the time that lies ahead works in the interest of unity as much as the period since the accession of Frederick the Great has done, and particularly the period since 1840, the year in which a national movement was perceptible for the first time since the war of liberation, then we can look to the future calmly and leave the rest to our successors. Behind the wordy restlessness with which people who do not know the trade search after the talisman that will supposedly produce German unity in a trice, there is generally hidden a superficial and, in any case, impotent lack of knowledge of real things and their consequences.

Source: G. Craig, *Germany 1866–1945*, Oxford: Oxford University Press, 1978, p. 20.

Document 22   THE EMS TELEGRAM

a) *Heinrich Abeken, a Prussian foreign office official, sent the following dis-patch to Bismarck on 13 July 1870 at 3.40 p.m.*

His Majesty writes to me: 'Count Benedetti spoke to me on the promenade, in order to demand from me, finally in a very importunate manner, that I should authorize him to telegraph at once that I bound myself for all future time never again to give my consent if the Hohenzollerns should renew their candidature. I refused at last somewhat sternly, as it is neither right nor possible to undertake engagements of this kind *à tout jamais*. I told him that I had as yet received no news, and as he was earlier informed from Paris and Madrid than myself, he could see clearly that my government had no more interest in the matter.' His Majesty has since received a letter from Prince Charles Anthony. His Majesty, having told Count Benedetti that he was await-ing news from the Prince, has decided, with reference to the above demand, on the suggestion of Count Eulenberg and myself, not to receive Count Benedetti again, but only to let him be informed through an *aide-de-camp*: 'That his Majesty has now received from the Prince confirmation of the news which Benedetti had already received from Paris, and had nothing further to say to the ambassador'. His Majesty leaves it to your Excellency to decide whether Benedetti's fresh demand and its rejection should be at once com-municated to both our ambassadors, to foreign nations, and to the Press.

b) *Bismarck edited it for publication as follows:*

After the news of the renunciation of the hereditary Prince of Hohenzollern had been officially communicated to the Imperial government of France by the Royal government of Spain, the French Ambassador further demanded of his Majesty, the King, at Ems, that he would authorize him to telegraph to Paris that his Majesty, the King, bound himself for all time never again to give his consent, should the Hohenzollerns renew their candidature. His Majesty, the King, thereupon decided not to receive the French Ambassador again, and sent the *aide-de-camp* on duty to tell him that his Majesty had nothing further to communicate to the ambassador.

Source: C. Grant Robertson, *Bismarck*, London: Constable, 1918, pp. 496–7.

Document 23   FRENCH PARTISANS, DECEMBER 1870

General Moltke describes the threat posed by French partisans and the tactics taken to counter them in a letter to his brother 12 December 1870. The dan-ger was that these tactics would prolong the war in France and increase the danger of foreign intervention.

The newly formed French armies have now all been gradually defeated on the open battlefield, but we are unable to be everywhere; minor ambushes cannot be prevented and are punished by pitiless severity. A handful of loafers singing the Marseillaise with guns and flags break into houses, shoot out of the windows and then run away out of the back doors, and then the town has to suffer for it. How lucky are those places which have a permanent enemy garrison in occupation . . .

Source: W. Andreas (ed.), Moltkes Briefe, Vol. 2, Leipzig: Bibliographisches Institut, 1922, p. 409 (translated by the author).

———————◆———————

MILITARY IMPATIENCE WITH BISMARCK, DECEMBER 1870 **Document 24**

Paul Bronsart von Schellendorff, chief of operations on the General Staff of the Prussian army, 1870–71, and war minister, 1883–89, records in his diary the army's irritation with Bismarck's determination to start negotiations with the French as soon as possible. Moltke, on the other hand wanted to occupy the whole of France and starve the Parisians into submission. As in 1866 Bismarck's insistence was on the priority of a political settlement to avoid the risk of foreign intervention.

7 December 1870
Count Bismarck is really beginning to be fit for a lunatic asylum. He has complained bitterly to the King that General Moltke has written to General Trochu and maintains that, being a negotiation with a foreign government, this should fall into his own sphere of competence. But General Moltke, as a spokesman of the High Command, has written to the Governor of Paris; the matter is therefore a purely military one. Since Count Bismarck asserts further that he had stated to me that he regarded the letter as dubious, whereas the contrary is the case, I have immediately reported to General Moltke that the chancellor's statement is not true and have asked to be relieved in future of oral missions to him. The King, to whom General Moltke spoke about this matter, of course finds the whole thing very disagreeable, and the war minister said, very naively, that we ought not to pursue the matter too far, since in view of the diametrically opposed statements of my report and of Count Bismarck the only conclusion would be that one of us had been lying. General Moltke can hardly be in any doubt which one of us this was.

It is lamentable how inefficient our ministry of war is . . . General Roon is lazy . . . I have . . . shown that we must and can do more . . .

Source: W.M. Simon (ed.), Germany in the Age of Bismarck, London: Allen & Unwin, 1968, p. 148.

———————◆———————

Document 25   ALSACE-LORRAINE

In 1891 Rémy de Gourmont dared criticize the French government's refusal to accept the loss of Alsace-Lorraine. His opinion was highly controversial, and as a result he was dismissed from his job at the Bibliothèque Nationale. The annexation of Alsace-Lorraine was to poison relations between France and Germany until 1919. The historian Volker Ulrich described the decision to annex the provinces as 'a severe mistake, perhaps the severest in Bismarck's career overall' (Lerman, 2004: 153).

Have they, in truth, become so unhappy, these corners of territory beyond the Vosges? Has one by chance made them change their language, their customs, their pleasures? . . . It seems to me that this has lasted long enough: this ridiculous image of the two little enslaved sisters, dressed in mourning and sunk to their knees before the frontier-post, weeping like heifers instead of tending their own cows. You may be sure that now, as before, they are gobbling their roasts with currant jelly, nibbling their salt pretzels, and guzzling their mugs of lager beer. Have no illusions: they are also making love and creating children. This new Babylonian captivity leaves me entirely cold.

Source: from KENNAN, GEORGE F.; *THE DECLINE OF BISMARCK'S EUROPEAN ORDER* © 1979 Princeton University Press, reprinted by permission of Princeton University Press.

Document 26   BISMARCK'S POWER

The wife of the British ambassador in Berlin, Lady Emily Russell, describes in 1880 Bismarck's domination of the Emperor and the Government. Much of what she says is perceptive. The letter was written at the height of Bismarck's power just after 'the new foundation of the Reich'. However, Bismarck's power was not as omnipotent as it appeared. The subsequent decade was to show that he effectively lost control of the Reichstag. Except for the years 1887–89, and ultimately, as his dismissal by William II indicated in 1890, his power was dependent on the good will of the monarchy.

The *initiated* know that the emperor . . . has allowed Prince Bismarck to have his own way in *everything*; and the great chancellor revels in the absolute power he has acquired and does as he pleases. He lives in the country and governs the German Empire without even taking the trouble to consult the emperor about his plans, who only learns what is being done from the Documents to which his signature is necessary, and which His Majesty signs without questions or hesitation. Never has a subject been granted so much irresponsible power from his sovereign, and never has a minister inspired a nation with more abject individual, as well as general, terror before. No wonder, then, that the crown prince should be worried at a state of things which he has not more personal power or influence to remedy than anyone else in Prussia, whilst Prince Bismarck lives and terrorizes over Germany from Friedrichsruh with the emperor's tacit and cheerful consent.

Bismarck has gradually appointed a ministry of clerks out of the government offices, who do as they are told by him, and he has so terrified the *Bundesrat*, by threatening to resign whenever they disagreed with him, that they now vote entirely in obedience to his instructions. He now expects that at the next general election he will, by careful management, obtain the absolute majority he requires to carry through his new taxation and commercial policy.

If Bismarck should ever die suddenly from indigestion, which his doctors fear and predict, the difficulty of reforming the general abuses which his personal administration has created will be great, and will impose a hard and ungrateful task on the sovereign, who will have to find and appoint the ministers capable of re-establishing constitutionalism in Prussia.

Source: G.E. Buckle (ed.), *The Letters of Queen Victoria*, Second Series, Vol. 3, London: Longman, 1926–30, pp. 169–70.

SPECULATION MANIA, 1871–1873 **Document 27**

The Berlin journalist and playwright, Felix Philippi, describes in his memoirs the frenzy of speculation on the Berlin Stock Exchange during the great bull market of 1871–73, which was fuelled by the French indemnity, the currency reform of 1871 and the availability of easy credit.

Everyone, everyone flew into the flame: the shrewd capitalist and the inexperienced petty bourgeois, the general and the waiter, the woman of the world, the poor piano teacher and the market woman; people speculated in porter's lodges and theatre cloakrooms, in the studio of the artist and the quiet home of the scholar; the *Droschke* [cab] driver on his bench and Aujuste [a girl's name] in the kitchen followed the rapid rise of the market with expertise and feverish interest. The market had bullish orgies; millions, coined right out of the ground, were won; national prosperity rose to apparently unimagined heights. A shower of gold rained down on the drunken city.

Source: G.A. Craig, *Germany, 1866–1945*, Oxford: Oxford University Press, 1978, p. 81.

Document 28   THE INDUSTRIALIZATION OF GERMANY

a) *Changes from rural to urban population*

	Total population	Percentage of population rural	Percentage of population urban*
1871	41,059,000	63.9	36.1
1880	45,234,000	58.6	41.4
1890	49,428,000	57.5	42.5
1900	56,367,000	45.6	54.4
1910	64,926,000	40.0	60.0

* Urban = population in a settlement of 2,000 or more.

b) *Occupational distribution (in per cent)*

	1843	1882	1907
Agriculture and forestry	60.84–61.34	42.3	34.0
Industry and crafts	23.37	35.5	39.7
Commerce and communications	1.95	8.4	13.7
Public and private services	4.5–5.0	5.8	6.8
Domestic service	–	8.0	5.8

c) *Population growth of the eight largest German cities*

City	1820	1870	1900	1910
Berlin	199,510	774,498	1,888,313	2,071,907
Breslau	78,930	207,997	428,517	517,367
Cologne	54,937	200,312	464,272	600,304
Essen	4,715	99,887	290,208	410,392
Frankfurt a.M.	41,458	126,095	314,026	414,576
Hamburg	127,985	308,446	721,744	953,103
Leipzig	37,375	177,818	519,726	644,644
Munich	62,290	440,886	659,392	665,266

Source: K. Pinson, *Modern Germany: Its History and Civilization*, New York: Macmillan, 1954, pp. 221–2.

Document 29   THE FLIGHT FROM THE LAND

A British Royal Commission reporting on, for comparative purposes, labour conditions in Central Europe in 1893 found that the standard of living for

German workers had greatly improved over the last decade. In the rural east, however, the flight from the land to the industrial centres in the west continued. This report shows that what Bismarck referred to as 'the Polish danger' was still very much a reality as it was feared that the inflow of Slavs, or rather Poles, would be a consequence of the exodus of the German population.

The general consensus of opinion in the country as a whole indicates a very great change for the better in the economic condition of the labourer during the last ten or twenty years. He is better fed and better clothed, better educated and better able to procure the means of recreation; nevertheless the migration statistics . . . indicate a continuous movement of the population from the agricultural east to the industrial west. Except in a few southern districts, such as Bavaria, where peculiar conditions prevail, the agrarian question proper, interpreted in Germany to mean the difficulty of procuring a sufficient supply of labour, scarcely exists in the west. With regard to the east, on the contrary, Dr Weber points out . . . that unless some means can be adopted for checking the outflow of the German population, there is every reason to fear that their places will be supplied by an inroad of Slavs, and that thus an element of disintegration already existing will be increased. . . . The inquiry instituted . . . by the Economic Club (*Verein für Sozialpolitik*) has brought out clearly the predominant influence of the social over the economic factors in agrarian discontent. The gulf which separates the employer from the employed in the east, and the lack of opportunity for acquiring land are, in the opinion of the members of the Economic Club reporting on the subject, mainly responsible for its depopulation. Up to the present time it has appeared almost impossible to supply the remedy, though the great landowners are sufficiently ready to divide much of their land into small holdings, if this or any other measure would secure them a permanent supply of suitable labour.

Source: T.S. Hamerow, *The Age of Bismarck, Documents and Interpretations,* New York: Harper Row, 1973, pp. 186–7.

———————◄●►———————

GRAIN PRICES

Document 30

Between 1875 and 1879 there was a series of bad harvests. German farmers were alarmed by the failure of prices for wheat and rye to rise dramatically to compensate them for poor harvests and to pay the interest on their heavy debts. They were also facing stiff competition from Russian imports. Hence their demand for protective tariffs.

The prices of wheat and rye (marks per ton) in Berlin, 1871–79

Year	Wheat	Rye
1871	216	159
1872	238	163
1873	251	175
1874	233	170
1875	193	151
1876	206	154
1877	227	153
1878	194	132
1879	198	133

Source: I.N. Lambi, *Free Trade and Protection in Germany, 1868–1879*, Stuttgart: Steiner, 1963, p. 133.

Document 31   THE FOUNDATION OF THE ASSOCIATION FOR THE REFORM OF TAXATION AND ECONOMY

As a result of the agrarian crisis, the Association for the Reform of Taxation and the Economy was formed. One of the aims of the organization was to consolidate the position of the Conservatives and the landed interest. This is emphasized by the following declaration which the constituent assembly of the Association accepted in February 1876.

In the field of economic and personal relations the absolute domination of Liberalism is to be broken and such institutions are to be formed which would be inspired by the conservative spirit and offer solid support to the Conservative Party.

The number of the followers of conservative principles is at present small. If we want to win over to conservatism wider circles, we must go along with the times. Indeed, we cannot betray our principles, but must at the same time follow the trends which move the people. We live in an era of material interests.

Source: I.N. Lambi, *Free Trade and Protection in Germany, 1868–1879*, Stuttgart: Steiner, 1963, p. 138.

GRASSROOTS SUPPORT FOR PROTECTION   **Document 32**

In February 1877 a small steering committee of Westphalian industrialists and agrarians met and drew up the following declaration which was then approved by an assembly of 400 representatives of Rhenish-Westphalian agriculture and industry on 10 March.

I   In view of the impending renewal of commercial treaties and tariffs, the depression which has lasted for many years necessitates that agriculture and industry proceed in the future with the same solidarity which exists in reality without prejudicing individual political ties.

II   For the promotion of general economic interests it is necessary:
   a)   to preserve and to develop home production as the first condition of general welfare;
   b)   the main factors for the attainment of this aim are low freight rates, well considered commercial treaties and tariffs, and a rational system of taxation, all based on actual conditions;
   c)   the discovery of the actual needs is to be reached through the questioning and consultation of experts;
   d)   the reform of the land and building tax and the mining tax which are to be covered through indirect taxation;
   e)   excepting the removal of direct and indirect export premiums enjoyed by foreign agricultural products, but which we spurn, German agriculture wants no further favours.

Source: I.N. Lambi, *Free Trade and Protection in Germany, 1868–1879*, Stuttgart: Steiner, 1963, pp. 135–6.

————————◄●►————————

CONDITIONS OF THE URBAN WORKING CLASS IN GERMANY, 1893   **Document 33**

The British Royal Commission of 1893, which looked for comparative purposes at the situation in Germany, provides accessible and invaluable data on the condition of the working classes in Germany and on the housing situation in the large cities. The continued migration of the rural population into the cities ensured housing shortages and high rents.

The Weaver's Budget given by Dr. von Schulze-Gaevernitz is as follows:

Weekly Budget of North German Weaver with Wife and four Children

Income	M	Expenditure	M
Wages of father	15	42 lbs rye bread (second quality)	5.60
Amount paid by children for board and lodging	7	30 **pints** [sic] potatoes	1.80
Total	22	2 lbs rolls	2.00
		2 lbs meal (second quality)	0.40
		¾ lbs meat (Sunday)	0.45
		½ suet	
		vegetables	3.40
		coffee	0.20
		2½ lbs butter	3.40
		6 pints skimmed milk	0.60
		rent	3.20
		sick and old age insurance	0.65
		school money	0.15
		Total	**21.85**

Pints Pre-metric measurement primarily for liquids, but was also used for dry substances such as potatoes.

[1 pint = 570 ml]
[1lb = 0.4536 kg]

In Berlin the conditions are specially bad, and the average number of persons inhabiting one tenement (*Grundstück*) has risen from 60.7 in 1880 to 66.0 in 1885. Subletting was shown by the census of 1880 to be exceedingly frequent, 7.1 per cent of the population took in persons who boarded and lodged with them, and 15.3 per cent took in persons to sleep (*Schlafleute*). One instance is given of a household taking 34 such night lodgers, in another case there were eleven, including two women. Thirty-eight per cent of the families taking night lodgers lived in a single room; one instance is mentioned in which a man and his wife with a family shared their one room with seven men and one woman. Though the worst kind of night shelters, known as 'Pennen', have now been suppressed by the police, it is still 'the opinion of experienced observers . . . that the evils existing in the large towns of England are less crying than in Germany . . .'

Source: T.S. Hamerow, *The Age of Bismarck, Documents and Interpretations*, New York: Harper Row, 1973, pp. 180–2.

REICHSTAG ELECTIONS, 1871–1890 **Document 34**

	1871		1874		1877	
	Votes	*Deputies*	*Votes*	*Deputies*	*Votes*	*Deputies*
Eligible voters	7,975,750		8,523,446		8,943,028	
Valid votes cast	4,134,299	397	5,259,155	397	5,535,785	397
PARTY						
Conservatives	548,877	57	359,959	22	526,039	40
Reichspartei[†]	627,229	67	431,376	36	426,637	38
National Liberals	1,171,807	125	1,542,501	155	1,469,527	128
Progressives	361,150	47	469,277	50	597,529	52
Center (Zentrum)	724,179	63	1,445,948	91	1,341,295	93
Poles	176,072	13	199,273	14	219,159	14
Social Democrats**	123,975	2	351,952	9	493,288	12
Guelphs	60,858	7	92,080	4	96,335	4
Danes	18,221	1	19,856	1	17,277	1
Alsace-Lorraine	234,545	15	234,545	15	199,976	15
Antisemites	–	–	–	–	–	
Other parties	66,670	–	36,636	–	14,153	

[†]Until 1871 the Free Conservatives. **After 1875 the German Social Democratic Party (SPD).

	1878		1881	
	Votes	*Deputies*	*Votes*	*Deputies*
Eligible voters	9,124,311	–	9,088,792	–
Valid votes cast	5,811,159	397	5,301,242	397
PARTY				
Conservatives	749,494	59	830,807	50
Reichspartei	785,855	57	379,347	28
National Liberals	1,330,643	99	746,575	47
Progressives	607,339	39	1,181,865	115[†]
Center (Zentrum)	1,328,073	94	1,182,873	100
Poles	210,062	14	194,894	18
Social Democrats	437,158	9	311,961	12
Guelphs	102,574	10	86,704	10
Danes	16,145	1	14,398	2
Alsace-Lorraine	178,883	15	152,991	15
Anti-Semites	–	–	–	–
Other parties	14,721	–	13,010	–

[†]Includes 46 Seats of the Liberal Union and 9 of the *Volkspartei*.

	1884		1887		1890	
	Votes	Deputies	Votes	Deputies	Votes	Deputies
Eligible voters	9,383,074	–	9,769,802	–	10,145,877	–
Valid votes cast	5,811,973	397	7,527,601	397	7,298,010	397
PARTY						
Conservatives	861,063	78	1,147,200	80	895,103	73
Reichspartei	387,687	28	736,389	41	482,314	20
National Liberals	997,033	51	1,677,979	99	1,177,807	42
Progressives[†]	1,092,895	74	1,061,922	32	1,307,485	76
Center (Zentrum)	1,282,006	99	1,516,222	98	1,342,113	106
Poles	206,346	16	221,825	13	246,800	16
Social Democrats	549,990	24	763,128	11	1,427,298	35
Guelphs	96,400	11	112,800	4	112,100	11
Danes	14,400	1	12,360	1	13,700	1
Alsace-Lorraine	165,600	15	233,685	15	101,156	10
Anti-Semites	–	–	11,496	1	47,500	5
Other parties	12,700	–	47,600	2	74,600	2

[†]Between 1884 and 1893 the *Freisinnige Partei.*

Source: K. Pinson, *Modern Germany: Its History and Civilization*, New York: Macmillan, 1954, pp. 572–3.

Document 35 ANNUAL EARNINGS OF WORKERS IN INDUSTRIES, COMMERCE AND TRANSPORT, 1871–1913

Year	Average annual income (in Marks) before deductions (tax etc.)	Cost of living index (1895 = 100)	Average annual income (in Marks) after deductions
1871	493	105.8	466
1875	651	112.7	578
1880	545	104.0	524
1885	581	98.6	589
1890	650	102.2	636
1895	665	100.0	665
1900	784	106.4	737
1905	849	112.4	755
1910	979	124.2	789
1913	1083	129.8	834

Source: M. Stürmer, *Das Ruhelose Reich: Deutschland, 1866–1918*, Berlin: Severin & Siedler, 1983, p. 41.

BISMARCK ATTACKS THE CATHOLIC CLERGY   **Document 36**

Bismarck regularly accused the Catholic clergy of being unpatriotic and hostile to the new Germany. During the debate on the School Supervision bill in the Prussian Landtag on 10 February 1872 he made the following attack on the Catholic clergy and Church in Germany.

The government cannot avoid the remarkable observation that the Roman Catholic clergy is national in all other lands. Only Germany makes an exception. The Polish clergy adhere to the Polish national movement, the Italian to the Italian . . . Only in Germany is there the peculiar phenomenon that the *clergy* has a more *international* character . . . The Catholic Church, even when she obstructs the development of Germany for the sake of foreign nations, is closer to its heart than the development of the German Empire . . . (Windthorst: 'Proof!') I cannot find an insult in that. (Call from the *Zentrum* and Right: 'Proof!') *Ach*, gentlemen, search your own hearts. (Long, lasting laughter.)

Source: M.L. Anderson, *Windthorst: A Political Biography*, Oxford: Oxford University Press, 1981, p. 159.

BISMARCK'S GUIDING PRINCIPLE IN DOMESTIC POLICY   **Document 37**

One of Bismarck's recent biographers has written that 'one of Bismarck's great strengths was that he could live with political ambiguity and the solutions he devised were never fixed or immutable' (Lerman, 2004: 267). In essence this speech to the Reichstag in 1881 bears testimony to this.

I have often acted hastily and without reflection, but when I had time to think I have always asked: what is useful, effective, right, for my fatherland, for my dynasty – so long as I was merely in Prussia – and now for the German nation? I have never been a doctrinaire . . . Liberal, reactionary, conservative – those I confess seem to me luxuries . . . Give me a strong German state, and then ask me whether it should have more or less liberal furnishings, and you'll find that I answer: Yes, I've no fixed opinions, make proposals, and you won't meet any objections of principle from me. Many roads lead to Rome. Sometimes one must rule liberally, and sometimes dictatorially, there are no eternal rules . . . My aim from the first moment of my public activity has been the creation and consolidation of Germany, and if you can show a single moment when I deviated from that magnetic needle, you may perhaps prove that I went wrong, but never that I lost sight of the national aim for a moment.

Source: A.J.P. Taylor, *Bismarck: The Man and the Statesman*, London: Arrow Books, 1961, p. 138.

Document 38   A LIBERAL ACADEMIC ASSESSES BISMARCK

Rudlof Haym (1821–1901) was a journalist, academic and writer. He had been elected to the Frankfurt Parliament in 1848. In the following 'Notes for a political speech' circa February 1881, Hyam draws up a Bismarck balance sheet and attempts to explain his paradoxical genius.

Prince Bismarck represents for me the incarnation of the national state. I do not always like his methods. Sometimes – I have in mind particularly universal and equal suffrage – he has gone too far in the direction of liberalism for my taste, at other times he has regrettable tendencies and sympathies towards conservatism, at yet other times he encourages interest-group politics which appeals to egoism and therefore slights the nobler motives in political life and must have a confusing and even corrupting effect. But in the face of all this I remind myself that nobody else has such a lively regard for the idea of making the young empire vital, permanent, and resilient, and that he is untiringly and successfully at work to realize this idea with sensible realism according to circumstances. All his twists and turns and inconsistencies can be explained by the power of this idea. Seen in this light, all the tortuous and often contradictory methods that he employs *vis-à-vis* the domestic factions, even his reckless experiments, become intelligible . . .

Source: W. Simon, *Germany in the Age of Bismarck,* London: Allen & Unwin, 1968, pp. 221–2.

Document 39   EXTRACTS FROM THE ANTI-SOCIALIST LAW, 1878

The Anti-Socialist Law of 1878 was perhaps the most important repressive law of Bismarck's chancellorship. After two attempts had been made on the life of Kaiser Wilhelm I in 1878, Bismarck seized the chance to call an election. The newly elected Reichstag passed the Anti-Socialist Law which banned all Social Democratic associations, meetings, and newspapers. Between 1878 and the law's lapse on 30 September 1890, about 1,500 people were sentenced to what totalled more than 800 years' imprisonment.

1 Societies which aim at the overthrow of the existing political or social order through social democratic, socialistic, or communistic endeavours are to be prohibited.

This applies also to societies in which social democratic, socialistic, or communistic endeavours aiming at the overthrow of the existing political or social order are manifested in a manner dangerous to the public peace, and particularly to the harmony among the classes of the population.

Associations of every kind are the same as societies . . .

4 The police are empowered:

1 To attend all sessions and meetings of the society.
2 To call and conduct membership assemblies.
3 To inspect the books, papers and cash assets, as well as to demand information about the affairs of the society.
4 To forbid the carrying out of resolutions which are apt to further the endeavours described in 1, par. 2.
5 To transfer to qualified persons the duties of the officers or other leading organs of the society.
6 To take charge of and manage the funds . . .

Whoever, knowingly or after public notice is given, acts in contravention of these regulations, or of the decisions based thereon, is to be punished by fine not exceeding one thousand marks, or with arrest or imprisonment not exceeding six months.

Source: LIDTKE, VERNON L.; *THE OUTLAWED PARTY* © 1966 Princeton University Press, 1994 renewed PUP reprinted by permission of Princeton University Press.

GERMAN GRAIN TARIFFS   **Document 40**

Tariffs discriminated against Russian imports and did much to harm Russo-German relations. They also drove up the cost of living for the German workers. They were levied as follows (marks per ton):

Product	1879	1885	1887
Wheat	10	30	50
Rye	10	30	50
Barley	5	15	25
Oats	10	15	40
Flour	20	75	105

Source: I.N. Lambi, *Free Trade and Protection in Germany, 1868–1879*, Stuttgart: Steiner, 1963, p. 230.

Document 41   RUMOURS OF A COUP

In early 1886 Bismarck was faced with a Reichstag *which blocked every attempt he made to put the* Reich's *finances on a firmer footing. He told the Prussian ministers that he was ready to 'violate the constitution if necessary'. Professor Mosler, who was on the left wing of the* Zentrum, *wrote in February 1886 'in strictest confidence to a friend' warning him of what might happen. However in the event Bismarck exploited the Bulgarian crisis and Boulanger's popularity in France to call an election in 1887 which was to give him a more cooperative* Reichstag.

Staatsstreich
A *coup d'état.*

Evil things are in the works. The recent threats of a ***Staatsstreich*** are meant seriously. If Bismarck does not get his Socialist Law and the whisky monopoly, he wants to dissolve the *Reichstag* and impose a new imperial constitution, whereby the *Reichstag* would result from the elections of the individual *Landtage*. With that, of course, he would be rid of the *Zentrum* and the *Freisinn* completely and in one blow. This person is, as you know, capable of anything – so I do not consider even this plan impossible.

Source: M.L. Anderson, *Windthorst: A Political Biography*, Oxford: Oxford University Press, 1981, p. 335.

Document 42   THE CONSERVATIVE BIAS OF THE PRUSSIAN CIVIL SERVICE IN THE 1880s

Albert von Puttkammer, the son of Robert von Puttkammer, the Prussian Minister of the Interior, who purged the Prussian administration of liberal civil servants in the early 1880s, paints what the historian Eckart Kehr describes as 'a pretty picture of this neofeudal bureaucracy'.

The nobility formed the nucleus of the Conservative party, and in keeping with its tradition, insisted on a considerable measure of loyalty to the king. The whole younger generation of public servants was impregnated with these views. Bourgeois elements vied with their aristocratic colleagues in openly displaying their convictions. Anyone familiar with personnel conditions in Prussian government offices must know that liberal political views had almost no exponents among government officials. The younger generation was conservative in its political views.

Source: E. Kehr, *Economic Interest, Militarism and Foreign Policy*, trans. and ed. G. Craig, Berkeley, CA: University of California Press, 1977, p. 119.

DISAGREEMENT BETWEEN WILLIAM II AND BISMARCK, JANUARY 1890   **Document 43**

Bismarck and William disagreed on the importance of the deportation clause in the new Anti-Socialist bill which was being debated by the Reichstag. *This clause provided for the regional banishment of Socialist agitators, but was unlikely to be passed by the* Reichstag. *It was this disagreement which was to lead to Bismarck's dismissal in March 1990.*

His Majesty was pleased to accede to the proposal of the secretary of state for the interior . . . that the *Reichstag* should be dissolved after tomorrow's debate on the third reading of the Socialist Law and to declare his intention of performing the dissolution himself. With respect to the decision of the *Reichstag* on this bill His Majesty was pleased to remark that the power of deportation was scarcely of so far-reaching an importance as to jeopardize the passage of the bill in case of its rejection. It was undesirable to close this *Reichstag*, which had performed much useful work, in disharmony, which might, moreover, have an unfavourable effect on the elections and on the maintenance of the *Kartell*. Perhaps it was possible to postpone a consideration of this question for the future.

The ministers having been asked for their individual views, the prime minister declared to begin with that it was scarcely possible any longer to secure the agreement of the federated governments to forgoing a part of the bill laid before the *Reichstag* and that moreover he would emphatically advise against taking any such step which would be the first step down the road of concessions. Such a step would be calculated to damage the prestige of the governments and to weaken their position. The Socialist Law contained the minimum that the governments required in the way of the use of force. Probably more would have to be asked for later. This possibility was precluded if it was now conceded that one could do with less. Even in the expected new strikes in the coal districts the power of deporting the agitators out of this area would be very useful. According to his political experience he assumed that it would have an undesirable effect on the elections if the law was defective owing to faults *committed by the governments*. The maintenance of the *Kartell* would not be endangered if the law was rejected.

Source: W. Simon (ed.), *Germany in the Age of Bismarck*, London: Allen & Unwin, 1968, p. 226.

BISMARCK DECLARES GERMANY A SATIATED POWER   **Document 44**

After the defeat of France, Bismarck was anxious to reassure Britain and the other European powers that Germany was a 'satiated' power. Bismarck's conversation in 1871 with the British Ambassador in Berlin was reported to London as follows:

He [Bismarck] neither desired colonies nor fleets for Germany. Colonies in his opinion would only be a cause of weakness, because colonies could only be defended by powerful fleets, and Germany's geographical position did not necessitate her development into a first-class maritime power. A fleet was sufficient for Germany that could cope with fleets like those of Austria, Egypt, Holland, and perhaps Italy, scarcely with that of Russia, but it could not be a German interest so long as she had no colonies to rivalize with maritime powers like England, America, or France. Many colonies had been offered to him, he had rejected them and wished only for coaling stations acquired by treaty from other nations.

Germany was now large enough and strong enough in his opinion, and even the Emperor William's insatiable desire for more territory had not led him to covet the possession of the Netherlands.

He had had trouble & vexation enough to combat the Emperor's desire to annex the German provinces of Austria, the population of which certainly desired to form part of the great German family, but that desire he would oppose so long as he was in power, because he preferred the alliance and friendship of Austria to the annexation of provinces that would add nothing to the strength and security of Germany and the loss of which would lessen the value of Austria as an ally.

The Swiss, for instance, were a German-speaking nation, but Switzerland was of greater value as an independent friendly neighbour to Germany than as a province of the German Empire.

Source: T.S. Hamerow (ed.), *The Age of Bismarck, Documents and Interpretations*, New York: Harper Row, 1973, pp. 142–3.

Document 45 BISMARCK DEFENDS THE DUAL ALLIANCE

In August 1879 Tsar Alexander wrote the so called 'Box on the ears letter' to William in which he warned him of the negative impact on Russo-German relations of Bismarck's pro-Austrian policy in the aftermath of the Berlin Congress. Only by threatening to resign did Bismarck manage to persuade William to agree to the Dual Alliance with Austria. Bismarck defended his actions later in his memoirs.

I was compelled by the threatening letter of the Czar Alexander to take decisive measures for the defence and preservation of our independence of Russia. An alliance with Russia was popular with nearly all parties, with the

Conservatives from an historical tradition, the entire consonance of which with the point of view of a modern Conservative group is perhaps doubtful. The fact, however, is that the majority of Prussian Conservatives regard alliance with Austria as congruous with their tendencies, and did so none the less when there existed a sort of temporary rivalry in Liberalism between the two governments. The Conservative halo of the Austrian name outweighed with most of the members of this group the advances, partly out of date, partly recent, made in the region of Liberalism, and the occasional leaning to *rapprochements* with the Western Powers, and especially with France. The considerations of expediency which commended to Catholics an alliance with the preponderant Catholic Great Power came nearer home. In a league having the form and force of a treaty between the new German Empire and Austria, the National-Liberal party discerned a way of approximating to the quadrature of the political circle of 1848, by evading the difficulties which stood in the way of the complete unification, not only of Austria and Prussia-Germany, but also of the several constituents of the Austro-Hungarian Empire. Thus, outside of the social democratic party, whose approval was not to be had for any policy whatever which the government might adopt, there was in parliamentary quarters no opposition to the alliance with Austria, and much partiality for it.

Source: Bismarck, *Reflections and Reminiscences*, Vol. 2, London: Smith, Elder, 1898, pp. 255–7.

SEPARATE PROTOCOL TO THE THREE EMPERORS' ALLIANCE, 18 JUNE 1881   **Document 46**

The Three Emperors' Alliance marked the defeat of the Pan Slavs and the revival of the Three Emperors' League. Through it Bismarck managed to postpone making a choice between Austria and Russia, but its short duration of three years suggested that it was in reality more a 'truce'.

1   Bosnia and Herzegovina.
    Austria-Hungary reserves the right to annex these provinces at whatever moment she shall judge opportune.
2   Bulgaria.
    The three Powers will not oppose the eventual reunion of Bulgaria and Eastern Rumelia within the territorial limits assigned to them by the Treaty of Berlin, if this question should come up by the force of circumstances. They agree to dissuade the Bulgarians from all aggression against the neighbouring provinces, particularly Macedonia, and to inform them that in such a case they would be acting at their own risk and peril.

3 Attitude of Agents in the East.

   In order to avoid collisions of interests in the local questions which may arise, the three Courts will furnish their representatives and agents in the Orient with a general instruction, directing them to endeavour to smooth out their divergences by friendly explanations between themselves in each special case; and, in the cases where they do not succeed in doing so, to refer the matters to their Governments.

4 The present Protocol forms an integral part of the secret Treaty signed on this day at Berlin, and shall have the same force and validity . . .

   (L.S.) Bismarck

   (L.S.) Széchényi

   (L.S.) Sabouroff

Source: W. Medlicott and D.K. Coveney, *Bismarck and Europe*, London: Edward Arnold, 1971, pp. 128–9.

Document 47   THE ATMOSPHERE AT ST PETERSBURG, AUTUMN 1886

Bernhard von Bülow, the German chargé d'affaires in Russia, described in a private letter of 15 November 1886 how the Russian government felt itself humiliated in Bulgaria even after the removal of Alexander of Battenberg. They viewed the election in July of Prince Ferdinand of Coburg as an Austrian victory.

Russia feels that she has disgraced herself without measure in Bulgaria. What has happened there in the last year – the Revolution in Philippopolis, Slivnica, Battenberg's return after the conspiracy of August 21, the manner in which he then abdicated, the behaviour of the Regency etc., – is viewed here as a series of humiliations. The sense of having produced this fiasco by one's own awkwardness only increases the touchiness. . . . The 'intelligentsia' is exasperated because the Panslav idea, which for twenty-five years has been regarded as an irreversible dogma, has turned out to be a great humbug . . . The Emperor is embittered because even after the removal of his arch-enemy Battenberg, things are going contrary to his expectations and wishes. Russia and the Tsar, in this mood, ask themselves on whom they should vent their wrath. On Bulgaria? The Panslavs warn against an occupation of Bulgaria, in which they see a mouse trap. On England? They would like to settle their scores with England only after Austria has been disposed of. On us? To be sure, we are hated here, and the Russians are not to be trusted. But this hatred flows more from a vague antipathy to what Germany represents than from political calculation. . . . On the other hand the Russians, thank God, fear us greatly. An early attack on us is unlikely. This of course does not exclude spurring the French on behind the scenes. I have already, in August, drawn attention to the intrigues of Zagulyayev,[1] Katakazi,[2] etc. These semi-official approaches will probably continue. The immediate object of Russian anger is Austria. I hear from every side: 'Il faut déplacer la question bulgare [The Bulgarian problem needs to be side-lined].' That means that Russia should extract herself from the Bulgarian swamp by a confrontation with Austria.

[1] An *attaché* at the Russian embassy at Paris
[2] Probably a Russian journalist in Paris

Source: from KENNAN, GEORGE F.; *THE DECLINE OF BISMARCK'S EUROPEAN ORDER* © 1979 Princeton University Press, reprinted by permission of Princeton University Press.

ANGRA PEQUENA **Document 48**

Adolf Lüderitz had founded a trading station at Angra Pequena in Namibia in 1883 and concluded treaties with the neighbouring chiefs, who ceded large tracts of country to the newcomers. In the belief that Britain was about to claim the area as a protectorate, Lüderitz transferred his rights over Angra Pequena on April 24 1884 to the German Imperial Government. Bismarck then announced the establishment of a Protectorate over Angra Pequena in a speech to the Budget Commission of the Reichstag, 23 June 1884.

It might perhaps involve the setting up of coaling stations and an extension of the consular system. These arrangements might eventually be used for other undertakings on the coast of Africa and the Pacific.

His earlier confidence that German undertakings would feel sufficiently safe under English protection was shaken, not *vis-à-vis* the British government, but by the behaviour of English colonial governments. He reminded them for instance that it had been necessary to remonstrate for years at the want of respect for the rights acquired by German landowners on the Fiji islands before the British occupation. And recently the Australian colonial governments had not only made excessive claims to independent territories in the Pacific, but had also proclaimed the principle that acquisitions of land in these regions which were made before an eventual occupation should be declared null and void.

If it were asked what means the German *Reich* possessed for protecting German undertakings in far-off places, the answer first and foremost would be the desire and interest of other powers to preserve friendly relations with her. If in foreign countries they recognized the firm resolve of the German nation to protect every German with the device *civis romanus sum*, it would not cost much effort to afford this protection. But of course if other countries were to see us disunited, then we should accomplish nothing and it would be better to give up the idea of overseas expansion . . .

Source: W. Medlicott and D.K. Coveney, *Bismarck and Europe*, London: Edward Arnold, 1971, p. 142.

Document 49   GERMAN HISTORIANS AS HISTORY

Eckart Kehr (1902–1933) was one of the first historians to emphasize the importance of social structure and economic interests in influencing political decisions, and has been called by Gordon Craig 'the father of modern German historical revisionism'. In a brilliant essay on 'Modern German Historiography, Kehr pointed out that German historiography reflects the course of German history.

The task of analysing the present state of German historiography is fraught with difficulty because it is so closely bound up with, and determined by, the general social and political development of the empire and the republic. Since the middle of the nineteenth century German historiography has been an almost perfect mirror image of the political-social situation. Speaking of one of the most famous works of German history, Mommsen's *Roman History*, which was honoured with a Nobel Prize in 1902, fifty years after the first edition, the distinguished historian Eduard Meyer said that one could learn more from the book about German liberalism in the 1850s than about the whole history of Rome up to the death of Julius Caesar. The history of German historical writing is a part of general German History. It does not stand by itself, but touches at every point general social and internal relationships.

Source: E. Kehr, 'Modern German Historiography' in *Economic Interest, Militarism and Foreign Policy*, trans. and ed. G. Craig, Berkeley, CA: University of California Press, 1977, p. 174.

Document 50   HANS-ULRICH WEHLER'S INTERPRETATION OF BISMARCK'S POLITICS
AFTER 1871

Wehler is one of the most famous members of the Bielefeld School, a group of historians who used the methods of the social sciences to analyse history. His main area of research is the Second Reich and he is a great proponent of the views that Germany took a Sonderweg *during these years. He is particularly critical of Bismarck's 'Bonapartism' and strategy of 'negative integration' in which Bismarck sought to unify Germany by subjecting various minority groups such as Roman Catholics, Alsatians, Poles, and Social Democrats to discriminatory laws.*

Bismarck's greater Prussian Imperial State, as founded in 1871, was the product of the 'revolution from above' in its military stage. The legitimacy of the young *Reich* had no generally accepted basis, nor was it founded upon a generally accepted code of basic political convictions, as was to be immediately demonstrated in the years of crisis after 1873. Bismarck had to cover up the social and political differences in the tension-ridden class society of his new Germany, and to this end he relied on a technique of negative integration. His method was to inflame the conflicts between those groups which were allegedly hostile to the *Reich*, **Reichsfeinde**, like the Socialists and Catholics, left-wing Liberals and Jews on the one hand, and those groups which were allegedly loyal to the *Reich*, the **Reichsfreunde**. It was thanks to the permanent conflict between these in- and out-groups that he was able to achieve variously composed majorities for his policies. The Chancellor was thus under constant pressure to provide rallying points for his *Reichspolitik*, and to legitimate his system by periodically producing fresh political successes. Within a typology of contemporary power structures in the second half of the nineteenth century Bismarck's regime can be classified as a Bonapartist dictatorship: a traditional, unstable social and political structure which found itself threatened by strong forces of social and political change, was to be defended and stabilized by diverting attention away from constitutional policy towards economic policy, away from the question of emancipation at home towards compensatory successes abroad; these ends were to be further achieved by undisguised repression as well as by limited concessions. In this way also the neo-absolutist, pseudo-constitutional dictatorship of the Chancellor could be maintained. By guaranteeing the bourgeoisie protection from the workers' demands for political and social emancipation in exchange for its own political abdication, the dictatorial executive gained a noteworthy degree of political independence *vis-à-vis* the component social groups and economic interests. And just as overseas expansion, motivated by domestic and economic considerations, had become an element of the political style of French Bonapartism, so Bismarck too, after a short period of consolidation in foreign affairs, saw the advantages of such expansion as an antidote to recurring economic setbacks and to the permanent direct or latent threat to the whole system and became the 'Caesarist statesman'.

Reichsfeinde
Enemies of the state.

Reichsfreunde
Friends of the state.

Source: from Wehler, H-U. Bismarck's Imperialism, 1862–1890, *Past and Present*, 1970, August, No. 48, pp. 122–3 by permission of the Past and Present Society.

Guide to Further Reading

This bibliography concentrates on the literature which is either written in or translated into English and therefore accessible to English-speaking readers. There are an enormous number of books devoted to the towering figure of Bismarck. In 1998 Karina Urbach calculated that there were at least some 7,000 books on him.

Standard biographies in English are O. Pflanze, *Bismarck and the Development of Germany*, 3 vols, Princeton University Press, Princeton, NJ, 1990 and L. Gall, *Bismarck, The White Revolutionary*, 2 vols, Allen & Unwin, London, 1986. More precise and recent biographies are B. Waller, *Bismarck*, Blackwell, Oxford, 1997, K.L. Lerman, *Bismarck*, Pearson, Harlow, 2004 and E. Feuchtwanger, *Bismarck*, Routledge, London, 2002. A.J.P. Taylor's *Bismarck: The Man and the Statesman*, Hamish Hamilton, London, 1955 has dated but remains a provocative and interesting work. C. Grant Robertson, *Bismarck*, Constable, London 1918 and W.N. Medlicott, *Bismarck and Modern Germany*, Athlone Press, London, 1965 are still worth reading. E. Crankshaw, *Bismarck*, Macmillan, London, 1981 is highly critical of Bismarck but does have some interesting insights, while A. Palmer, *Bismarck*, Charles Scribner's Sons, New York, 1976 is readable and more balanced in its assessment of Bismarck. Bismarck's own memoirs, *Bismarck, the Man and Statesman, Being the Reflections and Reminiscences of Otto Prince von Bismarck*, 2 vols, (trans. A.J. Butler), Smith Elder, London, 1898, are somewhat selective and at times 'economical' with the truth. These are supplemented by W. Littlefield (ed.), *Bismarck's Letters to his Wife from the Seat of War, 1870–71*, Appleton & Co., New York, 1903 and J. Penzler (ed.), *Correspondence of William I and Bismarck with Other Letters*, 2 vols (trans. J.A. Ford), Heinemann, London, 1903.

There are also a large number of books which provide a general background to German unification and the Second *Reich*. T. Nipperdey, *Germany from Napoleon to Bismarck, 1800–1866*, Princeton, Princeton UP., 1996 and

J. Sheehan, *German History, 1770–1866*, Oxford, OUP, 1989, are both strong on economic, social and cultural history. W. Carr, *A History of Germany, 1815–1990*, London, Edward Arnold, fourth edition, 1991 is well written and within its limits a comprehensive study covering the whole period. M. Fulbrook, ed., *German History since 1800*, Edward Arnold, London, 1997 contains some interesting and stimulating essays by leading historians on various aspects of nineteenth century German history. Many of these essays are repeated in J. Breuilly 19th Century *Germany, Politics, Culture and Society, 1780–1918*, Edward Arnold, 2001. David G. Williamson, *Germany since 1815: A Nation forged and Renewed*, Palgrave, Basingstoke, 2005 also provides a concise overview. There are several older surveys which are still worth reading, G. Mann, *The History of Germany, Since 1789*, London, Chatto and Windus, 1968; H. Holborn, *A History of Modern Germany*, 1840–1945 Vol. 3, London, Eyre and Spottiswoode, 1969 and K. Pinson, *Modern Germany. Its History and Civilization*, New York, Macmillan, 1966. A.J.P. Taylor, *The Course of German History*, London, Hamish Hamilton, 1945 is a provocative book worth reading if only because of its breathtaking generalizations! D. Blackbourn, *Germany 1780–1918*, London, Fontana, 1997 is a concise survey, which is very useful for both social and economic as well as political history. V.R. Berghahn, Imperial Germany, 1871–1914, Providence, R.I and Oxford, Berghahn Press, 1994 and G. Craig, *Germany 1866–1945*, Oxford, OUP. 1978 have some excellent chapters on Bismarckian Germany. Concise and very informative is M. Seligmann and R. McLean, *Germany from Reich to Republic, 1871–1918*, Macmillan, Basingstoke and London, 2000; H.-U. Wehler, *The German Empire, 1871–1918*, Berg, Oxford, 1985 is the classic structural study of the Empire, while W.J. Mommsen, *Imperial Germany, 1867–1918: Politics, Culture and Society in an Authoritarian State*, Edward Arnold, London, 1995 contains a series of perceptive essays about how the *Reich* 'modernized' without becoming a constitutional liberal state.

Brendan Simms, *The Struggle for Mastery in Germany, 1779–1850*, Macmillan, Basingstoke, 1998 provides an excellent and concise account of the growing Prussian-Austrian rivalry after 1815.W. Henderson, *The Zollverein*, Cass, London, 1968 (new impression), is still the classic work on the *Zollverein* in English. H.J. Voth, 'The Prussian Zollverein and the bid for economic superiority', in P.G. Dwyer (ed.), *Modern Prussian History, 1830–1947*, pp. 109–125, Pearson, London, 2001 is a brief but more up-to-date study. W. Siemann, *The German Revolution of 1848–49*, Macmillan, Basingstoke, 1998 is arguably the best single volume study of the revolutions in print.

The bitter conflict between the Liberals and the Prussian government over the Army bill is well covered in E. Anderson, *The Social and Political Conflict in Prussia, 1858–1864*, University of Nebraska Press, Lincoln, 1954 and T. Hamerow, *The Social Foundations of German Unification*, 2 vols, Princeton University Press, Princeton, NJ, 1969–72. The development of German nationalism and the process of German unification is analysed by John Breuilly, *The Formation of the First German Nation State, 1800–1871*, Macmillan, London, 1996 and Hagen Schulze, *The Course of German Nationalism: From Frederick the Great to Bismarck, 1763–1867*, Cambridge University Press, Cambridge, 1991. Light is shed on the *Grossdeutsch* alternative in N. Hope, *The Alternative to German Unification: The Anti-Prussian Party, Frankfurt, Nassau and Two Hessens, 1859–1867*, Franz Steiner, Wiesbaden, 1973.

The diplomacy of unification is analysed by W. Carr, *The Origins of the Wars of German Unification*, Longman, London, 1991 and W.E. Mosse, *The European Powers and the German Question, 1848–71*, Cambridge University Press, Cambridge, 1958. Edward A. Bucholz, *Moltke and the German Wars, 1864–71*, Palgrave, Basingstoke, 2001 is an illuminating study of Moltke's military genius and his conduct of the wars of unification, while Dennis Showalter, *The Wars of Unification*, Edward Arnold, London, 2004 provides a very useful military analysis of the three wars. The Franco-Prussian war is covered by M. Howard in his classic, *The Franco-Prussian War*, Rupert Hart Davis, London, 1962 and S.W. Halperin, 'The Origins of the Franco-Prussian War Revisited: Bismarck and the Hohenzollern Candidature for the Spanish Throne', *Journal of Modern History*, 45(I), 1973.

H. Böhme, *Deutschlands Weg zur Grossmacht*, Kiepenhauer & Witsch, Cologne, 1966 is invaluable for the economic dimension to German unity; but for English-language readers a very useful selection of the material, which Böhme used for this book, has been edited and translated: H. Böhme (ed.) (trans. by A. Ramm), *The Foundation of the German Empire*, Oxford University Press, Oxford, 1971; F. Stern, *Gold and Iron: Bismarck, Bleichröder and the Building of the German Empire*, Allen & Unwin, London, 1977, sheds light on the links between politics and high finance during the Bismarck period.

On the first two decades of the Second *Reich* there is a large literature. Nation-building is analysed in Abigail Green, *Fatherlands: State Building and Nationhood in Nineteenth-Century Germany*, Cambridge University Press Cambridge, 2001. H.W. Koch, *A Constitutional History of Germany in the Nineteenth and Twentieth Centuries*, Longman, London, 1984 provides a good overview of constitutional developments. G.G. Windell, 'Bismarckian Empire: Chronicle of Failure, 1866–1880', *Central European History*, 2(4), 1969 is interesting on the relations between the *Reich* and Prussia. M.L. Anderson, *Practising Democracy*, Princeton University Press, Princeton, NJ, 2000 is an invaluable study of universal franchise in Imperial Germany and the development of a democratic culture. The political parties are well covered. The Centre Party and the *Kulturkampf* are discussed in: E.L. Evans,

German Center Party, 1870–1933: A Study in Political Catholicism, Southern Illinois University Press, Carbondale, 1981; H.S. Smith, *German Nationalism and Religious Conflict: Culture, Ideology, Politics, 1870–1914*, Princeton University Press, Princeton, NJ, 1995; and R.J. Ross, *The Failure of Bismarck's Kulturkampf*, Catholic University of America Press, Washington, DC, 1998. M.L. Anderson, *Windthorst: A Political Biography*, Oxford University Press, Oxford, 1981 is an excellent biography and, by extension also, account of *Kulturkampf*.

The best accounts of German Liberalism are in J.J. Sheehan, *German Liberalism in the Nineteenth Century*, Methuen, London, 1982 and D. Langewiesche, *Liberalism in Germany*, Macmillan, London, 2000. J. Retallack, *Notables of the Right: The Conservative Party and Political Mobilization in Germany, 1876–1918*, Unwin Hyman, London, 1988 analyses the evolution of the Conservative Party. For the political mobilization of the peasantry the following articles are well worth reading: D. Blackbourn, 'Peasants and Politics in Germany, 1871–1914', *European History Quarterly*, 14, 1984, and R.M. Berdahl, 'Conservative Politics and Aristocratic Landholders in Bismarckian Germany', *Journal of Modern History*, 44, 1972. For the development of the SPD S. Miller and H. Potthof, *A History of German Social Democracy: From 1848 to the Present,* Berg, Oxford, 1986 and W.L. Guttsmann, *The Social Democratic Party, 1875–1933*, George, Allen & Unwin, London, 1981 are the standard histories. V.L. Lidtke, *The Outlawed Party: Social Democracy in Germany, 1878–1890*, Princeton University Press, Princeton, NJ, 1966 covers Bismarck's anti-socialist campaign.

For the economic background to the Second *Reich* during the Bismarck era, A. Milward and S.B. Saul, *The Development of the Economies of Continental Europe, 1850–1914*, Allen & Unwin, London 1977 and C. Trebilcock, *The Industrialization of the Continental Powers, 1870–1914*, Longman, London, 1981 put the growth of the German economy within the European context, while M. Kitchen, *The Political Economy of Germany, 1815–1914*, Croom Helm, London, 1978 is a useful guide to both developments in agriculture and industry in the nineteenth century. I.N. Lambi, *Free Trade and Protection in Germany, 1868–1879*, Steiner, Wiesbaden, 1963 is a useful account of the tariff debates in the 1870s, as is H. Böhme, 'Big Business Pressure Groups and Bismarck's Turn to Protectionism, 1873–79', *Historical Journal*, 10, 1967, while H. Rosenberg, 'Political and Social Consequences of the Great Depression of 1873–1896 in Central Europe', *Economic History Review*, 13, 1943 is inevitably dated, but is still a stimulating article.

International developments are covered in outline by: A.J.P. Taylor, *The Struggle for Mastery in Europe, 1848–1918*, Oxford University Press, Oxford, 1954; J. Lowe, *The Great Powers and the German Problem, 1865–1925*, Routledge, London, 1994; N. Rich, *Great Power Diplomacy, 1814–1914*,

McGraw-Hill, New York, 1992; K. Hildebrand, *German Foreign Policy from Bismarck to Adenauer*, Unwin Hyman, London, 1989; and L. Geiss, *German Foreign Policy, 1871–1914*, Routledge, London, 1976.

There is, of course, also more detailed literature on Bismarck's foreign policy after 1871. Bismarck is the hero in the classic W.L. Langer, *European Alliances, 1871–1890*, revised edn, A. Knopf, New York, 1951. W.N. Medlicott, *The Congress of Berlin and After*, Methuen, London, 1938 and *Bismarck, Gladstone and the Concert of Europe*, Athlone Press, London, 1956 are still well worth reading, as is his 'Bismarck and the Three Emperors Alliance, 1881–87', *Transactions Royal Historical Society*, 27, 1945. G.F. Kennan, *The Decline of Bismarck's European Order,* Princeton University Press, Princeton, NJ, 1979 and B. Waller, *Bismarck at the Crossroads: The Restoration of German Foreign Policy after the Congress of Berlin*, Athlone Press, London, 1974 explore the complex last decade of Bismarck's diplomacy. Austro-German relations in the 1870s are analysed by N. Bagdassarian, *The Austro-German Rapprochement, 1870–1879*, Farleigh Dickinson University Press/Associated Universities Press, Madison, NJ/London, 1976. M.E. Townsend, *The Rise and Fall of Germany's Colonial Empire*, Macmillan, New York 1930 (reprinted in 1966 by H. Fertig, New York) is still useful, but of course very dated; P. Kennedy, 'German Colonial Expansion: Has the Manipulated Social Imperialism been Antedated', *Past and Present*, 54, 1972 is an invaluable introduction to Bismarck's colonial policy. H.U. Wehler, 'Bismarck's Imperialism, 1862–1890', *Past and Present*, 48, 1970 is a brilliant case for the social imperialism argument, while A.J.P. Taylor, *Germany's First Bid for Colonies, 1884–1885*, Macmillan, London, 1938 argues that Bismarck was pursuing only diplomatic objectives.

For source material, W.N. Medlicott, and D.K. Coveney (eds), *Bismarck and Europe*, Edward Arnold, London, 1971 contains much useful material on Bismarck's diplomacy. Sources specifically on the Hohenzollern candidature crisis can be found in G. Bonnin (ed.), *Bismarck and the Hohenzollern Candidature for the Throne of Spain*, Chatto & Windus, London, 1957. 'Bismarck's Relations with England, 1871–1914', *German Diplomatic Documents, 1871–1914*, vol. 1, (trans. E.T.S. Dugdale), Methuen, London 1926, provide much material from a British perspective, while the first three volumes of N. Rich, and M.H. Fischer (eds), *The Holstein Papers*, 4 vols, Cambridge University Press, Cambridge, 1955–63, are also a mine of information. More general collections are: T.S. Hamerow (ed.), *The Age of Bismarck: Documents and Interpretations*, Harper Row, New York, 1973; D. Hargreaves (ed.), *Bismarck and German Unification*, Macmillan, London, 1991; W.M. Simon (ed.), *Germany in the Age of Bismarck*, Allen & Unwin, London, 1968; and L.L. Snyder (ed.), *Documents of German History*, Greenwood Press Publishers, Westport, CT, 1958.

There are some interesting sources on the problem of Bismarck's legacy in J.C. Röhl (ed.), *From Bismarck to Hitler: The Problem of Continuity in German History*, Longman, London, 1970. Bismarck's dismissal after William I's death is fully covered in Röhl, *Wilhelm II: The Kaiser's Personal Monarchy*, Cambridge University Press Cambridge 2004. There are a considerable number of articles and reviews which consider the Bismarck legacy. A start is the survey of the Bismarck historiography in K. Urbach, 'Between Saviour and Villain: 100 years of Bismarck Biographies', *Historical Journal*, 41, 1998. Other articles of interest are: A. Dorpalen, 'The German Historians and Bismarck', *Review of Politics*, 15, 1953; G.P. Gooch, 'The Study of Bismarck', in *Studies in German History*, Longman, London, 1948; O. Pflanze, 'Bismarck and German Nationalism', *American Historical Review*, 60, 1955; M. Stürmer, 'Bismarck in Perspective', *Central European History*, 4(4), 1971; and H.A. Schmitt, 'Bismarck as Seen From the Nearest Church Steeple: A Comment on Michael Stürmer', *Central European History*, 6(4), 1973.

References

Anderson, E.N. (1954) *The Social and Political Conflict in Prussia, 1858–1864*, Lincoln, NE: University of Nebraska.

Anderson, M.L. (1981) *Windthorst: A Political Biography*, Oxford: Oxford University Press.

Anderson, M.L. (2000) *Practising Democracy*, Princeton, NJ: Princeton University Press.

Berdahl, R.M. (1972) 'Conservative Politics and Aristocratic Landholders in Bismarckian Germany', *Journal of Modern History*, 44.

Berger, S. (1995) 'Historians and Nation-Building in Germany after Reunification', *Past and Present*, 148.

Blackbourne, D. (1997) *Germany, 1780–1918*, London: Fontana.

Böhme, H. (1966) *Deutschlands Weg zur Grossmacht*, Cologne: Kepenheuer & Witsch.

Bonnin, G. (ed.) (1957) *Bismarck and the Hohenzollern Candidature for the Throne of Spain*, London: Chatto & Windus.

Canis, K. (1996) 'Der Zweibund in der Bismarckischen Aussenpolitik', in H. Rumpler and J. Niederkorn (eds) *Der Zweibund, 1879*, Vienna: Österreichische Akademie der Wissenschaften.

Craig, G.A. (1978) *Germany 1866–1945*, Oxford: Oxford University Press.

Crankshaw, E. (1981) *Bismarck*, London: Macmillan.

Dittrich, J. (1970) 'Ursachen und Ausbruch des deutschfranzösischen Krieges, 1870–71', in T. Schieder and E. Deuerlein (eds) *Reichsgründung, 1870–71*, Stuttgart: Seewald Verlag.

Eley, G. (1986) *From Unification To Nazism*, London: Allen & Unwin.

Eley, G. (1992) 'Bismarckian Germany', in G. Martel (ed.) *Modern Germany Reconsidered, 1870–1945*, London: Routledge.

Evans, R.J. (ed.) (1978) *Society and Politics in Wilhelmine Germany*, London: Croom Helm, London.

Evans, R.J. (1987) *Rethinking German History: Nineteenth-Century Germany and the Origins of the Third Reich*, London: Unwin Hyman.

Evans, R.J. (1997) *Re-reading German History: From Unification to Reunification, 1800–1996*, London: Routledge.

Eyck, E. (1950) *Bismarck and the German Empire*, (trans. and abridged), London: Allen & Unwin.

Fischer, F. (1967) *Germany's Aims in the First World War*, London: Chatto & Windus.

Gall, L. (1970) 'Das Problem Elsass-Lothringen', in T. Schieder and E. Deuerlein (eds), *Reichsgründung, 1870–71*, Stuttgart: Seewald Verlag.

Gall, L. (1986) *Bismarck, The White Revolutionary*, Vol. 1, *1815–71*, Vol. 2, *1871–1898*, London: Allen & Unwin.

Geiss, I. (1976) *German Foreign Policy, 1871–1914*, London: Routledge.

Grant Robertson, C. (1918) *Bismarck*, London: Constable.

Green, A. (2001) *Fatherlands: State-building and Nationhood in Nineteenth-Century Germany*, Cambridge: Cambridge University Press.

Hahn, H-W. (1984) *Geschichte des Deutschen Zollvereins*, Göttingen: Vandenhoeck & Ruprecht.

Halperin, S.W. (1973) 'The Origins of the Franco-Prussian War Revisited: Bismarck and the Hohenzollern Candidature for the Spanish Throne', *Journal of Modern History*, 45(1).

Hamerow, T.S. (1969) *The Social Foundations of German Unification*, Vol. 1, 'Ideas and Institutions', Princeton, NJ: Princeton University Press.

Hamerow, T.S. (1972) *The Social Foundations of German Unification*, Vol. 2, 'Struggles and Accomplishments', Princeton, NJ: Princeton University Press.

Headlam, J. (1899) *Bismarck and the Foundation of the German Empire*, New York: Knickerbocker Press.

Henderson, W.O. (1968) *The Zollverein* (new impression), London: Cass.

Hildebrand, K. (1990) '"A System of Stopgaps?" Opportunities and Limits of German Foreign Policy in the Bismarckian Era', in G. Schöllgen (ed.) *Escape into War? The Foreign Policy of Imperial Germany*, Oxford: Berg.

Howard, M. (1962) *The Franco-Prussian War*, London: Rupert Hart Davis.

Kehr, E. (1977) *Economic Interest, Militarism and Foreign Policy*, (trans. and ed. G. Craig), Berkeley, CA: University of California Press.

Kennan, G.F. (1979) *The Decline of Bismarck's European Order*, Princeton, NJ: Princeton University Press.

Kennedy, P.M. (1972) 'Bismarck's Imperialism: The Case of Samoa, 1880–1890', *Historical Journal*, 15.

Kolb, E. (1970) *Der Kriegsausbruch 1870: Politische Entscheidungsprozesse und Verantwortlichkeiten in der Julikrise 1870*, Göttingen: Vandenhoeck & Ruprecht.

Krockow, C. von (1990) *Die Deutschen in ihrem Jahrhundert, 1890–1990*, Reinbeck, bei Hamburg: Rowohlt Verlag.

Langer, W.L. (1931) *European Alliances and Alignments, 1871–1890*, New York: Alfred A. Knopf.

Lerman, K. (2004) *Bismarck*, Harlow: Pearson.

Lidtke, V.L. (1966) *The Outlawed Party: Social Democracy in Germany, 1878–1890*, Princeton, NJ: Princeton University Press.

Mann, G. (1968) *The History of Germany since 1789*, London: Chatto & Windus.

Medlicott, W.N. and D.K Coveney (eds) (1971) *Bismarck and Europe*, London: Edward Arnold.

Meinecke, F. (1950) *The German Catastrophe*, (trans.), Cambridge, MA: Harvard University Press.

Milward, A.G. and S.B. Saul (1977) *The Development of the Economies of Continental Europe, 1850–1914*, London: Allen & Unwin.

Mitchell, A. (1977) 'Bonapartism as a Model for Bismarckian Politics', *Journal of Modern History*, 49(2).

Mommsen, W.J. (1995) *Imperial Germany, 1867–1918*, London: Edward Arnold.

Mosse, W.E. (1958) *The European Powers and the German Question, 1848–71*, Cambridge: Cambridge University Press.

Nipperdey, T. (1996) *Germany from Napoleon to Bismarck*, Princeton, NJ: Princeton University Press.

Palmer, A. (1976) *Bismarck*, New York: Charles Scribner's Sons.

Panayi, P. (2000) *Ethnic Minorities in Nineteenth and Twentieth Century Germany*, Harlow: Pearson.

Pflanze, O. (1955) 'Bismarck and German Nationalism', *American Historical Review*, 60.

Pflanze, O. (1990) *Bismarck and the Development of Germany*, Vol. 1 (2nd edition), *The Period of Unification, 1815–71*. Vol. 2, *The Period of Consolidation, 1871–80*. Vol. 3, *The Period of Fortification, 1880–1898*, Princeton, NJ: Princeton University Press.

Pinson, K. (1954) *Modern Germany: Its History and Civilization*, New York: Macmillan.

Ritter, G. (1969) 'The Sword and the Sceptre', *The Prussian Tradition, 1740–1890*, Vol. 1, Miami, FL: University of Miami Press.

Röhl, J.C. (1966) 'The Disintegration of the *Kartell* and the Politics of Bismarck's Fall from Power, 1887–90', *Historical Journal*, 9.

Röhl, J.C. (1967) *Germany without Bismarck: The Crisis of Government in the Second. Reich, 1890–1900*, London: Batsford.

Röhl, J.C. (ed.) (1970) *From Bismarck to Hitler: The Problem of Continuity in German History*, London: Longman.

Rosenberg, H. (1943) 'Political and Social Consequences of the Great Depression of 1873–1896 in Central Europe', *Economic History Review*, 13.

Sheehan, J.J. (1982) *German Liberalism in the Nineteenth Century*, Methuen, London.

Sheehan, J.J. (1989) *German History, 1770–1866*, Oxford: Oxford University Press.

Showalter, D. (2004) *The Wars of German Unification*, London: Hodder.

Silverman, D.P. (1972) *Reluctant Union: Alsace-Lorraine and Imperial Germany, 1871–1918*, University Park, PA and London: Pennsylvania State University Press.

Simms, B. (1998) *Struggle for Mastery in Germany, 1779–1850*, London and Basingstoke: Palgrave Macmillan.

Stern, F. (1977) *Gold and Iron: Bismarck, Bleichröder and the Building of the German Empire*, London: George Allen & Unwin.

Stürmer, M. (1971) 'Bismarck in Perspective', *Central European History*, 4(4).

Taylor, A.J.P. (1938) *Germany's First Bid for Colonies, 1884–1885*, London: Macmillan.

Taylor, A.J.P. (1954) *The Struggle for Mastery in Europe, 1848–1918*, Oxford: Oxford University Press.

Taylor, A.J.P. (1955) *Bismarck: The Man and the Statesman*, London: Hamish Hamilton (and 1961, London: Arrow Books).

Townsend, M.E. (1930) *The Rise and Fall of Germany's Colonial Empire*, New York: Macmillan.

Turner, H.A. (1967) 'Bismarck's Imperialist Venture: Anti-British in Origin?', in P. Gifford, W.R. Louis and A. Smith (eds) *Britain and Germany in Africa: Imperial Rivalry and Colonial Rule*, New Haven, CT: Yale University Press.

Urbach, K. (1998) 'Between Saviour and Villain: 100 years of Bismarck Biographies', *Historical Journal*, 41.

Voth, H.J. (2001) 'The Prussian *Zollverein* and the Bid for Economic Superiority', in P.G. Dwyer (ed.) *Modern Prussian History, 1830–1947*, Harlow: Pearson.

Waller, B. (1974) *Bismarck at the Crossroads: The Restoration of German Foreign Policy after the Congress of Berlin*, London: Athlone Press.

Wehler, H.-U. (1969) *Bismarck und der Imperialismus*, Cologne: Kiepenheuer & Witsch.

Wehler, H.-U. (1970) 'Bismarck's Imperialism, 1862–1890', *Past and Present*, 48.

Wehler, H.-U. (1985 [1973]) *The German Empire*, (trans. Kim Traynor) Oxford: Berg.

Wehler, H.-U. (1996) *Deutsche Gesellschaftsgeschichte, 1815–1845/48*, Munich: Beck.

Windell, G.G. (1969) 'Bismarckian Empire: Chronicle of Failure, 1866–1880', *Central European History*, 2(4).

Index